TARGETING TOP TERRORISTS

Columbia Studies in Terrorism and Irregular Warfare

COLUMBIA STUDIES IN TERRORISM AND IRREGULAR WARFARE
Bruce Hoffman, Series Editor

This series seeks to fill a conspicuous gap in the burgeoning literature on terrorism, guerrilla warfare, and insurgency. The series adheres to the highest standards of scholarship and discourse and publishes books that elucidate the strategy, operations, means, motivations, and effects posed by terrorist, guerrilla, and insurgent organizations and movements. It thereby provides a solid and increasingly expanding foundation of knowledge on these subjects for students, established scholars, and informed reading audiences alike.

Ami Pedahzur, *The Israeli Secret Services and the Struggle Against Terrorism*
Ami Pedahzur and Arie Perliger, *Jewish Terrorism in Israel*
Lorenzo Vidino, *The New Muslim Brotherhood in the West*
Erica Chenoweth and Maria J. Stephan, *Why Civil Resistance Works: The Strategic Logic of Nonviolent Conflict*
William C. Banks, editor, *New Battlefields/Old Laws: Critical Debates on Asymmetric Warfare*
Blake W. Mobley, *Terrorism and Counterintelligence: How Terrorist Groups Elude Detection*
Jennifer Morrison Taw, *Mission Revolution: The U.S. Military and Stability Operations*
Guido W. Steinberg, *German Jihad: On the Internationalization of Islamist Terrorism*
Michael W. S. Ryan, *Decoding Al-Qaeda's Strategy: The Deep Battle Against America*
David H. Ucko and Robert Egnell, *Counterinsurgency in Crisis: Britain and the Challenges of Modern Warfare*
Bruce Hoffman and Fernando Reinares, editors, *The Evolution of the Global Terrorist Threat: From 9/11 to Osama bin Laden's Death*
Boaz Ganor, *Global Alert: The Rationality of Modern Islamist Terrorism and the Challenge to the Liberal Democratic World*
M. L. R. Smith and David Martin Jones, *The Political Impossibility of Modern Counterinsurgency: Strategic Problems, Puzzles, and Paradoxes*
Elizabeth Grimm Arsenault, *How the Gloves Came Off: Lawyers, Policy Makers, and Norms in the Debate on Torture*
Assaf Moghadam, *Nexus of Global Jihad: Understanding Cooperation Among Terrorist Actors*
Bruce Hoffman, *Inside Terrorism*, 3rd edition
Stephen Tankel, *With Us and Against Us: How America's Partners Help and Hinder the War on Terror*
Wendy Pearlman and Boaz Atzili, *Triadic Coercion: Israel's Targeting of States That Host Nonstate Actors*

Targeting Top Terrorists

UNDERSTANDING LEADERSHIP REMOVAL
IN COUNTERTERRORISM STRATEGY

Bryan C. Price

Columbia University Press
New York

Columbia University Press
Publishers Since 1893
New York   Chichester, West Sussex
cup.columbia.edu
Copyright © 2019 Columbia University Press
All rights reserved

Library of Congress Cataloging-in-Publication Data
Names: Price, Bryan C., author.
Title: Targeting top terrorists : understanding leadership removal in counterterrorism strategy / Bryan C. Price.
Description: New York : Columbia University Press, [2019] | Series: Columbia studies in terrorism and irregular warfare | Includes bibliographical references and index.
Identifiers: LCCN 2018031736 (print) | LCCN 2018033612 (e-book) | ISBN 9780231547727 (e-book) | ISBN 9780231188227 (hardcover) | ISBN 9780231188234 (paperback)
Subjects: LCSH: Terrorism—Prevention.
Classification: LCC HV6431 (e-book) | LCC HV6431 .P737 2019 (print) | DDC 363.325/17—dc23
LC record available at https://lccn.loc.gov/2018031736

Cover art: © Shutterstock

Contents

Acknowledgments vii

1 Introduction 1

2 Organizations and Leaders 32

3 Leadership in Terrorist Organizations 74

4 Quantitative Analysis of Leadership Decapitation in Terrorist Groups 103

5 The Effects of Leadership Decapitation on Hamas 150

6 Conclusion: Policy Implications and Future Research 179

Appendix 191
Notes 199
Bibliography 241
Index 261

Acknowledgments

This book would not have been possible without the help of many people whom I admire and look up to. My dissertation committee at Stanford University deserves the lion's share of credit for shaping my views on this topic. I could not have asked for a better dissertation advisor or mentor than Martha Crenshaw, a scholar who has done so much in the field for the past five decades. Perhaps the best compliment I can pay her is that she is an even better person than she is a scholar, and I will be forever indebted to her for taking on a very green PhD candidate. My other committee members—Scott Sagan, Kenneth Schultz, and Glenn Carroll—deserve similar thanks and praise. I would have been unable to execute the quantitative analysis without the help of Thomas Brambor, whose ninja coding skills were only outmatched by his patience and generosity. I would also like to thank my team of amazing graduate students at Stanford who carried me across the finish line and who honed my argument in meaningful ways, including Aila Matanock, Amanda Robinson, Tim Johnson, and Rachel Stein.

For the past six years, I have been blessed to work with the most dedicated and talented terrorism scholars at the Combating Terrorism Center and the Department of Social Sciences at West Point. Although naming every faculty member, distinguished chair, senior fellow, and cadet is impractical, special thanks go to those who contributed to this book, such as Brian Dodwell, Don Rassler, Daniel Milton, Arie Perliger, Mohammed al-'Ubaydi,

Bruce Hoffman, and Assaf Moghadam. I will always be thankful for two amazing bosses—Colonel Suzanne Nielsen and Brigadier General Cindy Jebb. Thanks also go to the tireless efforts of the Columbia University Press editorial team and to the anonymous reviewers of my manuscript. Finally, I would like to thank my family, who have always supported me during my academic and military career. Without the love of my father Jay Price and my late mother Mary Price, my two brothers Jay and Sean, my wife Tonya, and my one and only daughter Samantha (aka Schmoopie), none of this would have been possible.

TARGETING TOP TERRORISTS

CHAPTER 1

Introduction

Late in the evening on May 1, 2011, President Barack Obama announced to the nation that Osama bin Laden was dead. Earlier that day, the president had ordered a team of elite military forces to go deep into Pakistan after the mastermind behind the September 11 terrorist attacks that had shocked the country and the world nearly ten years prior. During his speech, President Obama said that he had told his new CIA director, Leon Panetta, that getting bin Laden was the number one priority in the United States's counterterrorism strategy against al-Qaeda.[1] America broke out in spontaneous celebration, and pundits immediately began speculating about the symbolic and operational importance of the bin Laden killing. But what did bin Laden's death mean, if anything, for the future of al-Qaeda? More broadly, what does it mean when terrorist groups experience the sudden loss of their leader?

Decapitation tactics, which are designed to kill or capture the key leader or leaders of a terrorist group,[2] feature prominently in the counterterrorism strategies of many states, including Israel and the United States. Yet scant attention has been paid to whether these tactics are even effective. We know very little about the effects of leadership succession, and leadership decapitation in particular, on terrorist group behavior.

The logic behind leadership decapitation as a counterterrorism tool is simple. It is commonly known by the "snakehead" metaphor—that is, cut the head off the snake, and the body will eventually die. Kill or capture the terrorist leader, and the group will eventually wither away.

The counterterrorism field, however, is split in the debate about the effectiveness of this tactic. Some scholars believe that targeting the group's leadership reduces its operational capability by eliminating its most highly skilled members and forcing the group to divert valuable time and limited resources to protect its leaders.[3] Decapitation tactics are also intended to disrupt the terrorist group's organizational routine and deter others from assuming power.[4] Scholars have credited these tactics with creating intra-organizational turmoil and even organizational collapse, most notably the demise of Aum Shinrikyo and the Shining Path following the arrest of their leaders.[5] Despite questions about the legality and moral legitimacy of targeted assassinations,[6] the United States expanded, rather than contracted, its targeted killing program under the Obama administration.[7] Early indications from the Trump administration suggest that targeted killing operations via drone strikes will increase even more.[8]

Leadership decapitation is often an appealing counterterrorism tactic to domestic audiences for a variety of reasons,[9] but most scholars argue that it is ineffective at best and counterproductive at worst.[10] Whereas proponents of decapitation highlight cases where the tactic has contributed to the organizational collapse of terrorist groups, critics counter with examples in which decapitation has increased and intensified terrorist activity.[11] Critics argue that targeted killings are both morally and ethically wrong and warn that they may produce a backlash effect. Rather than reducing the terrorist threat, leadership decapitation is likely to increase the number of willing recruits for terrorist groups to exploit, allowing them to grow in size and popularity.[12] Decapitation tactics may be prominent in Israel and the United States, detractors say, but that does not mean they are necessarily effective. Israel arguably has the most liberal and robust targeted killing policy of any state, yet one scholar concluded that "no compelling evidence exists that targeted killings have reduced the terrorist threat against Israel."[13]

The few empirical analyses that evaluate the tactic's effectiveness have produced mixed results. Moreover, scholars have yet to produce a compelling theoretical justification that explains why decapitation tactics *should* work, nor have they given policymakers guidance about when decapitation tactics should be employed, if ever. So what are we to make of this controversial counterterrorism tactic?

This book is an attempt to provide answers to this question and other key questions that policymakers and academics have debated over time. Is leadership decapitation effective? Why should we expect leadership decapitation to be effective against terrorist groups when it has been largely a failure against other types of groups, such as drug cartels and heads of state? Is it effective against certain types of terrorist groups but not others? Does it matter whether a terrorist group leader is killed versus captured? Does the size, ideology, or age of the group increase its susceptibility to organizational death?

To answer these questions, this book uses an organizational approach to unpack the mystery of decapitation effectiveness. It emphasizes the pivotal roles individual leaders play within these organizations. Drawing on both the literature on terrorism and organizational theory, with a special emphasis on leadership, I propose a conceptual framework for identifying the types of organizations in which leaders should exercise the most influence over organizational performance. This functional typology of organizations suggests that leaders of violent, clandestine, and values-based organizations are more important in influencing organizational performance than leaders of nonviolent, nonclandestine organizations that place profit maximization above all other goals. Additionally, replacing leaders in violent, clandestine, and values-based organizations is more difficult. This finding provides a much-needed theoretical justification for the proposition that decapitation tactics should be effective against terrorist groups, and conversely, why decapitation may not be effective against other types of organizations.

Second, I examine the empirical record to put this conceptual framework to the test. In other words, leadership decapitation might work in theory, but does it work in practice? This book uses survival analysis, a statistical modeling technique that is popular in the field of biomedicine, to test whether decapitation tactics are effective in dissolving terrorist groups. It employs an original data set consisting of 207 terrorist groups that were operational between 1970 and 2008, and it includes over three hundred observations of leadership change within those organizations. The data set is the largest and most comprehensive of its kind on the topic, and it includes data on both of the administrations under President George W. Bush. It was during President Bush's two administrations that the successes of leadership decapitation strategies were repeatedly touted and embraced by the U.S. counterterrorism community; these strategies were subsequently embraced and escalated by the Obama and Trump administrations.

Third, following a large-N quantitative analysis of leadership decapitation's effects on terrorist group mortality, I dive into a case study analysis of how the tactic affects a particular group, Hamas. By examining a group that has endured multiple leadership decapitation events throughout its history, we can observe how the loss of key leaders influences the operational capability of the organization, its day-to-day activities, and its organizational culture.

Finally, this book provides a set of policy-relevant findings that counterterrorism officials can use to inform strategy and policy moving forward. These findings provide policymakers with sound recommendations about decapitation and when it will be the most effective in destabilizing groups, what methods of decapitation are preferred over others, and which groups are most susceptible. More importantly, this book provides policymakers with proper expectation management about what leadership decapitation can and cannot do. It even provides some alternative methods to killing or capturing the leader that can achieve the same effects produced by leadership decapitation.

In the final analysis, this is also a book about leadership. Although it emphasizes the unique role that leaders play in terrorist groups and how they affect organizational performance, this book examines how and why leadership matters in other organizations as well. It helps explain why losing leaders in other kinds of organizations does not produce the same effects that it does in terrorist groups. In short, it helps explain when being leaderless is meaningless and when it matters most. It is natural, then, to begin a book on leadership by reaffirming why studying leaders is a worthwhile endeavor in the first place.

Why Leaders Matter in Explaining Terrorist Group Behavior

Leaders exist in every organization. Leadership can exist in the form of one person or a group of people. They can be benevolent or malevolent, competent or incompetent, formal and informal. While the literature on leadership is prolific, the number of studies that attempt to quantify the causal effect that leadership has on outcomes of interest in the social sciences is quite small. In the mainstream media, leadership is a popular topic and one that ostensibly "matters" to most people. Walk into any chain bookstore and there will undoubtedly be a section dedicated to the subject. The media and the court of public opinion are often quick to assign praise or blame based on their determination of good or bad leadership, and many universities offer classes, if not entire curricula, devoted to leadership studies. However, leadership is not as rigorously studied in political science as it is in other disciplines such as sociology and psychology.

There are several reasons that the discipline of political science has focused less on leadership. First, studying the influence of individual leaders does not easily lend itself to general, large-scale theories, making many scholars hesitant to champion "great man" explanations.[14] Following Kenneth Waltz's lead from his book *Man, the State, and War*, many agree that other factors such as "the roar of the anarchic system, domestic politics, and institutional dynamics drown out the small voices of individual leaders."[15]

Second, the study of leadership is notoriously "fuzzy" and does not seem compatible with the "hard" science approach that political science sometimes aspires to emulate.[16] According to Pollack and Byman, some have even argued that studies of individuals in political science are "theoretically hopeless" because they "focus only on impersonal forces as the causes" of important events.[17] It is difficult, therefore, to develop meaningful and falsifiable hypotheses about leadership, and it is equally difficult to study leadership quantitatively. In other words, how do we know when leadership matters and when it does not?

Third, even those who study leadership in its "home field" of organizational theory find the subject problematic, especially when trying to explain how leadership affects organizational performance.[18] Thus, at the risk of oversimplification, studying the effects of leadership is just *hard*.

Scholarly works in political science using leadership to explain important outcomes were more prevalent before other research programs, such as rational choice, entered the discipline. Today, works emphasizing leadership over other factors are relatively scarce. Those that do emphasize leadership tend to focus on politicians and presidents in particular, such as Richard Neustadt's and Alexander George's seminal works on presidential personality and performance, or James Barber's predictive model of presidential performance based on character type.[19] This personalized view of presidential leadership was later critiqued by scholars who downplayed the importance of individual leadership, even at the presidential level, in favor of a more institutionalized approach that relied on a rational choice framework.[20]

According to this line of argument, the constraints and incentives of the leader's position, not the character or personality of the individual occupying that position, explained far more of the variation in many political outcomes.[21]

Thus the study of individualized leadership assumed an awkward place in the discipline and one that was not especially compatible with rational choice, which relies on the assumption that all the actors' preferences are known. What motivates individual leaders, however, is not always clear. Worse, motivations can differ between individuals holding similar leadership positions. As Robert Dahl noted in *Who Governs?*, "the goals and motives that animate leaders are evidently as varied as the dreams of men. . . . [T]here is no convincing evidence at present that any single common denominator of motives can be singled out in leaders of associations. . . . Hence, a choice among [a leader's] strategies is necessarily based more on hunch, guesswork, impulse, and the assessment of imponderables than on scientific predictions."[22] Other political scientists agreed with Dahl and concluded that "there is no 'rational theory of leadership.'"[23] Thus, as the rational choice research program proliferated within the discipline, more work in political science followed Waltz's lead in focusing on factors other than the so-called first image (Waltz's term for theories emphasizing the importance of individuals). Hermann and Hagan were unhappy with this change in the study of international politics over the past several decades, and they described what they thought was the rationale behind this trend:

> Because the systemic imperatives of anarchy or interdependence are so clear, leaders can choose from only a limited range of foreign policy strategies. If they are to exercise rational leadership and maximize their state's movement toward its goals, only certain actions are feasible. Consequently, incorporating leaders and leadership into general theories of international relations is unnecessary since such knowledge adds little to our understanding of the dynamics of conflict, cooperation, and change in international affairs.[24]

Leadership studies are more prevalent in the field of organizational behavior. These studies have primarily focused on the relationship between individual leadership and the performance (i.e., sales, earnings, and market share) of economic firms,[25] while others have examined leadership changes and the performance of church pastors,[26] city mayors,[27] and athletic teams.[28] Surprisingly, despite the conventional wisdom and overwhelmingly popular view that leadership matters, there is disagreement among academics about the causal relationship between leadership and organizational performance.[29] Some studies provide qualitative and quantitative evidence to suggest that top-level leadership has little, if any, meaningful influence on organizational performance,[30] while others suggest that it is vital to an organization's success or failure.[31]

While this debate remains largely unsettled, interest in identifying quantifiable effects of leadership has waned over the past three decades. Pfeffer's 1977 article, "The Ambiguity of Leadership," remains one of the most influential academic pieces on leadership studies and summarizes the inherent difficulties in discerning leadership's effects on organizational outcomes.[32] Pfeffer focused on three obstacles that make studying leadership difficult. Although the issues Pfeffer raised were well suited to explain the difficulties in proving a link between leadership and performance among economic firms, they do not apply nearly as well to leadership within terrorist groups. While these obstacles may have held back the quantitative study of leadership in economic firms, the absence of these obstacles suggests that leadership in terrorist groups is ripe for analysis.

First, Pfeffer argues that most leadership studies fail to account for the fact that leaders in many economic organizations are often selected for their positions of authority, and as a result, perhaps only certain, limited styles of behavior may be chosen. This would inject a selection bias into any findings. In the business world, leaders are often groomed for positions of higher authority and selected on the basis of their past performance and future potential. It is also not uncommon for successor CEOs in the business world to come from outside the firm, nor is it uncommon for CEOs to lead organizations across different industries.[33]

This does not happen very often in terrorist groups. Although terrorist group leaders sometimes split from their parent group to form new terrorist groups, as was the case when Ahmed Jabril broke away from the Popular Front for the Liberation of Palestine to start up the Popular Front for the Liberation of Palestine—General Command (PFLP-GC),[34] it would be odd for a terrorist group to bring in an "outsider" from another terrorist group to be its leader, even if the person was an excellent leader in another organization. Additionally, leaders in one type of organization, say, a radical Islamic terrorist group, do not cross over to lead other types of organizations, such as Marxist-Leninist or environmental terrorist groups. Although some leaders are undoubtedly selected from within terrorist groups based on their talents and skills, just as they are in many economic firms, the founders of terrorist groups cannot be pigeonholed into generalized types in the way we do with CEOs. In other words, there is no one "type" for terrorist leaders. In the data set of terrorist groups I have collected from 1970 to 2008, terrorist group leaders are an eclectic group. They include twelve-year-old boys and octogenarians, psychopaths and two recipients of the Nobel Peace Prize, high school dropouts and college professors. Some assume power based on their military experience, charisma, or organizational skills, while others are believed to hold mystical powers or are chosen to lead by some religious deity.[35] Thus the selection bias that negatively affects the study of leadership in economic firms does not seem to be an issue for studying terrorist group leaders.

Second, Pfeffer claims that it was too difficult to properly evaluate a leader's influence on organizational performance because once in the leadership position, the discretion and behavior of the leader were often constrained "by both the demands of others in the role set and by organizationally prescribed limitations on the sphere of activity and influence."[36] Pfeffer's work mirrors research done in organizational ecology that suggests that organizational performance and behavior are "largely functions of environmental forces, which are viewed as unrelenting and often intractable external pressures and constraints."[37] While these constraints are easily observable in the behavior of leaders in economic firms, terrorist group leaders face far fewer constraints from the outside world. As clandestine organizations, they are insulated from most of the external pressures that influence economic firms and political organizations. Unless the group is state sponsored, terrorist leaders do not have a boss higher up in the system, nor do they answer to a board of directors or shareholders. Terrorist leaders are not worried about perceptions of legitimacy by anyone outside the audiences they recruit from or are trying to influence. In other words, institutional isomorphism does not seem to be a powerful force in making all terrorist groups look and act like one another.[38]

Third, Pfeffer argues that leaders can typically affect only a few of the variables that determine organizational performance. However, terrorist group leaders wield enormous power and influence over group activity. Leaders of underground organizations that defy social norms and mores by killing innocent people to achieve a political objective often have enormous flexibility in creating the structure, activities, and identity of the organizations they command. They purposefully defy legal restrictions and government regulation, and they are not (normally) chained to decades of tradition.[39] Maybe more important, they are under less pressure to adhere to social and moral sanctioning when it comes to organizational structure or behavior.[40]

Pfeffer concludes that the link between leadership and organizational performance is essentially an open question, but not before making two points that indirectly suggest that studying leadership effects in terrorist groups may be a profitable exercise after all. Notwithstanding the inconclusive quantitative evidence of a causal link between leadership and organizational performance, studying the link is important if only for the simple fact that most people *believe* leaders affect organizational performance.[41] Since the concept of leadership is itself socially constructed, as long as people *think* that leadership matters, it is important to study its effects. "It may be that the romance and the myth surrounding leadership concepts are critical for sustaining follower-ship and that they contribute significantly to the responsiveness of individuals to the needs and goals of the collective organization."[42] In other words, if group followers believe their leader affects organizational performance, then studying leadership is still important, even if this belief is a myth, is wrong, or cannot be proven quantitatively. Additionally, Pfeffer is critical of many leadership studies that focus on low-level leaders and believes that "if leadership has any impact, it should be more evident at higher organizational levels or where there is more discretion in decisions and activities."[43] Thus studying the link between organizational performance and high-level terrorist group leaders should be a useful endeavor.

Scholars have studied leadership in revolutionary movements[44] and social movements.[45] These studies have argued that the dynamics between leaders and followers are different in these types of organizations and that leadership was a defining factor in the existence and success of certain movements. These works represent a move away from the notion that structural factors alone can account for certain outcomes[46] and introduce new concepts of leadership, such as the importance of "leadership capital."[47] Unfortunately, while these recent studies propose interesting hypotheses and have enhanced our theoretical understanding of leadership in different organizations,[48] they tend to rely exclusively on case study analysis and anecdotal pieces of evidence rather than empirically testing their hypotheses through large-N statistical analysis. There is nothing wrong with findings based solely on case study analysis, but statistical analyses may uncover general patterns that are difficult to see in case study analysis, not to mention findings that are generalizable across a broad array of organizations beyond the specific industry of the case study. An opportunity exists, therefore, to test hypotheses about the effectiveness of decapitation tactics and to determine whether they contribute to organizational decline across a large population of terrorist groups.

In sum, few works in political science have studied how individual leaders affect organizational performance, particularly since rational choice became such a popular research program. Some reasons that explain why include the growing popularity of other levels of analysis over the first image and the difficulties in finding a causal link between leaders and organizational performance in economic firms. While leaders have been more rigorously studied in social and revolutionary movements, the same cannot be said for leaders in terrorist groups. Moreover, the hypotheses generated in these studies are not tested against large-N data sets, making generalization across the universe of leaders in different organizational types problematic.

The Study of Terrorism: Three Levels of Analysis

The literature on terrorism has exploded in the years following the tragic events of September 11, 2001, but there is little consensus on the two questions scholars and policymakers are most interested in: what the causes of terrorism are and what factors lead to the decline of terrorism. Academics from various disciplines—political science, criminology, psychology, economics, organizational theory, sociology—have approached these questions using different levels of analysis and a host of advanced methodological techniques.[49] So what do we know, and which approaches are the most useful in answering these questions?

Causes of Terrorism

To answer the first question concerning the causes of terrorism, scholars have tended to focus on three levels of analysis: macro-level factors, organization-level factors, and what I will call the individual or "foot soldier" perspective.

MACRO-LEVEL FACTORS

In works that use macro-level factors to explain the causes of terrorism, variables of interest include poverty levels, religion, civil liberties, anti-American sentiment, unemployment, education, and ideology.[50] These studies often suffer from two major weaknesses. First, these macro-level explanations cannot adequately explain important exceptions to their general predictions. For example, studies trying to show that terrorist group members are disproportionately poor/uneducated or upper middle class/educated have problems explaining why the rolls of the Irish Republican Army were disproportionately working class with average education levels.[51] Those who claim that macro-level factors such as education and economic development are root causes of terrorism cannot explain why terrorism proliferated in Italy and Germany in the 1970s but not in France during the same time period, even though these states were similar across a broad spectrum of macro-level characteristics.[52] Second, these studies often have a difficult time explaining how so many people around the world can be exposed to these macro-level factors, yet so few end up engaging in terrorist acts.[53] The number of terrorists is miniscule when compared to the millions of people who are poor, uneducated, and who live in oppressive societies where political expression is restricted or denied. In light of these weaknesses, the literature on the causes of terrorism seems to be moving away from these general macro-level approaches.[54]

ORGANIZATION-LEVEL FACTORS

Other studies go a step down from the macro level and look at terrorism from an organizational perspective, emphasizing the influence of organizational behavior and group dynamics.[55] These studies often take an "open system" approach[56] in which researchers focus on both the internal and external aspects of the group, such as the organizational structure, social dynamics, group pathologies, and how the group perceives and adapts to a fluid and hostile environment.

Some of these studies ignore the role that individual leaders play within these organizations, and it is not uncommon for scholars to refer to "they" or "the group" when discussing organizational decision making, similar to the way structural realists treat states as unitary actors in international relations. This subtle distinction depersonalizes the process and wrongly implies that decisions made by the group are independent of those individuals wielding power within the group. For some types of organizations, this depersonalization seems appropriate. Large and complex organizations are often thought to behave in ways that are beyond the control or influence of one individual or even a small group of individuals. The complex and multi-organizational foreign policy decision-making apparatus of a state serves as one example where this assumption seems appropriate.[57] However, most terrorist groups face different constraints and incentives than other organizations, which means that the decision making of the leader or small group of leaders is more important in explaining group behavior in these organizations.

The organizational level of analysis has not been as widely applied as macro-level or individual-level factors, but this is starting to change, more so in the counterterrorism literature than in the literature pertaining to the causes of terrorism. After all, although there are obvious and important differences between terrorist groups and the types of organizations usually studied by organizational theorists, "terrorist organizations *are* organizations" facing similar constraints and challenges.[58] The idea that group-level factors may have more explanatory power than other macro- or individual-level factors is not a new one in the terrorism literature,[59] but scholars have paid more attention to this approach in the past decade.[60]

Some scholars argue that certain important topics in terrorism research, such as suicide terrorism, can *only* be explained by organizational factors. Ami Pedahzur challenges the notions that suicide terrorism can be explained by macro-level factors such as culture or religion, or that it can be explained as a grassroots phenomenon where people spontaneously "take to the streets and begin to set off explosive devices."[61] Instead, Pedahzur states, "One of the clearest conclusions of this study, as well as of other inquiries, is that suicide terrorism is a product of an organizational process."[62] According to Gambetta, "unlike self-immolations, which have been typically individual acts, *all suicide missions have been decided by and executed with the support of an organization.*"[63] Although the ones performing the suicide attack may not be especially skilled or engaged in the planning, Pedahzur states that "they are trained for this mission by an organization which has a set of goals."[64] "In fact, it is a highly calculated, top-down phenomenon."[65] Unlike other organizational theorists, Pedahzur explicitly emphasizes the leaders' role in the frequency and effectiveness of suicide terrorism, noting that leaders, not impersonal and external forces, decide when to start and stop the use of the tactic.[66] In many other organizations that perform suicide terrorism, the indoctrination of potential suicide attackers is focused on worship of and obedience to the group leader, not the ideological cause.[67]

INDIVIDUAL MOTIVATIONS AND "FOOT SOLDIER" BIAS

Finally, scholars attempt to explain terrorism from the individual's perspective, such as looking at an individual's motivations.[68] These accounts are often biased toward the rank and file of the terrorist organization, the "foot soldier," more than the leadership's perspective.[69] It should be noted that many of these works focus on why people *join* organizations rather than why they *found* them. Scholars choosing this level of analysis often use rational choice, psychological, or sociological approaches.

Rational choice explanations suggest that members of terrorist groups are competent utility maximizers who choose terrorism over other less attractive alternatives.[70] However, this framework cannot explain why groups behave in ways counter to what we perceive as being rational.[71] For example, why do groups turn to terrorism to achieve their political goals when former terrorist groups have so often failed?[72] Why do some groups engage in suicide bombing while groups with the same goals and constraints refrain from using this tactic? Why do some groups like the Baader-Meinhof Gang attack frequently and with reckless abandon, while other groups like the PFLP are meticulous and conservative in their attack profile, only striking when operational success is ensured? Why do some groups adhere to bargaining theory and compromise, thus improving their position, while others never do?[73] I argue that the decisions made by leaders in these organizations are the determining factors in most or all of these questions. Post uses the refrain "the cause is not the cause" to discourage us from reading too much into the ideological rhetoric of terrorist groups.[74] I agree and believe that terrorist group behavior is determined more by leadership decisions than by blind subservience to an ideological cause.

Scholars have also used psychological approaches to explain the causes of terrorism. Initially these studies tried to find common psychological traits of terrorist group members to show that they were somehow different from the rest of society,[75] but this line of inquiry has been largely debunked in recent years. Terrorists are not different in terms of personality from the rest of society, but they do have different belief systems, and this is where the psychological literature has centered its attention in recent years.[76] Unfortunately, what is important to this line of study is that the "majority of work to date has focused on explaining the individual's decision to resort to terrorism in the first place," while "much less attention has been given to how the psychology of the individual can influence the group."[77] Here the focus should be on leaders, not foot soldiers. McCormick argues that

> this is of particular importance in the case of underground organizations . . . which have been constructed around defining personalities. This is more common than is commonly assumed, particularly in the initial stages of a terrorist group's development. The individual psychology of a handful of individuals, in such cases, can often provide significant insights into group behavior in the face of changing circumstances.[78]

This account suggests two important points. First, we can learn more about terrorist group behavior by studying terrorist group leaders rather than foot soldiers, and second, terrorist group leaders inspire members to join.

Other explanations from economists and political scientists, such as the club model, explain group membership in a different way, but they too tend to focus on individual motivations. They argue that individuals join organizations, even radical Islamic terrorist groups, mainly because these organizations provide public goods that the state fails to provide in an efficient or sufficient manner.[79] Alternative accounts suggest that individuals join terrorist organizations mainly because of the social benefits conferred by the group. These individuals are thus "social utility maximizers" rather than "political utility maximizers."[80] While terrorist group members enjoy the social benefits of belonging, these accounts do not have a compelling explanation for why individuals do not join other types of organizations that provide similar public and social goods without the obvious risks that accompany membership in a terrorist organization. Additionally, a common omission in many of these explanations is the other, perhaps more important, half of the equation that explains why individuals join organizations—those responsible for recruiting individuals to join their ranks. Although some terrorist groups expand their memberships through walk-ins and volunteers, recruitment is most commonly performed by "enlistment officers" who actively recruit members to join their organizations.[81] Psychological accounts often discount this type of recruitment and place more emphasis on so-called self-radicalization instead of active recruitment by terrorist groups.[82]

Thus, in explaining why some groups resort to terrorism, scholars tend to privilege macro-level factors and the foot soldier perspective more than the leadership's role in decision making.[83] Maybe this is because it is difficult to develop falsifiable theories to show that individual leadership decision making trumps these other variables. One could argue that there are snippets of truth in all of the above explanations. For example, some people may join terrorist groups because of the need to fulfill social needs, some join because they are disenfranchised and angry with the political status quo, and some may do it after making rational calculations about costs and benefits. The problem with these accounts is that they place too much emphasis on the decision making of the individual "foot soldier" while treating the group and its leadership as passive agents, when in fact terrorist groups actively recruit and influence the foot soldier.[84]

Of course, some members join of their own accord after making rational cost-benefit analyses of their plight, but knowing what we know about voluntary group membership, prospective members can also join because they are inspired, cajoled, coerced, or recruited by the leaders of the terrorist group and their message.[85] The reasoning that explains why some people join and volunteer to work on political campaigns serves as a useful analogy. Of course, some do it because they receive social benefits from the organization (club model), because they have made some rational calculation that their lives will be better off if their candidate wins (rational/strategic model), or because they are emotionally attached to the cause (psychological approach), but another explanation could be that they volunteer simply because they are inspired by the candidate they support or were specifically recruited to join the team.

In short, there are no universally accepted answers to the question of what factors cause an individual to commit terrorist acts. But none of the given answers seem to emphasize leadership over other factors. Leadership influence is virtually absent in the macro-level approach, and most of the work done on individual-level factors focuses on those joining terrorist groups rather than those recruiting them. The organizational level of analysis holds the most promise for a proper emphasis on leadership because leaders play a pivotal role in determining most organizational characteristics, but few works have rigorously examined the role that leaders play in terrorist groups.

How Terrorism Declines

This book contributes most directly to counterterrorism policy, and more specifically, to understanding how terrorist groups end. Although studies examining the causes of terrorism outnumber those analyzing how terrorism ends, interest in the latter topic has increased in the past decade. Similar to the lack of consensus surrounding the root causes of terrorism, there is a significant amount of disagreement about how terrorism declines. For example, what does an effective counterterrorism strategy look like? What are the metrics that should be used to determine success or failure? Are the counterterrorism policies currently employed making the threat of terrorism worse instead of better? Can states do anything meaningful within their power to dissolve terrorist groups?[86] At the time of this writing, there are no clear answers to these questions.

Building on earlier work by Crenshaw,[87] Cronin is the leading scholar in this subfield. Her 2006 *International Security* article, "How al-Qaida Ends," set the stage for future study on the decline and demise of terrorist groups.[88] Prior to Cronin's work, a common critique of this line of research was its reliance (some would say overreliance) on case studies of individual groups to explain how terrorism ends. A Canadian intelligence publication lamented that

> even in what little work has been done on terrorist group decline, analysts focus most frequently on one particular group and the precise conditions which led to its demise, decline, disappearance, or defeat. Such studies tend to emphasize particular context and environment-specific factors which are difficult to reduce to common principles or factors that can be applied across the board.[89]

In addition to the global threat posed by international terrorism since 9/11, the experience of the United States in Iraq, Syria, Afghanistan, Libya, Yemen, and East Africa has also contributed to the urgency in finding quick, viable, and cost-efficient answers to how terrorism ends. This urgency was expressed by former secretary of defense Donald Rumsfeld in a memorandum to his senior staff in October 2003:

> Are we capturing, killing or deterring and dissuading more terrorists every day than the madrassas and the radical clerics are recruiting,

training and deploying against us? Does the U.S. need to fashion a broad, integrated plan to stop the next generation of terrorists? The U.S. is putting relatively little effort into a long range plan, but we are putting a great deal of effort into trying to stop terrorists.[90]

Are we any closer to answering Rumsfeld's questions fifteen years later? Most would say no, but why?

Evaluating optimal counterterrorism strategies is difficult. First, even if we were certain of the ingredients that facilitate the decline of terrorism, it is difficult to ascertain a clandestine group's operational status for obvious reasons. Inactivity can be misperceived as a group in decline, while a flurry of activity can signal a group's resurgence when it is really in its final death throes and acting out in desperation.[91] A period of inactivity by a terrorist group could be the result of effective counterterror strategies, but it could also mean that the group is temporarily dormant for other reasons, such as long planning cycles, recruiting campaigns, or the need to procure additional resources before attacking again.[92]

Second, establishing and evaluating metrics for winning the war on terrorism is a formidable task.[93] As noted counterterrorism scholar Daniel Byman laments, "successful counterterrorism is notoriously difficult to measure."[94] Thus, how should we answer Rumsfeld's question? What should serve as metrics for success—number of incidents? Terrorist fatalities? Friendly fatalities? Opinion polls? Total destruction of the group? How does one evaluate and weigh short-term versus long-term trends? Each metric has its own disadvantages. Additionally, unlike for other government policies, where it is possible to compare and contrast the effects on certain populations using natural experiments, lab simulations, or ready-made control groups, there is no getting around the counterfactual problem in counterterrorism. In other words, in order to accurately depict the effect that certain counterterrorism strategies have on ending terrorist groups, we would have to understand how these groups would fare in the absence of any government response.[95] This point is important because some scholars argue that terrorist groups have a natural tendency to implode and that the best counterterrorist policies would be better served if they focused on amplifying this natural tendency instead of trying to destroy groups outright.[96] Finally, determining the second- and third-order effects of counterterrorism policies, what is often referred to as "blowback," may be more difficult than establishing even the baseline metrics for success.[97]

So how do terrorist groups end? Cronin suggests that terrorist groups can end in six ways:[98]

1. The group's leaders are killed or captured.
2. The group is vanquished by force.
3. The group achieves its stated goals.
4. The group moves toward a legitimate political process.
5. The group implodes and/or loses popular support.
6. The group moves to criminality, insurgency, or cataclysmic war.

It is significant that Cronin's first scenario in which terrorist groups can end is that the group's leaders are killed or captured. The benefits of killing or capturing the top leader are attractive and intuitive, in large part because the metrics of decapitation are easy to understand and quantify. If killing or capturing the leader quickly leads to dissolution of the group, then these strategies are also extremely appealing because of their cost-effectiveness, assuming the leader can be killed or captured with fewer resources than it would take to destroy the entire group. For these reasons, Cronin says there is "little wonder that governments like to target the top,"[99] but she claims that "the effects of capturing or killing a terrorist leader have varied greatly."[100] Like most scholars who have studied the effectiveness of decapitation, Cronin lists a few of the prominent cases in which decapitation has apparently succeeded in ending the group or failed.[101] Because decapitation strategies were only a small part of her overall study on how terrorism ends, she offers several variables that may affect success or failure when removing a terrorist leader, but a systematic test is badly needed in order to draw any meaningful conclusions.

Cronin's conclusion that "sometimes decapitation works, sometimes it does not" is unsatisfactory because it tells us very little about why this is the case. Even though we know little about what happens when a leader is removed from a terrorist group, many scholars have strong opinions about the subject. Often these opinions are not based on the empirical record, and if they are, they are often based on one or two examples that get repeated incessantly in the debate. For instance, a professor at an American university recently wrote that he was adamantly against targeted killings of terrorist groups "not so much . . . on moral grounds but for the practical reasons that it *usually* results in rampaging, out-of-control followers, brings to power more militant, replacement leaders, and encourages the counter-assassination of our own leaders." This opinion, like many others on the topic of leadership decapitation, was presented as fact even though no supporting evidence accompanied it. Academic debates on the utility of decapitation strategies, however, have not prevented Israel and the United States from putting them front and center in their counterterrorism strategy.

Decapitation Tactics in Historical Context

Decapitation tactics are not new. Putting decapitation tactics into historical context is important because policymakers are often apt to base their decisions on historical precedent, particularly when it comes to combating security threats. This is why leaders are often chided for "trying to fight the last war" instead of developing and employing solutions better suited to confronting today's security challenges.

The idea that killing a leader will dissolve the group dates back thousands of years. One needs to look no further than the Bible to draw the same conclusion Cronin did two millennia later. In the book of Apocrypha, a widow named Judith famously defeated an entire army simply by decapitating the army's general, literally and figuratively. According to the story, Judith manipulated her way into the tent of Holofernes, the commander of the Assyrian army that was besieging the city of Judah. Judith supposedly seduced the general with her beauty and copious amounts of wine, and then beheaded him with his own sword. Once she displayed the general's head on the city wall, the Assyrian army fled in disarray to Damascus, and she successfully saved the city of Judah. The historical accuracy of this account may be in dispute, but it is important because of its symbolism and the fact that it reflects the logic inherent in contemporary decapitation strategies. To be fair, one could draw the exact opposite conclusion by citing the story of Jesus. His arrest and persecution had the exact opposite effect on the Christian movement and is a telling example that decapitation can backfire when a charismatic leader is glorified as a martyr for the larger movement.

Centuries later, decapitation tactics (as well as tactics to prevent our own leadership decapitation) played an influential role in military and foreign policy after the United States emerged from its isolationist shell at the beginning of World War II. Pape argues that leadership decapitation has been a cornerstone of U.S. air campaigns ever since American planes bombed German government buildings in World War II.[102] He argues that leadership decapitation has thus been a central feature in every air campaign since, including in North Korea, Vietnam, Libya, and Iraq during the first Gulf War:

> According to this strategy, a nation's leadership is like a body's brain: destroy it and the body dies; isolate it and the body is paralyzed; confuse it and the body is uncontrollable. The logic of decapitation is part punishment and part denial. As a punishment strategy, it aims to overcome a key weakness in such strategies: the increased ability of governments to repress dissent in war. As a denial strategy, it aims to extend the logic of operational paralysis to "strategic" or national decision-makers.[103]

During the early days of the Cold War, fear of a nuclear or conventional attack aimed at decapitating the other superpower's leadership nodes drove both the United States and the Soviet Union to extreme lengths to ensure redundancy in their command and control systems.[104] Moreover, some argued that if a nuclear war ever broke out, decapitating the USSR's leadership with our first (and potentially only) nuclear salvo "may offer the best hope of escaping annihilation."[105] Covert decapitation strategies aimed at other hostile state leaders were popular for the United States at the time, despite their mixed results. Covert operations that succeeded in bringing about the political outcomes the United States desired, such as the CIA-engineered coup in Guatemala in 1954, line one side of the ledger, while embarrassing and unsuccessful attempts to kill Cuban leader Fidel Castro and influence the Cuban revolution line the other.[106] Leadership decapitation was also a central (and controversial) pillar in U.S. counterinsurgency strategy in Vietnam under the Phoenix program in the late 1960s and early 1970s.[107] In 1986, a U.S. airstrike targeted the headquarters building of Libyan leader Muammar Qaddafi, but Qaddafi survived.[108] In 1998, the United States launched seventy-five cruise missiles in Operation Infinite Reach, an unsuccessful attempt to kill Osama bin Laden in Afghanistan, following the embassy bombings in Kenya and Tanzania.[109]

Beginning with the 2002 National Security Strategy, the United States made it "our first priority to disrupt and destroy terrorist organizations of global reach and attack their leadership; command, control, and communications; material support; and finances."[110] The 2003 *National Strategy for Combating Terrorism* (*NSCT*) elaborated on the logic behind targeting terrorist group leaders:

> At the top of the structure, the terrorist leadership provides the overall direction and strategy that links all these factors and thereby breathes life into a terror campaign. The leadership becomes the catalyst for terrorist action. The loss of leadership *can* cause many organizations to collapse. Some groups, however, are more resilient and can promote new leadership should the original fall or fail.[111]

This measured tone about the success of decapitation strategies mirrors Cronin's, but it is equally as unsatisfying, mainly because it tells us little about what differentiates the groups that are resilient in the face of decapitation from those that ultimately collapse. It is also important to note that in the *NSCT*'s graphic depiction of "The Structure of Terror," the leadership is separate from the organization as a whole, sitting atop the organizational pyramid.[112] A re-creation of this illustration is found in figure 1.1.

Figure 1.1 The structure of terror

The 2006 *National Strategy for Combating Terrorism* also gives prominence to attacking terrorist group leaders. According to this document, the first way in which the United States can stop terrorist attacks before they occur is to target the

> leaders who provide the vision that followers strive to realize. They [leaders] also offer the necessary direction, discipline, and motivation for accomplishing a given goal or task. Most terrorist organizations have a central figure who embodies the cause, in addition to several operational leaders and managers who provide guidance on a functional, regional, or local basis. The loss of a leader *can* degrade a group's cohesiveness and *in some cases* may trigger its collapse. Other terrorist groups adapt by promoting experienced cadre or decentralizing their command structures, making our challenge in neutralizing terrorist leaders even greater.[113]

The most detailed account of the importance of decapitation in our current counterterrorism strategy comes from the 2006 *National Military Strategy for the War on Terrorism*. Like the previous documents, it cites targeting the leadership as the first key element in the war on terror. However, it emphasizes not just the killing or capturing of terrorist leaders but also attacking the social construction of terrorist group leadership:[114]

> This resource is vulnerable to the military, intelligence, law enforcement, and informational instruments of national power. Military, intelligence, and law enforcement instruments focus on capturing or killing key terrorist leaders, while informational instruments focus on degrading their standing with their followers and potential recruits. Leadership provides the following focus for targeting: strategic vision/motivation; operational guidance/direction; and tactical direction.[115]

In sum, leadership decapitation is a central part of U.S. counterterror strategy today. Its primacy in every one of the previously cited documents is indicative of the importance American policymakers place on the role terrorist leaders play within their respective organizations. In fact, in 2009, members of the House Intelligence Committee exposed a secret CIA program that had been operational since 2001 under the Bush administration to dispatch small paramilitary teams to foreign countries in order to kill senior al-Qaeda terrorist leaders.[116] But despite the importance placed on leadership decapitation in many of the top U.S. national security documents, little research has been done to show that this is an effective strategy. Additionally, although decapitation is the first strategy discussed in these documents, policymakers are often quick to temper and silence those suggesting that decapitation can be a silver bullet to win the war on terror.[117]

Previous Work on Decapitation Effectiveness

Although several scholars have evaluated the effectiveness of decapitation strategies in countering terrorism, few have done so in a systematic fashion, and they often fail to spell out the theoretical reasons that explain variation in the effectiveness of these strategies. According to Cronin, work on decapitation effectiveness is in its infancy. "Past experience with the decapitation of terrorist groups, however, is just beginning to be studied in a systematic way and, as we shall see, the relationship between decapitation and a group's demise is not straightforward."[118] (In general, most of this work focuses on case studies that support a specific conclusion, whatever that may be.)[119] Others try to explain the effectiveness of decapitation strategies within a particular country such as Israel[120] and Afghanistan.[121] These country- and region-specific studies add to our understanding of decapitation, but generalizing their findings across all groups has not been done before.

Similar to the findings from the case study method, the few works that have tried to quantitatively measure decapitation effects on terrorist group behavior also find contradictory evidence that can support both sides.[122] For example, Gupta and Mundra found that targeted killings and other types of violent provocations were poor predictors of the number of suicide attacks of three different groups in the Palestinian territories from 1993 to 2003. Unlike targeted killings and other violent provocations, political provocations accurately predicted the number of suicide attacks.[123] Kaplan et al. found that targeted killings in Israel from 2001 to 2003 increased the "terror stock" or recruitment of terrorist groups, which ultimately led to an increase in the expected suicide bombing rate.[124] Both of these studies looked at a narrow sample of terrorist groups in a relatively short period of time, not to mention their exclusive focus on suicide terrorism, so it is difficult to extract any meaningful generalizations about decapitation effects across other groups, at other times, using terrorist tactics in addition to suicide terrorism.

Three works, however, have tried to test decapitation's effectiveness against larger numbers of groups and across longer periods of time, but all are either methodologically flawed in some way or test hypotheses against small data sets that are not representative of the broader population of terrorist groups.

Langdon and her colleagues examined nineteen guerrilla, terrorist, religious, and revolutionary groups from 1750 to the present day that boasted more than one hundred members.[125] They concluded that "the leadership of a group can generally change or be seriously challenged without threatening the group's survival."[126] Langdon and her team, however, based their findings on an extremely small sample that is ill-suited to deriving statistically significant results. Moreover, their study attempts to explain variation in decapitation effectiveness across several different types of organizations that have very little in common over a period stretching more than 250 years. As an odd example, two of the groups in their sample are the Shining Path, one of the most dangerous and violent terrorist groups in South America, and the Mormon Church in the United States, an organization that, needless to say, has a less than notorious track record for perpetrating violence. Additionally, Langdon et al.'s decision to limit their sample to groups with over one hundred members does not make for a particularly representative sample because many terrorist organizations are believed to be rather small.[127]

Mannes measured the change in the frequency of attacks before and after a top terrorist leader was killed or captured.[128] Although Mannes should be commended for explicitly stating his coding criteria and publishing the list of terrorist groups in his study (a rarity, it seems, for many researching this topic), only seventy-one groups populate his data set, and he does not have a method for dealing with right-censored data.[129] Finally, the decision to study the frequency of attacks two years prior to decapitation and two years after may not allow for a long enough lag time to witness the interorganizational changes taking place after a decapitation event.

There are several reasons that a longer time frame may be more appropriate. First, in their study of suicide attacks within Israel and the Palestinian territories, Gupta and Mundra found they could not predict the frequency of attacks using violent provocations (i.e., decapitation strategies) with any statistical significance for two-thirds of the groups they studied from 1991 to 2003.[130] Therefore, explanations for the variation in the frequency of attacks lie elsewhere. Second, the aspects that a leader influences other than operational capability, such as changing organizational culture or how a group recruits new members,[131] may take time to manifest, thus increasing the time group members need to formulate (and act upon) a meaningful evaluation of their leader. As a result, an increase or decrease in the number of attacks may not pick up the fact that the group is imploding from within or acting out in desperation.[132] Third, planning cycles can sometimes take years, especially for the more complex "spectaculars" performed by groups like al-Qaeda. According to several accounts, planning for the 9/11 attacks began as early as seven years prior to 2001. It is unlikely they would have been called off in the event bin Laden was killed or captured in the two years prior to September 11.[133] Additionally, there is speculation that a number of so-called retaliation attacks conducted by terrorist groups after a leader has been killed or captured are actually justified by the groups ex post facto following the decapitation event and would have occurred anyway because of extended planning cycles.[134]

The most comprehensive attempt to test leadership decapitation effectiveness thus far is that by Jenna Jordan.[135] She concludes that decapitation strategies are not only ineffective but may also be counterproductive, extending the survival time of groups that would have dissolved otherwise.[136] Jordan's dependent variable is whether or not the group survived more than two years after experiencing a leadership decapitation event. Here Jordan may be setting too high a standard for counterterrorism policies. Limiting the time horizon to two years is a reasonable time horizon to evaluate a policy, but I believe there are two reasons to consider longer time horizons. First, limiting the evaluation period to two years only looks at the short-term effects of decapitation on the terrorist group. This is a problem if one believes the effects of decapitation on a terrorist group persist (or can persist) longer than two years. Second, if we agree that there are no "silver bullet" solutions in counterterrorism, then we should not rely solely on "silver bullet"–like time horizons to evaluate counterterrorism policies. Although examining the short-term effects is definitely important, policymakers should also consider the long-term effects of the policies they employ. If politicians have a bias, especially politicians in Western democracies, it is to base decisions on their short-term results rather than their long-term value.

Additionally, Jordan's argument is weakened in other ways. First, her definition of what constitutes a leader is too broad: "Leadership is defined as either the top leader of an organization or any member of the upper echelon who holds a position of authority within the organization."[137] For many terrorist groups, this distinction is very difficult to accurately determine. Information about the top leader in a terrorist group is often difficult to acquire, let alone information about those "holding a position of authority within the organization." Jordan employs a database with 290 observations of decapitation among ninety-six terrorist groups from 1945 to 2004, but unlike Mannes, she does not explain her reasons for selecting the groups that she analyzed, nor does she include a list of groups in her appendix.[138] Jordan uses logistic regression, and as a result, she cannot account for right-censored observations within the data set.[139] In other words, Jordan cannot say what ultimately happens to those groups that have had their leaders decapitated within the two years prior to her study ending, nor can she say what may happen to the terrorist groups that are still active but have not experienced decapitation when her study ends.[140] Other types of models, such as survival models (also called event-history models or hazard models), are capable of mitigating these types of problems.[141]

The Plan Ahead

Leadership should be an important variable in explaining the behavior of terrorist groups, including why they form and dissolve. The organization should be the unit of analysis in determining why this is so. The influence of terrorist leaders is nonexistent in macro-level explanations of terrorism, and the individual approach focuses too much on the foot soldier and does not capture the leader-follower dynamic that is so powerful in terrorist organizations.[142] Although terrorist leaders are instrumental in the formation of groups, this is difficult to predict ex ante. It is easier to provide evidence to explain how they are involved in the dissolution of terrorist groups.

The first task in this book is to justify the argument that leaders are important in explaining terrorist group behavior. The organizational features of terrorist groups are fundamentally different than they are in other organizational types. These features allow leaders in these organizations to affect organizational performance to a large degree. What theoretical evidence supports the assumption that the removal of a terrorist leader will have more of an impact on a terrorist group than the removal of a CEO from an economic firm? Using concepts from the literature on organizational theory and leadership, I develop a functional typology of organizations where leaders matter most. This is the focus of chapter 2.

In chapter 3, I focus on terrorist groups and their leaders. Terrorist leaders are different from their followers in many ways, and this difference has important implications for the effectiveness of decapitation strategies. I also introduce the literature on leadership succession and show how it applies to our understanding of terrorist organizations. Finally, I explain why group duration should be an important dependent variable in evaluating counterterrorism policy, and I then present hypotheses to be tested in the next chapter.

I focus on group duration for several reasons. First, I believe it is an important and understudied dependent variable. Although the conventional wisdom in the field suggests that 90 percent of all terrorist groups last less than a year and the remaining 10 percent last less than a decade,[143] few studies have actually used empirical evidence to support such claims.[144] In fact, Rapoport's untested assertion became the conventional wisdom, when it really should never have been treated as a research finding in the first place. I explain why in chapter 4.

Second, since recent U.S. national security strategies specifically identify disrupting and destroying terrorist groups as a primary goal in U.S. counterterrorism efforts, group duration is important because it has been argued that "terrorism is rarely abandoned as long as the organization using it continues to exist."[145] Although some academics and policymakers promote strategies aimed at taming terrorist groups and rehabilitating them into becoming legitimate organizations by entering the political process, U.S. counterterrorism strategy, while recognizing the need to address the political grievances that contribute to terrorism, unmistakably adopts an offensive focus. The 2006 *NSCT* explicitly states that "the fight must be taken to the enemy, to keep them on the run."[146] Additionally, the United States has traditionally promoted a tough stance of not negotiating with groups that resort to terrorism.[147] Terrorist groups like Hamas that have entered state politics as legitimate actors have not stopped using terrorism as a tactic, even after winning a majority of parliamentary seats in several elections. If states had to rank-order their most preferred outcome when it comes to terrorist organizations that threaten the security of the state, I believe policymakers would rank destruction of the group over rehabilitating them, as rehabilitation would most likely be a long and uncertain process in almost every case.

Third, studying terrorist group duration is important because once groups have conducted terrorist acts, "psychological pressures and organizational politics are likely to encourage the continuation of violence even if it becomes counterproductive in an instrumental sense."[148] Even if a terrorist group remains intact yet renounces terrorism, however, the skills and knowledge it acquired to function clandestinely are well adapted to performing other illicit activities, such as drug trafficking, diamond smuggling, or kidnapping for ransom.[149] The Shining Path's past activity in the Peruvian drug trade serves as one of several examples of groups using their clandestine experience for purposes other than political terrorism, and it shows why governments often require complete disarmament and demobilization of the group.[150]

I test the hypotheses generated in chapter 3 in the next chapter by using an original data set that includes 207 terrorist organizations and their leaders from 1970 to 2008 and spans sixty-five countries. I discuss in detail how I collected and coded the data and how this data set is different from previous data sets. I also explain the difficulties and shortcomings of data collection in this field and present some descriptive statistics of the groups in my data set. After controlling for a number of organization- and state-level factors, I test these hypotheses using a Cox proportional hazards model to determine whether decapitation events increase or decrease the mortality rate of terrorist organizations. I also explain how other factors affect terrorist group duration, such as the type of method chosen for decapitation (killing versus capturing the leader), the frequency of leadership turnover, the roles played by allied and rival groups, and the difference between removing the organization's founder as opposed to successor leaders.

Finally, to better understand the micro-level processes that occur after leadership decapitation in terrorist groups, I conducted an in-depth case study of Hamas from 1987 to the present day. Hamas represents a "least likely" case that shows the scope and limits of my theory. Despite experiencing several decapitation events, Hamas remains an active group today. Although this could plausibly be seen as a favorite case for critics of decapitation strategies, the Hamas case study provides evidence that shows how decapitation affected the group's willingness to sign cease-fires and its ability to conduct terrorist attacks.

I conclude with a chapter that summarizes the main findings and policy recommendations and also suggests where research in counterterrorism should head in the future, including possible extensions to the methods used in this book as well as new ways to exploit the original data set presented here. In the end, the most important takeaway from this analysis is that leadership decapitation is not a panacea for U.S. counterterrorism.

Although it will likely always remain an attractive tool for policymakers because it is domestically popular, enjoys bipartisan support, and provides tangible metrics that the government is actually doing something, it is a controversial tool with substantial disadvantages. My intention with this book is not to champion the tactic of leadership decapitation, but to provide policymakers with more nuanced information about what this tactic can and cannot do. As with evaluating any policy or tactic, decision makers should consider both the short- and long-term implications and conduct a cost-benefit analysis based on the final results.

Limitations

With that said, two major problems confront any serious analysis of decapitation tactics and their impact on terrorist group behavior and duration. First, it is difficult to accurately determine whether killing or capturing a terrorist group leader is the most important variable in ending terrorist groups. For example, consider a terrorist group that has been experiencing organizational decline for a host of other reasons that are unrelated to leadership and on its "last legs," so to speak. If such an ill-fated group ended soon after its leader was killed or captured, it would be foolish to interpret leadership decapitation as the sole reason, or even the most important reason, for the group's demise. Additionally, some may argue that only "bad" or incompetent terrorist groups allow their leaders to be killed or captured, and that decapitation is therefore a symptom of a group dysfunction rather than a causal variable that facilitates the demise of the group sooner than expected.

Since opening the organizational "black box" of terrorist groups is often more difficult because of their clandestine nature than it is for conventional political organizations and economic firms, dissecting which variables cause organizational decline in terrorist groups is problematic. In order to account for a potential omitted variable problem and show that losing a leader was a causal variable in an organization's decline instead of a symptom of a dysfunctional group, I differentiated cases of leadership succession to include incidents where the leader was killed or captured as well as cases where the leader was removed for other reasons unrelated to a state's counterterrorism strategies. For example, I coded for leaders that were thrown out of the organization by group members, leaders who stepped down for personal reasons to include voluntary resignations, and those who died from natural causes, car accidents, and plane crashes.

If leadership decapitation is, in fact, a symptom of dysfunctional organizations, and not, as I believe, an event that creates the conditions for organizational decline, then we should expect to find no correlation between leadership removal via these other means and organizational decline. To put it another way, if we believe decapitation is somehow correlated with groups that would have ended anyway, then we should find no such correlation with groups whose leaders have died in power because of natural causes and unforeseen accidents. After all, if one assumes that dying of natural causes or dying in a car accident or plane crash is a random event that could happen to any terrorist group leader, then there should be no discernible pattern indicating that these types of groups are more likely to end than other groups. However, I found a positive correlation between group death and leaders who die of natural causes and accidents. Although it is impossible to completely rid any study of omitted variable problems, I believe this is compelling evidence that leadership succession is an important variable in causing organizational decline and is independent of other group characteristics.

The second limitation of this book is somewhat related to the one already detailed. How does one differentiate between cases where a state purposefully crafts and executes an operation aimed solely at killing or capturing a terrorist group leader, such as the carefully planned and executed targeted killing campaign waged by Israel against Hamas and Hezbollah or the U.S. mission to kill or capture Osama bin Laden, and cases where killing or capturing a terrorist group leader is part of a larger operation aimed at destroying the entire group? In the latter example, killing or capturing the leader may not even be the primary goal of the operation. Therefore, is it fair to attribute organizational decline to operations in which the leader is killed or captured along with the majority of the group in a large-scale effort in the same way we would in cases where the leader is assassinated by a sniper's bullet?

Unfortunately, because of issues of data availability, this is a difficult problem to solve in decapitation studies. States have incentives to take credit for any operation that kills or captures a group's leader and act as though leadership decapitation was the focus of their mission, even if it was really the result of blind luck instead of prior planning. If the state's military or security forces happen to kill or capture the terrorist group leader in an operation, the state will most likely pretend that the operation was designed from the outset with this objective in mind. Therefore, it is difficult to parcel out the operations that are primarily focused on killing or capturing the group's leader and those intended simply to destroy the group or its capabilities. In the original data set in this study, a majority of the cases where a leader was killed or captured also involved the killing or capture of other group members, but very few involved catastrophic cases where a majority of the group was killed or captured.[151] Although I do not control for these nuances in coding decapitation events, these limitations are important to consider when evaluating this study and one that I hope future researchers can resolve.

CHAPTER 2

Organizations and Leaders

In March 2017, *Forbes* magazine named Theo Epstein the world's greatest leader.[1] He bested other world leaders such as Pope Francis and Angela Merkel and business icons Jack Ma of Alibaba and Jeff Bezos of Amazon. Unless you are a sports fan, you have probably never heard of Theo Epstein. He is, however, credited with leading the Boston Red Sox to their first World Series title in 86 years before leaving for Chicago, where he led the seemingly star-crossed Cubs to their first World Series win in 108 years. Yet Epstein never filled out a lineup card. He never threw a pitch, made a diving catch, or hit a game-winning home run. In fact, he never even put on a uniform. Epstein was the general manager of both organizations, a front office job that is primarily responsible for assembling all of the players and coaches on the team.

The Cubs valued Epstein so much that the organization gave him a five-year contract for $50 million in 2017. To put this into perspective, Kris Bryant, the team's star player and the 2016 National League MVP, was paid just over $1 million in 2017.

When Epstein found out that *Forbes* named him the world's greatest leader, he thought it was ridiculous. "Um, I can't even get my dog to stop peeing in the house," he quipped to a reporter. "If [Cubs player Ben] Zobrist's ball is three inches farther off the line, I'm on the hot seat for a failed five-year plan. I'm not even the best leader in our organization."[2] Although Epstein was likely being self-deprecating for effect in that interview, he raises an interesting question about how we think about the relationship between leaders and organizational outcomes. Was Epstein's leadership as the general manager of the Chicago Cubs *that* important? How much credit does Epstein deserve for the Cubs' wins? How much blame does he deserve for their losses?

Before one can say that leaders matter in terrorist groups, we need to answer whether leaders matter when it comes to organizational performance in any organization. If so, when do they matter, and in what contexts will they matter most? The findings in this chapter suggest that leaders matter in explaining organizational behavior, but they matter more in some organizational types than in others.

The literature on leadership has mainly focused on how leaders affect organizational performance in specific types of organizations, such as economic firms, political organizations, the military, and sports teams. The conclusions drawn from these more conventional organizational types are often applied to organizations that are less frequently studied. However, although all organizations share at least some defining characteristics, organizations can differ in important ways, and little has been written about how leaders affect performance across different types of organizations, particularly illicit, clandestine organizations such as terrorist groups. Some findings from research on the more conventional and frequently studied organizations can be seamlessly applied across all organizations, while others cannot. Unfortunately, this problem can lead to misinformed policy decisions.

Thus, in order to understand how leaders affect outcomes in different types of organizations, this chapter proposes a typology of organizations based on three dimensions: whether violence is a central part of the organization's core purpose, whether the organization operates clandestinely, and to what extent values and ideology are central to the organization's core purpose versus to what extent it is interested in profit maximization. These dimensions affect organizational behavior and the influence leaders wield in important ways. They have an impact on how intense the loyalty is between leaders and followers, the skill sets needed to thrive (and survive) as the overall leader, and the organization's culture, learning capacity, and ability to adapt to leadership succession.

This chapter proceeds as follows. First, I explain the literature on leadership and organizational behavior that serves as the genesis for this typology. Next, I present the typology and its different dimensions, explain how each affects important aspects of leadership influence, and propose examples of organizations that fit each idealized type. Third, I conduct focused comparisons of organizational types that differ only in one of the three dimensions while holding others constant. Fourth, I discuss how these organizational types cope with the stress and instability caused by leadership succession and outline the organizational types in which replacing the leader should be most difficult. This chapter provides a theoretical foundation and framework that not only explain why certain organizational types are more affected by leadership succession than others but also suggests that terrorist groups feature certain organizational characteristics that make them especially susceptible to instability when they lose a top leader.

Why a Functional Typology of Where Leaders Matter Most?

The organizational typology presented here explains why leaders matter more in some organizational contexts than others. It is based on concepts from several different subfields within the organizational theory literature. As discussed in the previous chapter, scholars studying leadership have essentially agreed to disagree about the extent to which leaders influence organizational performance.[3] A plausible reason for this lack of consensus lies in the three different ways the literature looks at leadership effectiveness.

First, early scholars used attribution theory to suggest that leaders possessing certain traits and characteristics were more successful than those without these traits.[4] At the risk of oversimplifying this line of research, one could say that this approach subscribed to the idea that leaders were born, not made. Put another way, leaders with the requisite traits were successful; those that did not possess them were ineffective.

Second, behavioralists in the 1950s bucked against this trend and argued that it was the leaders' behavior, not their innate traits, that ultimately determined leadership effectiveness. This approach led to studying the effectiveness of different leadership styles and approaches, such as the hard-line autocratic style or the more democratic version of participative leadership. Here, leaders may not be born with specific traits, but they could be effective if they behaved in a certain way. Both the attribution and behavioral approaches, however, "suffer[ed] from a tendency to look for simple answers to complex questions."[5] Additionally, this "early research mostly ignored how leaders influenced people by appealing to their ideological values, helped interpret the meaning of events, and facilitated adaptation and change in a turbulent environment."[6]

More recently, leadership scholars have focused on a more nuanced approach based on contextual factors that include the individual organization and its environment. This third approach, commonly referred to as the situational approach or contingency theory, moved away from the "one-size-fits-all" nature of previous approaches, but it is often criticized for being so situationally dependent that it cannot explain leadership in broader, more general terms. Scholars using this approach focus on the aspects of leadership that apply to one specific organizational type or environment but not others.[7]

Today, scholars of leadership have made attempts to resolve the common critique that the situational approach is too specific to be of general use. For example, some have tried to ascertain which type of leadership will be most effective across larger swaths of organizational types than specific firms or industries. Building on Max Weber's conception of the three different sources of authority—rational-legal, traditional, and charismatic—James MacGregor Burns, a noted twentieth-century leadership theorist, proposed the concept of transformational leadership.[8] According to Burns, it is useful to conceive of two types of leadership: transactional and transformational leadership. Transactional leadership appeals to the self-interests of both leaders and followers. "Transactional leaders induce followers to behave in ways desired by the leader in exchange for some good desired by the follower."[9] In economic firms, business owners exchange pay and status for work effort.[10] In politics, politicians exchange policy promises for votes and campaign contributions. Transformational leadership, like transactional leadership, must appeal at some basic level to the self-interests of both leaders and followers, but central to this type of leadership is the emphasis on values and emotion. Transformational leadership thus transcends short-term goals of both leaders and followers and essentially asks followers to do more for less in pursuit of goals that are less "specific, tangible, and calculable."[11] All transformational leaders are therefore transactional leaders in some sense, but not all transactional leaders can be transformational. Moreover, some organizational types are more conducive to transactional leadership than they are to transformational leadership and vice versa.[12]

Thus the situational approach is relatively new to the leadership literature, and there are many opportunities for additional research. Compared to the hundreds of studies done on leadership traits and behaviors, Yukl argues that "there have been relatively few studies on specific types of leadership . . . and the situations where they are relevant."[13]

This point, and a particular finding from organizational theorist Glenn Carroll, served as my primary motivation to develop a typology of organizations to explain leadership effectiveness. Carroll wrote an article in 1984 that challenged previous studies of leadership succession and its impact on organizational performance, namely because previous works failed to consider the organizational context of the succession event.[14] Carroll argued that previous work on the organizational performance of baseball teams, measured in team wins before and after the team's manager was replaced, was not applicable to leadership succession in economic firms.[15] Thus, if leadership succession affects organizational performance differently in sports teams than it does in economic firms, there should be differences across other types of organizations as well, such as terrorist groups. In fact, a common criticism of the leadership literature, especially the literature focusing on leadership effectiveness, speaks to this point. One of the noted shortcomings in the literature is that "researchers have not controlled, or taken into account organizational variables in research designs," even though "organizational variables sharply influence behavior and performance."[16] As a result, "failing to control for, or incorporate organizational variables confounds research results."[17]

The literature on political organizations also motivated an interest in constructing this typology, particularly the work of Terry Moe on the American presidency. Paralleling the literature on leadership in the middle of the twentieth century, scholars in American politics were using leadership styles to explain the variation in organizational performance of U.S. presidents. According to scholars of this era such as Richard Neustadt and Alexander George, modern presidents could no longer rely solely on their institutional powers to get their way. Instead, "the power of the president was the power to persuade," thus making the president's reputation and prestige the new coin of the realm.[18] Personality and leadership style suddenly mattered more than presidents' institutional power, and they could help explain why some presidents were successful in implementing their agendas while others floundered.[19]

Moe disagreed and suggested that the president's role as an *institutional* actor, not his personality or individual leadership style, was a better predictor of behavior and outcomes.[20] To Moe, it was the position, not the individual, that ultimately mattered most in determining presidential behavior. All modern presidents operate within the same institutional structure and therefore face similar constraints, including a limited time to get things accomplished, institutional checks and balances, and the principal-agent problem of controlling the bureaucracy. As a result, all presidents, regardless of their individual personalities, leadership styles, or political ideologies, use the most efficient resources available to them—politicization of the bureaucracy and centralization of more control under their immediate purview—to cope with these constraints. It is important to note the qualification—that presidents choose the most efficient resources *available* to them, not the most efficient resources. As Moe states, the "American public bureaucracy is not designed to be effective."[21] Rather, the bureaucracy is a reflection of the structure of the system and of the constraints and resources of the actors within it.

We know that organizations have different structures, face different institutional and environmental constraints, and differ in their ability to marshal resources to mitigate these constraints. To be sure, the American public bureaucracy would look a lot different if political leaders had other resources and operated under a different set of constraints, such as a parliamentary system, for example. Moreover, political organizations are but one type of organization, and it would be a mistake to generalize the influence presidents wield over the bureaucracy to the influence leaders wield in other types of organizations.[22] As Carroll noted, comparing leadership effectiveness in economic firms and baseball teams is problematic because the organizational context is simply different. If this is true, and I believe it is, then comparing leadership effectiveness in other types of organizations should be equally as problematic. Yet this has not stopped some scholars from criticizing decapitation strategies in counterterrorism policy on the grounds that they have not worked in other organizational types in the past. For example, decapitation tactics have largely failed against state regimes,[23] drug cartels,[24] and religious organizations such as the Mormon Church and the Christian Scientists, cults, and insurgencies.[25] Thus many people who are critical of decapitation tactics base their arguments on evidence and anecdotes from other organizations that are really quite different from terrorist groups. Organizations like state governments and drug cartels are different types of organizations that vary across multiple dimensions, and as I will show next, these dimensions have meaningful implications on leadership influence within each type.

The Three Dimensions That Matter Most

In which organizations are leaders able to substantively influence organizational performance? Put another way, where do leaders matter most? The typology put forth in this book categorizes different types of organizations across three dimensions. By no means are these the only dimensions through which organizational types may differ. I believe, however, that these dimensions matter most in explaining leader influence in organizational outcomes. Following Carroll, I focus on different organizational contexts. Following Moe, I focus on the institutional and environmental constraints that leaders face and the solutions they have available to mitigate them. The three dimensions are violence, clandestineness, and the degree to which the organization is values based versus profit based.

Violence

Not surprisingly, violent organizations are those that incorporate physical force into their core purpose.[26] Examples include militaries, police forces, drug cartels, street gangs, terrorist groups, warlords, mercenaries, and private military companies such as Blackwater. The differences between violent organizations and nonviolent organizations can be found in the nature of the leader-follower dynamic within the organization, how influential leaders are in affecting organizational performance, and the skill sets needed to both thrive and survive as a leader in this kind of environment.

It should first be noted that in the psychology literature, social identity theory suggests that there will be a baseline level of cohesion that exists in all organizations simply because of the distinction made between in-group and out-group members.[27] Therefore, all groups will exhibit some level of bonding and cohesion, at least enough to overcome the collective action problem, or they will cease to exist eventually.[28] This holds true for both violent and nonviolent organizations.

Beyond this base level of group cohesion, however, we should expect violent organizations to be more cohesive than their nonviolent counterparts for two different but related reasons: the fact that they use violence and the fact that they often live in danger of being victims of violence themselves. The fact that they use violence has an effect on the organization, in and of itself, even if the group does not face any danger of having violence perpetrated against it.[29] Cohen argues that armed groups in Sierra Leone often relied on gang raping of civilians as a method of socialization to enhance group cohesion.[30] The Lord's Resistance Army, a violent organization operating in Uganda and Sudan, is an example of a violent organization that developed cohesion through participation in violent acts even though organization members operated in an environment where they faced very little resistance and were not in fear of being victims of violence themselves. This group became (and remains) notorious for its brutality, including many senseless incidents of rape, murder, and torture against a population that was virtually powerless to defend itself. The use of violence in these types of organizations creates a bond and cohesiveness that are not as commonly seen in nonviolent organizations.

Additionally, because many violent organizations operate in environments where they too can become victims of violence, organizational bonding and cohesion are enhanced in another way. Whereas the use of violence can be seen as a collective bonding event, as already shown, similar to a rite of passage in which group cohesion is enhanced simply through members participating in the act, living under the constant threat of violence forces group members to rely on one another for their individual security. For violent organizations that operate "in the face of external danger and pursuit, [the group] is the only source of security."[31] This threat could come from either the state or rival groups. It can even come from the environment in which the group performs its tasks.[32] Of course, some organizations are more at risk than others. A manual from the U.S. military reads: "While members of some professions engage in dangerous tasks daily, only members of the Armed Forces can be ordered to place their lives in peril anywhere at any time. The obligations they undertake, risking life and well-being for the greater good, are in many ways extraordinary."[33] Regardless of the source of the violent threat, the important thing to note is that in these hostile environments, a group member's fate often rests in the hands of another member, a situation that results in more intra-organizational trust and cohesion.

Not only are the bonds between individual members more cohesive in violent organizations, but the bonds between leaders and followers in these organizations are more intense as well. The occupational hazards of violent organizations can include injury and death, and as a result, the leader-follower dynamic is different than in other organizations.[34] Decisions made by leaders can have fateful consequences for group members and vice versa.

Since trust and cohesion are essential elements in preserving both individual and organizational survival, leaders exercise more influence and control over more aspects of their subordinates than they do in nonviolent organizations. Leaders in violent organizations often wield "awesome decision-making and punitive powers" that would seem intrusive in other organizational settings.[35] The well-known images of drill instructors reprimanding new recruits at a military boot camp or police academy serve as examples of the intense nature of the leader-follower dynamic in these organizations, as do the bloody initiation ceremonies performed by street gangs or the loyalty tests required of new terrorist group and drug cartel members. In violent organizations, followers are often labeled as subordinates; in nonviolent organizations, they are often labeled as employees. This distinction may be subtle, but it is important in properly characterizing the leader-follower dynamic in these organizations.

The requisites for leadership in violent organizations are often different from those in nonviolent organizations. For example, it is not uncommon for street gang leaders to be the physically largest, most violent, and strongest members in their organization.[36] These traits would seem odd if they determined leadership roles in economic firms or political organizations. Leadership traits that are preferable in violent organizations are sometimes not compatible in nonviolent organizations. Noting that both Winston Churchill and Charles de Gaulle were removed from office following World War II, former president Richard Nixon observed in his book on leadership that "the qualities that make a man a great leader in war are not necessarily those that the people want in peace."[37]

Because membership in violent organizations often entails not only performing acts of violence but also exposing oneself to violence, a behavior that goes against our natural survival mechanism, leadership in these organizations is often more inspirational and motivational than in other organizations. Unlike the more formal and traditional forms of authority that are common in many nonviolent organizations, "charisma is the warrior's basis of authority."[38] The expectations that followers have of their leaders in violent organizations are also often higher than those of leaders in nonviolent organizations. The most cogent example of this comes from war, where leaders deemed incompetent or detrimental to unit success were sometimes killed by their own subordinates during firefights, a term popularized as "fragging" during the Vietnam War.

Again, this type of extreme follower behavior is certainly rare or nonexistent in nonviolent organizations. When company employees deem Larry from accounting or Jane from human resources as incompetent leaders, their lives are not in jeopardy.

The fact that violent organizations are often more cohesive than nonviolent organizations has important implications for leadership succession as well. Grusky found that leadership succession is likely to cause greater instability in organizations where members have established extremely close ties to one another.[39] Since violent organizations can lose their leaders quite frequently because of the occupational hazards of operating in hostile environments, and since this environment also forces groups to be naturally more cohesive, leadership succession in violent organizations should cause more instability than it does in nonviolent organizations. Of course, some violent organizations diligently plan for these succession contingencies ahead of time. In the U.S. Army, for example, it is standard practice to train subordinates to assume leadership roles two ranks above their own. This is because in combat, the probability of losing a leader is higher than in most organizations, and in the heat of battle, replacing that leader with a competent successor can often determine mission success or failure, not to mention the prevention of friendly loss of life. In violent organizations where the loss of a leader occurs less frequently and under less chaotic circumstances, such as a local police force, the need to plan for an unanticipated leadership succession is less important. Regardless of the preparation involved prior to succession, losing a leader because of injury or death is an understandably traumatic event even for the most prepared organizations, and especially so for the most cohesive organizations. Thus, we should expect leadership succession to be more unstable in violent organizations than in nonviolent organizations.

These distinctions about leadership in violent and nonviolent organizations lead to the following propositions:

Proposition 1: Leaders are more important in affecting organizational performance in violent organizations than in nonviolent organizations.

Proposition 2: The organizational context that violent organizations operate within is more conducive to transformational leadership than transactional leadership.

Proposition 3: Leadership succession is more likely to cause more instability in violent organizations than it does in nonviolent organizations.

Clandestineness

Clandestine organizations operate underground to avoid being discovered by either the state or mainstream society.[40] Examples of clandestine organizations include cults, drug cartels, smuggling networks, organized crime syndicates, terrorist groups, and even nonillicit groups such as the Free Masons in the United States. Of course, some of these groups can be more clandestine than others. In other words, some groups may operate deep underground where every aspect of the organization is kept hidden from the public, whereas other groups could have their members live relatively normal lives and conduct only some of their business underground. An example of a group operating deep underground would be a terrorist organization in an extremely oppressive state. In this case, the group operates underground because it *has* to.[41] Outsiders learning of its existence would surely seek to destroy it.

On the other hand, a group can also operate clandestinely not because it *has* to, but because it *chooses* to. It may or may not be an illicit organization. Certain organizations might operate clandestinely because they fear the outside world or because they wish to isolate themselves for cultural or normative reasons. Examples of these groups include the Skull and Bones organization at Yale, the ultra-orthodox Jewish population in Israel,[42] or religious cults like the Unification Church and the Heaven's Gate organization in the United States.[43] Some of these nonillicit groups even go on to become terrorist groups. For example, Aum Shinrikyo operated as a nonillicit, clandestine organization for almost a decade before conducting its first terrorist attack in 1994. The group even ran legal but covert operations, including uranium mining from an Australian compound in the years prior to its infamous subway attack in Japan.[44] For purposes of analytical clarity, I focus more on illicit clandestine organizations in this chapter.

The differences between clandestine organizations and those operating out in the open are important for several reasons. First, there is more organizational uncertainty within clandestine groups than in nonclandestine organizations. The lack of transparency prevents outsiders from learning about the organization and forces prospective members to learn about the organization from those within the group, and often the group's leaders. Second, because of the incessant need for operational security, especially for illicit organizations, clandestine organizations are generally less institutionalized.

This has important implications for organizational learning, adaptation, and leadership succession. Finally, operating underground and in seclusion can lead to a dysfunctional organizational culture and poor decision making.

EFFECTS OF UNCERTAINTY AND CLANDESTINENESS

Organizations that operate clandestinely face a great deal of uncertainty. Illicit organizations that operate underground and live in a hostile environment are constantly in danger of being infiltrated, compromised, and destroyed by outsiders. Because of this uncertainty, followers depend on their leaders for their safety and security more so than in other types of organizations, and especially in illicit and violent ones. In these organizations, "having entered a world of conspiracy and danger, the members are bound together before a common threat of exposure, imprisonment, or death. Theirs is truly a common fate."[45] Since members of clandestine organizations are often isolated and detached from society, followers are more reliant on leaders to give them information and to help them frame reality. In her study of underground organizations in Germany and Italy, della Porta found that "the risks of being discovered induced members to concentrate decision making in the hands of a small group of clandestine leaders."[46] In these tight-knit organizations, members "tend to believe only information from sources they trust, and the only trustworthy person would be someone who shared their beliefs. Leaders exercise a dominant influence."[47] (In these organizations, leaders "play a key role in sense-making and sense-breaking.")[48]

To combat the stress and uncertainty that often accompanies living underground, clandestine organizations tend to be more cohesive and develop closer bonds than nonclandestine organizations. In della Porta's study, "affective ties were even more important in the underground than in legal organizations."[49] Life in the underground can "build intensely personalized loyalties of rank and file toward the leaders, far beyond the depersonalized and symbolic loyalty given to 'the people upstairs' " of more conventional, aboveground organizations.[50] After all, cohesion and loyalty to the group are essential for building group trust and maintaining operational security. This, however, also makes clandestine groups more susceptible to some psychological dysfunctions that hamper group decision making and inhibit organizational learning.

Leaders of clandestine groups have incentives to enforce uniformity and compliance, but this often leads to groupthink, particularly in smaller organizations, and a lack of creative thinking on the part of group members.[51] Since membership in clandestine groups is, by nature, more selective than membership in other types of organizations, the cost of entry is usually large enough to discourage the faint of heart. For those that make it into the group, the cost of exiting could be even greater, particularly in violent, clandestine groups that operate illicit networks.[52] In their three-year field study of gangs in St. Louis, Decker and Van Winkle found that "the beating administered at the time of leaving the gang was more severe than at the time of entry."[53] For terrorist groups, "deviations from the group's way of thinking are seen as signs of lack of faith and commitment."[54] Challenging decisions made in these organizations "is tantamount to challenging the legitimacy of the movement."[55] Before joining some drug cartels, leaders demand that new recruits provide the names and addresses of immediate family members to make them think twice before crossing the group or cooperating with authorities if they are ever caught.[56] Thus it is not difficult to see why group members in clandestine organizations want to fit in and avoid rocking the boat. Although she was referring to terrorist organizations, the following passage from Crenshaw describes how dissent could be perceived in many clandestine groups:

> The dynamics of interaction within the terrorist organization prevent members from challenging collectively-held belief systems or for the group as a whole to change. In particular, the tendencies toward cohesion and solidarity present in all primary groups lead to the suppression of dissent and the internalization of group standards and norms. Individuals become extremely dependent on the group. Deliberate organizational strategies may be designed to enforce uniformity and to insulate the group from reality. Challenges to orthodoxy are threats to individual identity and group existence.[57]

Since decisions made in clandestine groups usually come from the top, members are thus hesitant to disagree and offer alternatives, even if these alternatives are superior to the leaders' plans. Again, this organizational feature of clandestine groups serves to enhance the position of leaders over their followers.

EFFECTS OF CLANDESTINENESS ON ORGANIZATIONAL LEARNING

This emphasis on group cohesion not only hampers decision making in clandestine organizations but can also inhibit organizational learning. Organizational learning, in this sense, refers to the "process through which members of a group acquire new knowledge that can be applied in strategic decision-making, tactical planning, and operational activities."[58] If the desire to fit in is so overwhelming, then this may reduce the ambition and desire of group members to innovate and offer solutions to critical problems. This is why, in addition to the tendency for clandestine groups to operate as networks with autonomous or semi-autonomous cells, organizational learning and innovation may be difficult. Thus, "given the compartmented, clandestine nature of illicit networks, where robust information sharing across network nodes can be problematic, there are compelling reasons to believe that traffickers and terrorists do not learn and may be condemned to commit the same mistakes repeatedly."[59] Since creating and maintaining effective lines of communication is difficult even for nonclandestine organizations, the cellular structures commonly found in many illicit clandestine groups only exacerbate the problem, creating "inherent barriers to information flow within the organization and handicap[ing] learning for the group as a whole."[60]

Depending upon the stability of the environment and the type of organizational culture established by the group's leadership, organizational learning may be less of a problem for some clandestine groups than others.[61] Organizations will find it easier to collectively learn in stable environments where the risk of engaging in learning activities is low. For example, when al-Qaeda was operating within Afghanistan prior to 2001, it could invest heavily in organizational learning—training camps, training manuals, meetings, and so on—without worrying much about operational security because of the safe haven provided by the Taliban, the ruling regime at the time. The group could learn, make mistakes, and engage in trial and error without too much interference from outsiders. In fact, the only substantial interference al-Qaeda endured prior to 9/11 was an ineffective cruise missile attack by U.S. forces following the twin East Africa embassy bombings in 1998 that targeted abandoned training sites in Afghanistan and Sudan.

As previously stated, however, clandestine organizations rarely operate in stable environments, nor are the risks of engaging in learning activity always low. To be sure, organizational learning became much more difficult for al-Qaeda after the United States invaded Afghanistan in October 2001. Additionally, the external environment is but one element that influences organizational learning. Organizational culture also plays a role, and organizational culture is determined primarily by the group's leadership.[62] According to Jackson, the two most important factors that contribute to a pro-learning culture within an organization are a group's tolerance for risk and leadership that makes organizational learning a priority.[63] Not only do leaders influence and determine organizational culture to a large extent, but they also have the final say in regards to risk taking. For example, is the organization afraid to conduct acts with high probabilities of failure? Leaders in these organizations not only determine whether or not to act but also play a large role in determining how the organization reacts and learns from failures, if it learns at all. Leaders who create organizational cultures that reward innovation and incremental learning are more survivable than groups that punish risk taking and failed ventures.[64] In fact, "fail fast" is a mantra often heard in today's business lexicon to encourage organizations to take risks in the name of learning more than their competitors.

Illicit clandestine organizations, such as terrorist organizations or drug cartels, are constantly pursued by outsiders wanting to destroy the group. This situation creates the necessity for constant change within these organizations regarding how they conduct their business. Terrorism scholar Bruce Hoffman uses an interesting metaphor to describe this perpetual need for change: "Al Qaeda is much like a shark, which must keep moving forward no matter how slowly or incrementally, or die. Al Qaeda must constantly adapt and adjust to its enemies' efforts to stymie its plans while simultaneously identifying new targets."[65] Other types of clandestine organizations can easily relate.

Unlike their nonclandestine counterparts, clandestine organizations are more reluctant to establish long-term and well-documented routines to improve organizational efficiency. Rules govern behavior in clandestine organizations just like they do in other organizations, but they are rarely codified.[66] Nonclandestine organizations can institutionalize how they conduct business—their tactics, techniques, and procedures (TTPs)—in ways that clandestine organizations cannot because of operational security concerns. Jackson posits that "any codified or explicit knowledge maintained by a group can represent a significant vulnerability."[67] In describing the need for constant change within drug cartels, Kenney states:

> Hostility provides the most vulnerable actors in the system with a compelling motive to change their practices: their organizational survival demands it. Targeted groups that fail to change phone numbers, safe houses, and other elements of their operational "signatures" may find themselves selected out of the system, courtesy of the enforcement networks that exploit their knowledge of existing practices to track them down and eliminate them.[68] . . . Because they operate in hostile environments, trafficking enterprises often refrain from codifying their rules in written documents. Instead, rules are embodied in informal, intersubjective understandings among participants about "the way things are done around here."[69]

These "intersubjective understandings" are often determined by the group's leadership and disseminated to followers. This lack of institutionalization enhances the importance of veteran members within the group because without codified rules and regulations, new recruits are often dependent on group veterans to show them the most efficient methods. This makes sense considering that it is difficult to get open source material on how to start a religious cult or drug cartel from scratch, the best way to destroy a building, or how to communicate covertly.

This is not to say that clandestine organizations never attempt to codify rules and regulations, establish training manuals on how to conduct business, or produce paperwork that makes their organizations more efficient. They sometimes do, but they do so at their own peril. Ultimately, they run the risk of outsiders learning more about their organizations and using this knowledge to destroy them. To keep knowledge from being transferred outside the organization, clandestine groups structure their organizations so as to "both minimize the chances of such transfer and to reduce the potential damage if it does occur."[70] Al-Qaeda is an example of an organization that tried to institutionalize organizational learning by producing thousands of documents and manuals, but many of these are now in the hands of counterterror analysts, such as those in the Harmony database at West Point's Combating Terrorism Center and the documents used in the Terrorist Perspectives Project at the Institute for Defense Analyses.[71] These "treasure troves" of information, like the information found at the Sinjar camp in northwestern

Iraq in 2007, were invaluable to U.S. counterterrorism efforts in Iraq and have given counterterror analysts new insights into how al-Qaeda operated.[72] Groups wanting to improve their organizational learning by codifying rules, norms, and TTPs face a difficult trade-off: institutionalization may improve organizational learning and thus organizational effectiveness, but it may also lead to more effective counterterrorism efforts, thus reducing the chances of group survival.[73]

This point has important policy implications for bringing down illicit, clandestine groups because, as Kenney states, "over time, extremists develop the sort of experiential *metis* that is difficult to codify in knowledge-based artifacts.[74] For this reason the capture of senior militants matters, and governments can—at least temporarily—degrade the capabilities of terrorist networks by apprehending their most experienced members."[75] Timing is critical here. As more time passes and organizations age, more information can be passed between veterans and new members. If enough time passes, most or all of the "experiential *metis*" that veterans possess can be passed down to other members, and the cycle continues. If veteran members are caught or killed prior to this occurring, however, we can expect the learning curve to be steeper because groups will require time, as well as more violent activity, to regenerate comparable levels of experience. If veteran members get caught or killed *after* they have passed down their experiential *metis*, then the organization should be demonstrably less affected by leadership decapitation.

CLANDESTINENESS AND LACK OF CONSTRAINTS

As a result of this disinclination to institutionalize, leaders of clandestine organizations are free from many of the institutional constraints that bind leaders in organizations operating above ground. Leaders in nonclandestine organizations must adhere to the rules and regulations of the system and of their individual organization, whatever they may be, or risk being sanctioned. Presidents in the U.S. political system are constrained by constitutional checks and balances. Business leaders must adhere to federal, state, and local laws as well as the regulations governing their industry. In voluntary social and religious organizations, leaders adhere to traditional norms and social mores. Even the most charismatic and transformational leaders in nonclandestine organizations must operate within the rules of the game to get things accomplished.

In contrast, operating rules and procedures in many clandestine groups "are set in sand, not stone."[76] As previously stated, clandestine organizations often operate in hostile environments (whether this is actually the case, such as with illicit groups, or just perceived, as in the case of some religious cults). As a result, leaders within these organizations have tremendous flexibility to structure their organizations as they see fit, without having to adhere to too many rules and regulations. Unlike the "institutional environment that constrains—and slows down—its sovereign competitors," clandestine terrorist groups and drug cartels, "as illegal non-state actors who operate outside the rule of law, . . . lack comparable restraints." What rules they *do* institute are "informal, flexible, and generally free from legal review and external oversight."[77]

And it is not just the legal rules and regulations that clandestine groups ignore. According to Crenshaw, "terrorists of both right and left seem to see themselves as a morally superior elite to whom conventional standards of behavior do not apply."[78] David adds, "Terrorists, almost by definition, are not constrained by established norms."[79] Tucker argues that religiously motivated terrorist organizations and groups with "charismatic, all-powerful leaders" are "less subject to societal norms."[80] Of course, some norms, especially cultural and social norms, will still apply in clandestine organizations.[81] Clandestine group leaders cannot buck every social and cultural norm lest they run the risk of not having any followers, but they are definitely less constrained in a number of ways—legally, socially, and morally—than leaders in nonclandestine organizations. According to Zawodny, a scholar with personal experience with the Polish underground during World War II, "an organization that is so independent from society that it has no fear of society's response presents a dangerous situation—the terrorists operate under *no* constraints."[82] Although Zawodny may have gone a bit too far in saying underground organizations such as terrorist groups operate without *any* constraints, it is safe to say that underground organizations do indeed have more discretion to break from the norm than their aboveground counterparts. And as a result of this increased discretion, leaders play a crucial role in determining the organizational culture, learning capacity, and establishment of institutional norms within their groups. They wield influence over all aspects of their organizations, influence that would make many of their counterparts in nonclandestine organizations surely envious.

Thus, because of the deference imparted to leaders as a result of groupthink, the lack of institutionalization because of operational security concerns, and the absence of the institutional constraints and societal norms that bind leaders in other organizations, I submit the following proposition about leaders in clandestine organizations:

Proposition 4: Leaders are more important in affecting organizational performance in clandestine organizations than in nonclandestine organizations.

Values-Based Versus Profit-Based Organizations

Organizations can also vary across an ideological dimension, with organizations that are purely driven by profit existing at one end and organizations driven primarily by values at the other end. In other words, one can imagine a continuum in which organizations that have values-oriented goals as their core purpose existing at one extreme and organizations completely devoid of these goals at the other. Examples of the former could include political parties, social movements, public service organizations, religious organizations, and cults. These types of organizations can represent a broad range of values. For example, some political organizations may be interested in establishing a political order based on a particular ideology, whereas other political organizations might be more oriented toward a single issue. These single-issue organizations might focus on eradicating a specific disease like AIDS or may be solely interested in a humanitarian issue like genocide, human rights, or children's health. Examples of profit-driven organizations could include mercenaries, private military companies, drug cartels, and economic firms. For some of these organizations, values and ideology are their raison d'être, while for others they are inconsequential to the group's overall purpose.

This dimension is important because leaders in values-driven organizations often require a different skill set than their counterparts in non-values-driven organizations. Transformational or charismatic leaders are thought to be more effective in ideological organizations than they are in nonideological organizations.[83] In other words, charismatic leaders are more important to the success of ideological organizations because there is often a need to articulate "a vision that draws an emotional and enthusiastic response"[84] since the goals may not always be "specific, tangible, and calculable."[85] Thus it is usually not enough for leaders in ideological organizations to be subject matter experts in their field or competent managers if they want to recruit and maintain membership within their organizations; they must be able to communicate, evoke confidence, and serve as role models for their followers.[86] They not only manage; they motivate and inspire.

Scholars explaining change in organizational performance in the business world sometimes use different terminology to describe this distinction between transformational and transactional leadership, but the concept is essentially the same. In their review of management turnover in economic firms, Furtado and Karan use the terms *firm-specific capital* and *general human capital* to explain why leadership succession is difficult in some firms and not others.[87] A firm can expect to have problems when managers with "firm-specific capital" leave their organization, whereas no significant change should occur when managers with only "general human capital," the type of capital that is easily transferable between firms and quickly substitutable, leave the organization. Put another way, managers who possess good managerial skills can be easily replaced, while those with intricate knowledge of the organization cannot. There is less mobility between leaders in ideological and values-driven organizations than there is in profit-driven economic firms. An excellent politician and leader in the Republican Party is unlikely to be replaced by one from the Democratic Party, even if the Democratic candidate is a better overall politician and leader. Leaders in these types of organizations have much more "firm-specific capital" than their counterparts in nonideological organizations. Thus, transactional leadership is more analogous to "general human capital" and competent management, whereas "firm-specific capital" is more analogous to transformational leadership. The former is easier to replace, while the latter is generally more difficult to replace.

Similar to clandestine organizations, ideological organizations often operate under more uncertainty than nonideological organizations. As a result, "when followers' efforts are directed toward implementation of ideological goals and values, or when their efforts are directed toward creating or delivering some social good," followers are more dependent on their leaders' vision and framing.[88] This is in contrast to many nonideological organizations, which clearly do not lend themselves to this type of charismatic leadership. In nonideological organizations, or "institutions directed exclusively to economic ends," with "roles requiring highly routine, non-thinking effort," charismatic leaders would theoretically be less effective.[89] In these organizations, the demands for leadership are based more on performance than on values, and the image of leaders as role models is considerably less important than their managerial competency, and maybe even irrelevant. Although it has been stated before, it is important to reiterate that all transformational leaders must act as transactional leaders in some capacity in order to succeed, but not all transactional leaders have what it takes to be transformational leaders, nor do they need to be transformational to succeed in their organization.[90]

Within values-based organizations, ideological salience will vary across group leaders and followers, and ideology will be more salient with first-generation members than with younger, nth-generation members. For example, Shapiro argues that lower-level terrorist group members are often less committed than their leaders.[91] Furthermore, "the leadership may possess more complex and differentiated belief structures than do followers."[92] In fact, in some ideological organizations, "the basis for the authority of leaders may lie precisely in the ability to articulate beliefs held implicitly by followers. Or authority may derive from the relevance of the leader's background to the general belief system."[93] Crenshaw cites the problems the Red Army Faction (RAF), a terrorist group in the 1970s that espoused a variant of Marxist ideology, had with leadership succession in its organization. When Andreas Baader, the group's top leader, was arrested and jailed with other high-ranking leaders within the group, second-generation leaders with less impressive ideological credentials tried to assume power but could not, even though these potential successors may have had better organizational and managerial skills. In fact, after Baader and his core leaders were captured, "no subsequent leaders possessed their degree of control, and the organization was divided by rivalries between managerial and ideological leadership styles."[94]

Leaders in values-based organizations are responsible for framing the group's ideology, and in some cases, they are responsible for *creating* it, as they do in some religious cults. Since charismatic leadership in some capacity is usually a necessary condition in the formation of purely ideological groups, removing the leadership in these organizations may cause more instability than in nonideological organizations, especially if successor leaders do not possess the charismatic skills of the former leader or if former leaders failed in the "routinization of charisma" prior to the changeover.[95] In the latter cases, removing the leadership can have serious implications if followers have not internalized their leader's ideological/values-driven goals and the means to achieve those goals, particularly if they are overly complicated and difficult to understand.

The Solar Temple, a religious sect, and the terrorist group Aum Shinrikyo exemplify these types of ideological organizations with complicated belief systems that required significant framing and translation from their leaders. The Solar Temple melded neo-Christian mystical beliefs of the Holy Grail and the Knights Templar with Egyptian thanatology, oriental folk medicine, and ecological apocalypticism.[96] Equally as eclectic, the Japanese group Aum Shinrikyo combined Indian and Tibetan Buddhism with Christian apocalypticism and New Age medical practices, none of which are easily compatible with one another.[97] Not surprisingly, after the leaders of the Solar Temple committed suicide and the leader of Aum Shinrikyo was arrested, these groups either lost direction or ceased to exist. The Solar Temple is no longer active, and Aum Shinrikyo changed its name to Aleph but lost over 90 percent of its membership during the 1990s.[98]

Thus, because values-based organizations have goals that often require additional framing, interpretation, and sometimes translation in order to be accepted by followers compared to nonideological organizations, and since ideological salience is more pronounced in first-generation leaders than follow-on leaders, leadership succession in these groups is likely to cause more instability.

The other extreme is those organizations that are primarily profit driven. The core purpose of these organizations is to maximize profit. This facet is important because it alters the primary incentives for both leaders and followers, and it requires a different leadership skill set to run such organizations. The extent to which an organization is profit driven is often inversely proportional to how values driven it is, although this does not have to be the case.

Although all organizations must procure a baseline level of resources to perform their core tasks, groups often differ in how much emphasis they place on the bottom line. For example, most economic firms must find ways to produce a net profit or they are eventually selected out of the system. For other groups, such as hard-core ideological and value-oriented groups, profit is secondary to the cause or value they are promoting or defending. There are even organizations that perpetually fail, regardless of the metric used to determine success, yet somehow survive for lengthy periods of time.[99]

The prototypical organization that maximizes profits is the economic firm. On the other end of the spectrum are volunteer groups, social clubs, and religious organizations. While some of these latter organizations want and need to make money in order to function, one could argue that they are more concerned with other purposes, such as performing good deeds, promoting group camaraderie, or celebrating faith with others.

It is across this values-based/profit-based dimension where Bass's distinction of transformational versus transactional leadership is clearest.[100] Both leaders and followers in profit-maximizing organizations are often motivated primarily by self-interest. Transactional leaders in economic firms exchange salaries and job titles for work effort and production. Transactional leaders in organized crime run protection rackets in which they provide physical security to local businesses for a fee. Here the fundamentals of supply and demand are vital to organizational decision making. However, in organizations where profit is not the driving factor behind organizational decision making, metrics of success are rarely conceptualized in terms of profit. Kenney's work on drug cartels and terrorist groups illustrates this point. Both types of organizations are violent and operate clandestinely; however, cartels are more interested in profit, whereas terrorist groups, by definition, always have a political motive behind their actions.

> The *raison d'etre* of trafficking networks is to produce, process, and transport illicit drugs in pursuit of satisfactory profits, while minimizing their exposure to unnecessary risks. Unlike terrorist groups, trafficking enterprises generally do not seek to instill fear and dread in civilian populations, or to implement political change. . . . Narcos are only interested in politics to protect their narrow economic interests and keep themselves out of jail—and their families out of harm's way. . . . Unlike drug trafficking, there is no economic "demand" for terrorism. . . . Nor is the creation of wealth central to the motivation of extremists, as it is for drug traffickers.[101]

This has important implications for leadership succession and replenishing the rank-and-file members. One of the arguments for why the so-called war on drugs has been such a failure for the United States is that the drug trade is such a lucrative business. American counterdrug efforts have done little to affect the supply and demand that perpetuate the industry. In fact, one of the proposed solutions to stopping the illegal drug trade is to make drugs legal, thereby removing the profit from the industry, which would theoretically decrease demand. As Kenney notes, decapitation strategies against drug cartel kingpins have been an abysmal failure. Once the kingpin is arrested, there are numerous underlings ready and willing to take his place because the incentives of the job significantly outweigh the risk involved. Leaders in these organizations can count on a steady stream of followers because it is such a lucrative business.

In organizations where profit is not the driving factor behind supply and demand, particularly in industries that are not particularly profitable, other factors serve as incentives to maintain their existence. As previously stated, when profit is not the driving factor in an organization, ideology sometimes is, and this requires a different type of leadership. Whereas profitable organizations can often count on a virtually endless supply of new members to join their ranks, the same cannot be said for organizations that do not appeal as readily to people's self-interests. Often members in ideological organizations have to be motivated, inspired, or activated by the leadership before they join. Again, Kenney illustrates this point when he compares the replenishment of terrorist organizations, where profit maximization does not enjoy primacy over other goals, to drug cartels, where it obviously does:

> When extremist networks replace fallen comrades, as they often do, they rely more on the uncertain supply of new militants to the cause than on the promise of lucrative earning drawn by robust demand in drug markets. Hence the phoenix effect may be more subdued in terrorist networks disrupted by government authorities than it is in trafficking enterprises.[102]

In terms of attracting followers, if profits are not enough to lure new members into the organization, then what does? In some organizations, the social benefits conferred by group membership are sufficient. In certain circumstances, the salience of the cause may be the primary motivation in joining. In other cases, the group has to actively recruit members to join its ranks and "sell" the incentives of joining the group in ideological terms or offer other incentives that are not intuitively obvious to the follower.

For leaders in profit-maximizing organizations, performance-based metrics often trump values-based metrics in determining leader effectiveness. A CEO who does not produce enough profit for the company may be fired by an unhappy board of directors, and his employees may also leave the organization to join one that is more profitable. In non-profit-maximizing organizations, values-based metrics are more important than they are in profit-maximizing organizations in relative terms, and they may be even more important than performance-based metrics such as profit in absolute terms. Take, for example, the case of Cathedral High School in Los Angeles. In 1984, Cathedral High sat on prime real estate, a location that was worth approximately $10 million. To make up for underenrolled schools in the district, including Cathedral, and to increase badly needed revenue for the Los Angeles Archdiocese, the archdiocese decided to sell the school in 1987. Cathedral was to merge with the other three schools in the district. But the deal was never completed, mainly because of the tremendous outcry of support from thousands of alumni and community members who protested that the school was too valuable in terms of community pride and nostalgia. As a result, the archbishop who pushed the initial idea to sell the school lost face in the community and subsequently retired. Even though the plan made excellent economic sense and would have led to windfall profits in what was a promising seller's market in Los Angeles, his successor tabled the proposal and the underenrolled school continued, even as the archdiocese continued to hemorrhage money.[103] This is not a unique case. Organizations make decisions all the time that economists would deem inefficient in terms of maximizing profits. But in organizations with core purposes other than maximizing profits, leadership effectiveness will be measured by followers in terms of values-based criteria rather than profits.

Recruiting is easier when organizations can appeal to the self-interests of potential members. For organizations that focus on maximizing profits, whether they are economic firms, drug cartels, "blood" diamond traders, or prostitution rings, new members will continue to join as long as the opportunity to make lots of money exists. This holds true even in the face of danger, when the occupational hazards of the job include injury, incarceration, and even death. A lower-level member of a drug cartel quoted in Kenney's book exudes this mentality: "Say one guy gets popped—you go work for another group or another guy."[104] When scholars surveyed a bunch of street gang members on their most important reason for remaining with the group, making money was the number one response.[105]

This is usually not the case in organizations that are motivated by values or the pursuit of a specific cause. For organizations that emphasize factors other than profit maximization, recruitment may be more difficult because the appeal of membership may be less intuitively obvious than it is in profit-maximizing organizations. This means that leaders will have to play a more proactive role in recruiting and retaining their current members. In addition, followers will judge leaders in these organizations on criteria that are more subjective than the ability to simply turn a profit. These values-based judgments create more room for leaders and followers to disagree.

The previous discussion leads to the following propositions:

Proposition 5: Leadership succession is more likely to cause instability in ideological/values-based organizations than in nonideological/profit-based organizations.

Proposition 6: The organizational context that ideological/values-driven organizations operate in is more conducive to transformational leadership than it is for nonideological/profit-driven organizations.

Proposition 7: Profit-maximizing organizations will have an easier time replenishing new leaders and followers and maintaining the members they currently have than organizations that are values driven.

The 3-D Model

So far, this study has analyzed organizational types that vary across three dimensions: violence, clandestineness, and whether the organization is mostly values based or profit based. Each dimension has different implications for the leader-follower dynamic within the various organizations. Figure 2.1 is an illustration of what these organizational types would look like in a three-dimensional model. It provides a functional typology of organizations that shows where leaders matter most in affecting organizational performance.

It is functional because it can help policymakers visualize and understand the theoretical justification behind decapitation strategies and why they may be less effective against some types of organizations, such as drug cartels and state regimes, and more effective against other types, such as religious cults and terrorist groups.

The organizational types that appear in each individual cube are idealized notions and meant for illustrative purposes only. Each dimension should be thought of as a continuum rather than a bifurcated threshold.[106] Separating them into individual boxes is done for analytical clarity. For example, groups involved in starting social movements may be clandestine initially and then move above ground over time as they gain momentum and public support. Others never go underground and operate in the open from the outset. The Solidarity movement in Poland during the Cold War is an example of a group that started underground initially, gained

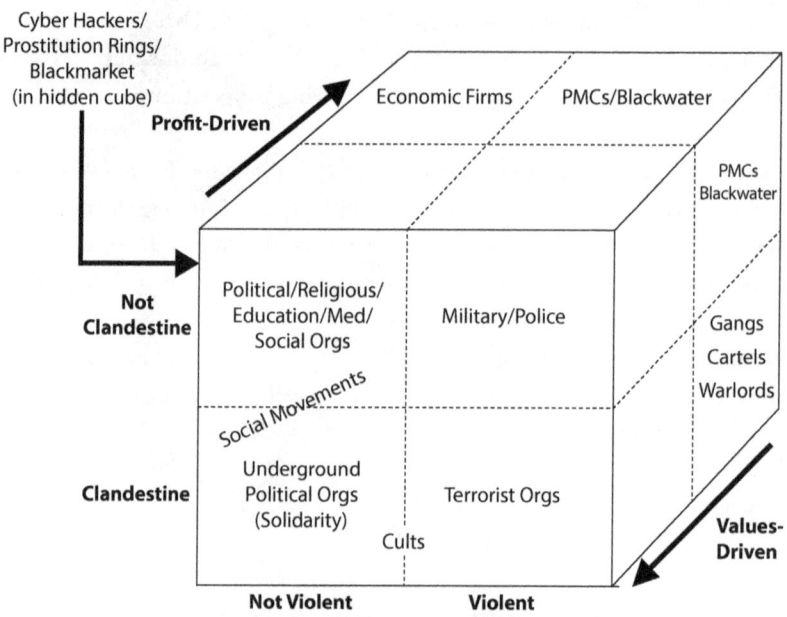

Figure 2.1 3-D model of organizational types and how they differ across three dimensions

momentum and support over time, and eventually operated out in the open as a legitimate political party.

Not only can organizational types (economic firms, political groups, etc.) move back and forth along the continuum, but organizations within each organizational type can do the same. In other words, organizations within each organizational type can differ along these same three dimensions. For example, as Cronin noted, some violent groups that start out as terrorist organizations can morph into criminal organizations without any meaningful political motivation behind their behavior, such as Abu Sayyaf in the Philippines, the FARC in Colombia, or more recently, the Shining Path in Peru.[107] In these cases, ideology became less important over time, while profit maximization gained in importance. Another example would be economic firms that are ideologically minded. These firms want to maximize profit as a core goal, but they may constrain their activities to environmentally or socially responsible practices and procedures. This is becoming more common and can be seen in a variety of industries, such as the diamond trade, organic and free-range farming, and "dolphin-free" tuna fishing.[108] There are even mutual fund companies that invest solely in these types of organizations (see, for example, the Forum for Sustainable and Responsible Investment at www.ussif.org). The overarching goal of these mutual funds is to make as much money as possible, but to do it in a socially, ethically, or environmentally friendly manner. With that said, I believe the current locations of organizational types represent where most of the organizations within each specific type would fall.

Putting It All Together

The previous section looked at how organizations vary across three dimensions, but it did so in isolation from the other dimensions. When we look at organizational types in this 2 × 2 × 2 structure, some interesting insights emerge, especially when looking at comparisons between organizations that differ on only one dimension. Based on the assumptions of leadership effectiveness and leadership succession from the literature previously cited, it is possible to see where leadership is more important in affecting organizational performance. This allows us to predict what organizational types will be most affected by leadership succession.

Varying the Violence Dimension
While Holding All Others Constant

In the beginning of the chapter, I posited that leadership will have more of an effect on organizational performance in violent organizations than in nonviolent organizations. Although there are always exceptions to the rule, it seems rather intuitive that a leader in a violent organization will have more influence than a leader in a nonviolent organization. This should hold true even after controlling for other organizational factors, such as tenure, size of the organization, resources, and the competency of both the leader and followers within the group. Additionally, leadership succession in violent organizations is more likely to be what some in the military refer to as a "significant emotional event" than leadership succession in a nonviolent organization.

As a useful thought experiment, one can imagine the degree of influence a military commander has over his organization compared to that of a supervisor in a local post office. Both organizations fall within the purview of the U.S. government, and both are not clandestine or motivated purely by profits, yet the company commander and the post office manager differ markedly in the degree to which they can influence organizational performance. Part of the reason has to do with their individual institutional contexts. Company commanders can unilaterally reward and punish soldiers in their units without the authority or approval of superiors within the chain of command, and they can control virtually every aspect of their soldiers' lives. These commanders can dictate their subordinates' work schedules, sleep schedules, educational and promotion opportunities, what they wear, where they live, and what they do in their off-duty time. The postal worker can do some of the same, but to a much lesser degree. And some of these aspects—such as controlling where postal workers live or what they do in their free time—would be completely out of bonds for a postal supervisor. Moreover, it is easy to see how a charismatic individual could single-handedly affect the morale and esprit de corps of a military unit, thus improving the unit's chances of success on the battlefield, but it is less obvious how an exceptionally charismatic individual could significantly affect how postal workers would deliver the mail differently than they would in the absence of such charismatic leadership. Because of the discretion granted to military leaders, changes of command are significant emotional events that can have significant consequences in organizational performance.[109] Conversely, changing out a post office manager is most likely less traumatic to the organization and will create less instability in terms of organizational performance.

Thus, generally speaking, leaders in the organizational types on the violent side of the three-dimensional model can affect organizational performance more than they can on the nonviolent side. Additionally, leadership succession will be more precarious on the right side than it will be on the left side.

*Varying the Clandestine Dimension
While Holding All Others Constant*

Second, I proposed that leaders in clandestine organizations will have more of an effect on organizational performance than those in nonclandestine organizations because of uncertainty, a disinclination to institutionalize, and the relative absence of constraints on leaders.

To help illustrate this point, imagine the differences in leadership influence between a private military company (PMC) and a drug cartel. Both organizations are violent and very interested in maximizing profits. Without the opportunity to make enormous profits, leaders and followers in these organizations would most likely be doing other things. In fact, many members of PMCs come directly from military careers, lured by the additional money they can make doing the same jobs they performed in the armed services. Neither group is ideologically oriented or values based, but drug cartels operate clandestinely while PMCs do not.

We should expect the PMC to have detailed contracts for clients and employees like any other regulated economic firm. And like other national militaries or security firms, these groups will most likely have common standing operating procedures (SOPs), training manuals, and a codified doctrine composed of tactics, techniques, and procedures that govern how they fight. Newcomers to the unit should be able to quickly learn the chain of command and understand how different elements of the unit contribute to the organization's overall goals. In fact, one would expect a PMC to look very similar to a military unit or private security firm in a lot of ways, including the existence of a distinct hierarchical structure, with the only difference being that PMCs fight for hire. There are even job opportunities in PMCs that one can only get if one has had specific types of training in the military.[110] It also should be noted that employees in these organizations have rights and legal recourses against unethical or immoral behavior by their leaders. Just like other economic firms or even the U.S. military, employees can take their leaders to court and seek out third parties to adjudicate contract disputes.

On the other hand, the leader of a drug cartel cannot mimic the structure and SOPs of other underground networks because this information is usually not available via open sources and because doing so increases the chance that law enforcement will learn how to defeat these networks if they are all structured similarly. As a result, we should expect more variation in how drug cartels look structurally, relative to the variation in how PMCs are structured. Moreover, we should expect the drug cartel to be less institutionalized in terms of chain of command, doctrine, and publication of its SOPs. This information is more likely to be verbal, implicit, and based more on what Kenney calls experiential *metis*—learning by doing, rather than textbook theory or doctrine. Unlike in PMCs, employees in drug cartels have little recourse against leaders who violate contracts or behave unethically or immorally. Employees can theoretically go to the authorities in these circumstances, but this is unlikely for obvious reasons, mainly because going to the authorities not only could incriminate the informant but also often leads to violent repercussions against informants and their families. In fact, the notion that "snitches get stitches" is often explicitly conveyed to new recruits, and even if it is not, it is definitely implicit in the organizational culture. As a result of these factors, leaders in drug cartels have more discretion in how to structure and run their organizations than leaders in PMCs.

Turning back to the three-dimensional model in figure 2.1, we can now say that leaders in the organizational types on the bottom half of the cube, the half denoting clandestine organizations, can affect organizational performance more than they can in organizations that populate the upper or nonclandestine half. Additionally, because of the well-defined procedures for leadership succession and the lack of institutionalization, leadership succession should be more precarious and increase instability within the organizations on the lower half of the cube than it will on the upper half.

Varying the Values-Based Versus Profit-Based and Clandestine Dimensions

Finally, since it was noted earlier that ideology is often inversely proportional to profit when determining primacy in an organization's priorities, we will look at how leaders affect organizational performance in organizational types at either end of the spectrum. To perform this thought experiment, the focus will first be on violent organizations only. Two comparisons are worth mentioning here; the first compares a pair of nonclandestine groups across this dimension, and the second compares a pair of clandestine groups.

The U.S. military and PMCs like Blackwater are both violent organizations that perform similar functions, such as the counterinsurgency mission in Iraq after 2003. I argue that the U.S. military could be seen as being more values based than Blackwater, and conversely, Blackwater can be seen as being more profit based than the U.S. military. Profit is generally not the primary motivating factor for people joining the uniformed services, and the U.S. military makes its commitment to certain values explicit, especially to new recruits. An example would be Field Manual 1 (FM-1), a document that the U.S. Army hails at its "capstone" manual and that is thought to convey "what the Army is, what the Army does, how the Army does it, and where the Army is going." This document emphasizes why dedication to certain values differentiates the profession of arms from other types of organizations:

> Members of the American military profession swear to support and defend a document, the Constitution of the United States—not a leader, people, government, or territory. That solemn oath ties military service directly to the founding document of the Nation. It instills a nobility of purpose within each member of the Armed Forces and provides deep personal meaning to all who serve. The profession holds common standards and a code of ethics derived from common moral obligations undertaken in its members' oaths of office. These unite members of all the Services in their common purpose: defending the Constitution and protecting the Nation's interests, at home and abroad, against all threats.[111]

In contrast, Blackwater's descriptions of its employment opportunities on its now-defunct web page lacked any mention of values, morals, and noble purposes. Instead, its explanation of its employment opportunities read much like what one would expect from an economic firm. For example, Blackwater provided several "critical points" to understand before applying for a position. Its first critical point read, "BSC (Blackwater Security Consulting) does not hire you; we contract you as an independent contractor. BSC will provide a 1099 at the end of the year to IC's (Individual Contractors) that documents all funds paid during the year. The IC has made provisions for all the tax issues. BSC provides overseas insurance (Defense Base Act) when working on a U.S. Government contract." Additionally, Blackwater said it was searching for potential employees whose "personalities must be such that everyone fosters a positive team environment, a willingness to work over the eight hours a day on team projects, and focus on presenting a unified team appearance and attitude to the customer."[112] The content and tone of each organization's employment pitch could not be more different.

In short, the military and other types of values-oriented organizations attempt to appeal, at least at some level, to people's values, morals, and organizational goals that are more important than individual, transactional goals. Conversely, profit-based organizations appeal mainly to people's self-interests. Even though both perform similar functions, the U.S. military uses words like *nobility of purpose* and *moral obligations*, while Blackwater uses words like *contract* and the *customer*.

This subtle distinction had important implications for success and failure in the counterinsurgency mission in Iraq, and it underlies many of the arguments against using private contractors in interstate conflict.[113] The U.S. military framed the counterinsurgency mission in Iraq and Afghanistan as a battle to win the hearts and minds of the local populace, and it was especially cognizant of the perception Iraqi citizens had about the coalition's use of violence.[114] Blackwater and other PMCs, however, were paid to do a job and to fulfill their contract, and were thus less concerned with how the local populace perceived their actions, especially in the long term.

An example of this problem can be seen in how Blackwater and other PMCs performed the convoy escort mission in Iraq compared to the military; the former were perceived to be much more liberal with the use of force.[115] Although they were legitimate, aboveground organizations, PMCs operated without many of the legal and bureaucratic rules and regulations that constrained the U.S. military in Iraq. As a result, Blackwater and other PMCs in Iraq often earned a negative reputation for their recklessness and violence. Brigadier General Karl Horst, deputy commander for the Third Infantry Division and someone who had personal experience with PMCs in Iraq in 2005, described PMCs this way: "These guys [PMCs] run loose in this country and do stupid stuff. There's no authority over them, so you can't come down on them hard when they escalate force. They shoot people, and someone else has to deal with the aftermath."[116] In addition to the infamous incident involving Blackwater in which twenty Iraqi civilians were killed in September 2007, PMCs were associated with a host of abuses in Iraq, yet few were ever prosecuted by the law.[117]

Some, including prominent Iraqis, place the blame for America's collective inability to quell the counterinsurgency specifically on PMCs. Fahmy Howeydi, one of Iraq's most influential journalists, went beyond labeling Blackwater and other PMCs as "mercenaries" and compared them to al-Qaeda, another group seen as coming to Iraq to exploit the security vacuum solely for profit.[118] Another journalist from *Al Jazeera* acutely identified the difference between the U.S. military and PMCs in Iraq, and highlighted the distinction important to this chapter, when he described U.S. private military contractors as "an army that seeks fame, fortune, and thrill, away from all considerations and ethics of military honor."[119]

The same distinction between values-based and profit-based organizations can also be seen in clandestine organizations. Kenney's comparison of terrorist groups and drug cartels is particularly illustrative here, and many of the differences between these two organizational types have already been detailed. Both types are clandestine and violent, but they differ in terms of profitability and ideology. Terrorist groups, by definition, are ideological. They perform acts of violence to achieve political objectives. As Kenney noted, "there is no economic 'demand' for terrorism," but there is a powerful one for drug cartels.[120] Drug cartels are ideologically neutral and not politically motivated. President George W. Bush even alluded to this distinction between values and profit motivation during the State of the Union address shortly after the September 11 attacks in 2001. Bush said, "Al Qaeda is to terror what the mafia is to crime. But its goal is not making money, its goal is remaking the world—and imposing its radical beliefs on people everywhere."[121]

Following these assumptions, leaders should affect organizational performance in both types of organizations because they are violent (right half of the cube) and operate clandestinely (lower half of the cube). However, because terrorist groups are ideologically motivated and less concerned with maximizing profits as their core purpose, leaders in these organizations are more influential than their drug cartel counterparts. This is because the incentives for group membership are often less intuitively obvious in terrorist organizations than they are in drug cartels, and the incentives for joining ideological groups often have to be translated, massaged, nurtured, and, for lack of a better word, "sold" to recruits and current members to maintain membership levels. Members join drug cartels to make money, not to fight for some higher purpose or achieve political ends. If there were no money to be made, drug cartels would not exist. Although it could be argued that members sometimes join terrorist groups for money, this is not the norm. As mentioned in the first chapter, people join terrorist organizations for a variety of reasons, including commitment to a cause, the social benefits conferred by group membership, peer pressure from friends and family, or persuasive recruitment methods by the groups themselves. But most of the reasons, however, are unrelated to money.

Leadership Succession

Because leaders often have the capacity to change organizational goals, strategy, and organizational culture, transferring leadership authority is an important event in many organizations, regardless of type. These events "are critical junctures for organizations"[122] and are referred to in the literature on organizational theory as "crisis events."[123] Even when new leaders have no intention of changing anything within the organization when they take over, the process can still be enormously disruptive simply because of the uncertainty and anxiety a change at the top creates among followers.[124]

In the previous section, following Grusky and others, I proposed that leadership succession would cause more uncertainty in organizations exhibiting high levels of cohesion. Violent organizations are thought to be more cohesive than nonviolent ones, and clandestine organizations are thought to be more cohesive than aboveground organizations. Thus, we should expect leadership succession to create more instability in violent and clandestine organizations than in nonviolent, nonclandestine organizations. Additionally, I proposed that leadership succession would create more instability in values-oriented organizations than in profit-oriented organizations.

Therefore, we should expect leadership succession to cause the most instability in violent and clandestine organizations that are primarily value oriented. Conversely, we should expect to see leadership succession to cause the least instability in nonviolent, nonclandestine organizations that are profit oriented. Referring to the idealized organizations within the cube, this means that leadership succession should cause the most instability in terrorist groups and the least instability in economic firms. Groups that share some dimensions but are not diametrically opposed across all dimensions should also differ in the instability caused by leadership succession.

Can instability within organizational types be measured and compared? This is difficult to do, especially considering that one can define instability in a number of ways. Most of the work done on the effects of leadership succession in economic firms measures instability in terms of organizational performance, which in turn is based on net profit,[125] the value of the company's stock,[126] and the overall growth of the organization.[127] Since these metrics are not appropriate in determining organizational performance in other types of organizations, other metrics have been selected. Scholars studying sports teams have looked at the percentages of games won before and after a leadership succession event,[128] while terrorism scholars have looked at the probability that the group dies within a certain period of time[129] and the frequency of attacks before and after a decapitation event occurs.[130]

Additionally, the bulk of the literature on leadership succession focuses on what some have called "voluntary turnover," meaning the leaders have been laid off or dismissed from positions of authority by others, or they simply retired on their own, rather than "involuntary turnover,"[131] meaning that leaders are removed from office by unanticipated events such as "heart attacks, plane or automobile crashes, suicides, and similar causes."[132] In most economic firms, voluntary turnover is more common than involuntary turnover. However, this is not the case in other organizational types such as terrorist groups, where leadership succession is more likely to be initiated by involuntary turnover in the form of death or arrest. For example, for the 207 terrorist groups in my data set that have committed at least four attacks and killed at least one person from 1970 to 2008, over 75 percent of all leadership turnover (involving only the top leader) was the result of involuntary removal (i.e., the leader was either arrested or killed by the state). Thus, in addition to the problems involved with comparing different metrics of organizational performance (profit versus duration, for example), comparing leadership succession across organizational types can also be problematic because few studies examine cases of leadership succession that include involuntary turnover.

However, although rare, leadership succession caused by involuntary turnover *does* occur in economic firms, and surprisingly, two separate teams of scholars have examined its effects. In 1985, Johnson, Magee, Nagarajan, and Newman performed a statistical analysis of the changes in abnormal stock returns before and after the sudden deaths of fifty-three senior executives from a diverse group of economic firms over an eleven-year period.[133] A year later, Worrell, Davidson, Chandy, and Garrison performed a statistical analysis of abnormal stock returns occurring before and after the sudden deaths of key executives (CEOs and chairmen of the boards of directors) from 1967 to 1981.[134]

Both sets of scholars found similar results. Johnson and his team of scholars could not find any statistically significant evidence that leadership succession due to involuntary turnover had any systemic effect on the market, a finding that was consistent with earlier studies of leadership succession in economic firms.[135] Similarly, Worrell and his team of scholars found that sudden death did not cause any statistically significant influence in stock returns for the population as a whole.[136] However, in accordance with much of the previous discussion about leadership influence, Worrell et al. found that the deaths of organizational founders, "hands-on key executives," and executives serving as both CEO *and* chairman, as opposed to those who were CEOs answering to a board of directors, were more likely to create uncertainty and negative reactions within the market.[137] Worrell et al. also found that when the executive's death was more sudden, such as in the case of a heart attack or car accident rather than a prolonged illness, the market reacted more negatively. In other words, the deaths of founders and CEOs who also happened to be the chairman on the board of directors, the two types of leaders with the most influence within the organization and the ones subject to the weakest and least amount of constraints, were more likely to cause instability in the marketplace than nonfounders and those serving in positions of lesser authority.

The null findings in both papers are important to this study because they help support the argument that leaders have more influence in some organizational types than in others. They only partially validate the argument because they only show that leadership succession does not have a meaningful impact on organizational performance in economic firms. They do not say anything about leadership succession in other types of organizations (this will be covered later in the book). They also suggest that leaders with more power (i.e., founders and leaders serving as both CEO and chairman) and fewer constraints (founders who do not have to worry about the precedent of former leaders and leaders who do not have to answer to a board of directors) have more influence on organizational performance. Furthermore, the fact that market reactions were negative depending upon how sudden the executive's death was supports the proposition stated earlier in this study that institutionalizing and anticipating leadership succession matters in terms of organizational performance. When leadership succession is uncertain, for whatever reason, whether it is due to sudden death or because the organization is disinclined to institutionalize, as in the case of illicit and clandestine organizations, organizational performance can and does suffer.

Although no scholars have systematically studied the effects of leadership succession in other types of organizations, especially when it is initiated because of involuntary turnover, we can still make some general inferences. For example, policymakers have targeted the leadership in the war on drugs, organized crime, and terrorist groups. What does the empirical evidence say about this tactic's effectiveness against these organizations? Furthermore, does the success of this tactic depend on whether the organizational environment is more conducive to transformational or transactional leadership?

Strategies of leadership decapitation have been a disappointing failure for U.S. counterdrug officials and policymakers. When the United States decided to actively engage the Colombian cocaine cartels as part of the "war on drugs" during the 1990s, it employed a relatively simple two-phase strategy to be executed over the course of twelve years from 1990 to 2001.[138] The first phase was called the "kingpin strategy." It specifically targeted the top leaders in the Medellin, Cali, and Atlantic Coast cartels and was supposed to be the prelude to Colombian president Pastrana's *Plan Colombia*, a shorter phase aimed at the supply-side factors of drug production and trafficking.[139] The "kingpin strategy" succeeded in decapitating many of the Colombian cartels, including Pablo Escobar, the notorious head of the Medellin cartel. However, killing and capturing the cartel leaders "did little to reduce the drug trade."[140] In fact, following Escobar's death on December 2, 1993, the price of cocaine dropped precipitously, production drastically increased, and more trafficking routes opened up into the United States than ever before. Instead of being crippled, "the cocaine business actually increased due to Pablo's death."[141] Thus "the ostensibly successful kingpin strategy had done nothing to reduce the supply of cocaine leaving Colombia."[142] Whenever a top cartel leader was arrested or killed, another one was eagerly waiting to take his place. It did not matter whether the kingpin was a charismatic leader or not, nor did it matter if his successor was charismatic. Escobar's death also made it easier for smaller organizations to join in. Although the kingpin strategy succeeded in tactical terms, it failed miserably in strategic terms, and it ended up expanding rather than slowing down the drug trade.

For many street gangs, like drug cartels, leadership is almost strictly transactional. A majority of the gang members interviewed by Decker and Van Winkle explicitly identified their leaders as those who could "deliver."[143] One gang member simply put it, "If you sell dope, you get the power. If you don't sell dope, you [are] just one of the boys."[144] As a result, "because of the situational nature of leadership, persons moved in and out of this role" regularly, without any significant effects on the organization.[145] Thus Decker and Van Winkle concluded the following: "The functional quality assigned to leaders within these gangs suggests that leadership is not a product of motivational skills (i.e., charismatic leaders) or organizational skills (bureaucratic skills) but rather emerges from the ability to satisfy everyday needs of the gang."[146]

Terrorist groups, on the other hand, are generally motivated by purpose rather than profit. And as a result, leaders play a more important role in these organizations because they help define, shape, and, at times, change this purpose as conditions change. In fact, terrorist leaders are sometimes so influential that when they call a stop to terrorist activity and command their groups to disband, the groups sometimes do. Pere Bascompte of the Spanish group Terra Lliure is an illustrative example of a leader who publicly renounced terrorism after years of armed struggle. In the case of Terra Lliure, hard-core members of the group defied the leadership and performed two minor attacks in the months following the announcement, but peace ensued thereafter.[147] It is amusing to imagine a kingpin making a public announcement asking his cartel to stop its activities on the grounds that it was now immoral, let alone have the group comply with his demands. Thus decapitation strategies have enjoyed arguably more success against terrorist group leaders than they have against kingpins and leaders in other organizational types.

Transformational Versus Transactional Leadership

Interestingly, this typology is also a graphical representation of where transformational leadership will be most prevalent (see figure 2.2). I argue that transformational leadership, the type of leadership that appeals not only to people's self-interests but also to their values and emotions, is more prevalent in violent, clandestine, and values-based organizations. This suggests that transformational leadership should be highest in terrorist groups and other similar types of organizations. It will be more commonly seen in political organizations, the military, religious sects, social movements, and voluntary social organizations. In fact, it is not difficult to quickly conjure up examples of individual leaders exhibiting a transformational leadership style in each of these organizational types. Individual leaders from a variety

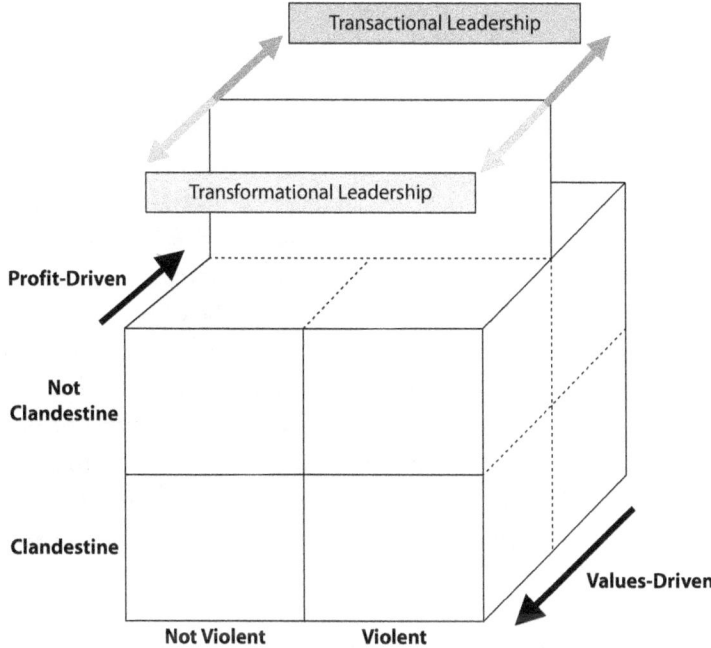

Figure 2.2 The 3-D model and transformational versus transactional leadership

of organizational types like Adolf Hitler, Charles Manson, George Patton, and David Koresh may come to mind.

As a check, we should expect economic firms to be the least likely organizational type to feature transformational leadership. Although there are certainly examples of charismatic figures within economic firms, particularly the entrepreneurial types, these organizations are more likely to feature transactional leadership. In many of these groups, leaders lead more by managerial competence than by motivating and inspiring group members through their individual example. They appeal directly to people's self-interests and exchange salary and status for work effort. When the exchange is completed or not accepted by one of the parties, it is not uncommon for either party to move on to another job, another boss, or another employee. In terms of leadership in these organizations, when the whistle blows at the end of the workday, so does the leader's influence on the employees. The same is usually not true in organizations where transformational leadership thrives.

Conclusion

For leadership decapitation to work as a counterterrorism policy, two conditions must be met. First, leaders need to be important to the overall success of the organization. If they are not, there is no reason to expect that organizational performance will suffer in their absence. Second, leadership succession must be difficult. If leaders are easy to replace, the benefits of targeting high-ranking leaders may not be worth the costs.

The typology presented in this chapter represents a theoretical justification for proposing that leadership decapitation will destabilize certain organizational types more than others. Allowing the universe of organizational types to vary across the three dimensions provides insight as to where leaders should theoretically wield the most influence in affecting organizational performance. Additionally, it separates organizational types into the two spheres where we are more likely to see transformational leadership and transactional leadership. This has important implications for the effectiveness of decapitation strategies because it suggests that replacing transformational leaders may be more difficult than replacing transactional leaders.

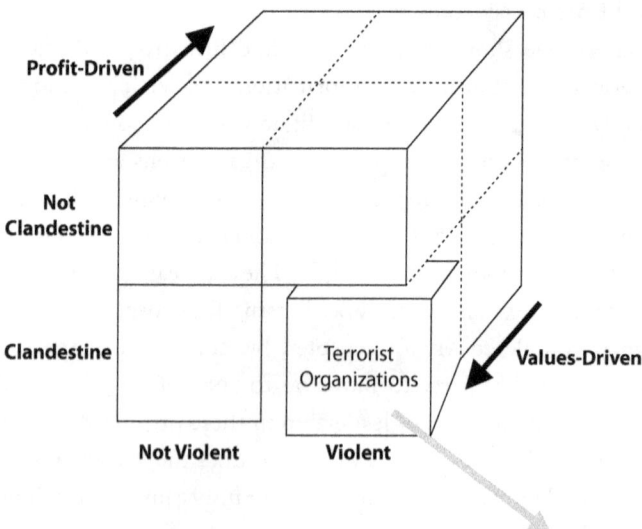

Figure 2.3 Focusing on terrorist groups

After identifying the organizational characteristics that should amplify a leader's influence on organizational performance, I would posit that leaders in violent, clandestine, and values-oriented organizations should be well positioned to affect organizational performance to a large degree. Figure 2.3 is an illustration of where terrorist groups exist according to this typology. Since terrorist groups feature all of these characteristics, leaders in these organizations should play a very important role. In the next chapter, I look exclusively at terrorist group leaders and investigate the conditions under which their removal should have the greatest impact on organizational survival.

CHAPTER 3

Leadership in Terrorist Organizations

In the immediate months after the United States invaded Afghanistan to oust the Taliban and destroy al-Qaeda in 2001, elite U.S. forces teamed up with local Afghan militias that were friendly to the Americans and wanted to remove the Taliban as well. Their mission was to kill Osama bin Laden, the notorious al-Qaeda leader and enemy number one for the United States. Bin Laden and his men were hastily trying to leave Afghanistan for the friendly confines of Pakistan, and U.S. forces were hot on their trail.

The officer in charge of the U.S. Delta Force contingent that led the mission, Dalton Fury(a pseudonym), recounts the tense moments when they not only had bin Laden's exact location but were also approximately two thousand meters away from him.[1] In fact, they were so close they could hear bin Laden's voice giving commands to his men over short-range, line-of-sight, handheld radios. In an interview with *60 Minutes* in 2008, Fury was asked how the Afghan fighters under his charge reacted when they heard it was Osama bin Laden's voice over the radio. Fury responded:

> Osama bin Laden is many a Muslim's hero. These guys, in my opinion, were more in awe of Osama bin Laden than they were willing to kill him. When they heard him talking on the radio, they would gather around the individual that held that hand-held transistor, he would hold it up in the air, almost as if he didn't want the connection to

break, almost like they could see the ridgeline that Osama bin Laden happened to be talking from, like they could almost see him and feel his presence. And they just stood there with wide eyes, somewhat in awe, that here is a leader of the jihad, the leader of al Qaeda, and they are actually hearing his voice over the radio.[2]

In fact, shortly after this event, the Afghan contingent accompanying Fury's men negotiated a cease-fire with bin Laden's forces, much to the Americans' chagrin. When Fury's team refused to comply with the cease-fire and tried to continue the fight, the Afghan militia turned their weapons on the Americans, creating an awkward moment in the battle.[3] Bin Laden would live to fight another day.

Although bin Laden is undoubtedly the most iconic terrorist leader of our era, he is but one of many terrorist leaders who can be described as transformational. Subordinates not only follow these types of leaders and put themselves and their families at great risk, but they also obey orders to kill innocent civilians in the name of a political cause. Terrorist leaders are a special breed, and leadership in these unique organizations is the focus of this chapter.

Chapter 2 presented the argument that the influence of leaders varies according to the types of organizations they lead. This chapter focuses exclusively on leadership in terrorist organizations and, more specifically, the unique organizational characteristics of terrorist groups that amplify the influence of their leaders. Terrorist groups are violent, clandestine organizations that are driven primarily by values in pursuit of their goals. As a result, terrorist group leaders have different incentive structures and fewer constraints than leaders in other organizations. Because these organizational characteristics also make leadership succession particularly difficult and more chaotic for terrorist groups than for other organizations, leadership decapitation should be, theoretically speaking, a viable and attractive counterterrorism option for many states.

This chapter first takes the three dimensions outlined in the previous chapter—violence, clandestineness, and the degree to which an organization is values based versus profit based—and analyzes how they apply to terrorist organizations. An in-depth analysis of these dimensions suggests that states should invest most of their resources on destabilizing terrorist groups at the organizational level rather than at the macro and individual levels. None of these levels of analysis should be excluded in crafting a state's counterterrorism policy, but organization-level factors should enjoy primacy. After considering the advantages and disadvantages of leadership decapitation as a counterterrorism tool, I present several hypotheses to be tested in the next chapter that shed more light instead of more heat on what is already a fiery debate regarding the efficacy of leadership decapitation.

Terrorist Leaders as Violent and Charismatic Leaders

As the heads of violent organizations, terrorist group leaders make life-and-death decisions not only for the audiences they target but also for group followers. Terrorist groups operate in hostile, stressful environments, and disobeying orders from a terrorist leader can often result in death. This is true even for groups with wildly different ideological goals. For example, in the Revolutionary Armed Forces of Colombia (FARC), the penalty for desertion is death, even for children.[4] Likewise, the Islamic State is known for its brutal treatment of those defecting from the caliphate.[5] An interview with a low-level member of Hamas who had been captured conveys the degree of obedience that is often demanded of group followers in terrorist organizations, even for low-level leaders:

> The rank and file were ready to follow through fire and water. I was subordinate to just one person, my relations with him were good, as long as I agreed to all that was asked of me. It was an organization with a clear hierarchy, and it was clear to me that I was at the bottom of the ladder and that I had to do whatever I was told. Commanders in the Hamas are commanders in every way. A commander's orders are absolutely binding and must not be questioned in substance.[6]

In other organizations, such as the Liberation Tigers of Tamil Eelam (LTTE) in Sri Lanka, group leaders even threaten their own members with execution if they disobey orders, including orders to perform suicide bombings.[7]

Leaders of violent organizations also rely more on charisma than leaders in other organizations. While leaders in other organizations depend on more conventional forms of authority, such as Weber's rational (legal or formal) authority or traditional forms of authority, "charisma is the warrior's basis of authority."[8] Since terrorist groups have no legal standing and are not considered "traditional" organizations, terrorist leaders often rely on charismatic authority to attract and keep followers.[9] Although Weber never specifically referenced terrorist groups in his work, the conditions he described for charismatic authority seem to fit the authority that terrorist leaders rely on perfectly. "According to Weber, charisma occurs when there is a social crisis, a leader emerges with a radical vision that offers a solution to the crisis, the leader attracts followers who believe in the vision, . . . and the followers come to perceive the leader as extraordinary."[10] Other organizational theorists describe authority in similar terms. Burns suggests that authority is determined by either transformational leadership or transactional leadership, where the former rests on appeals to the followers' self-interests and the latter appeals to the followers' values and emotions.[11] Transformational leadership is thus comparable to or synonymous with charismatic leadership.

Deikman claims that dependence on charismatic leaders is "supported and enhanced by three cult behaviors: compliance with the group, avoiding dissent, and devaluing the outsider."[12] However, these behaviors are not unique to cults; all three are often found in violent organizations as well, and they are very prominent in terrorist groups. Charismatic leaders are also said to advocate "a vision that is highly discrepant from the status quo, but still within the latitude of acceptance by followers."[13] Since terrorist leaders advocate killing civilians in the name of their political cause, they definitely convey a "vision that is highly discrepant from the status quo." In fact, charismatic terrorist leaders are sometimes able to attract large memberships despite their seemingly unrealistic visions, such as the apocalyptic future that Shoko Asahara of Aum Shinrikyo advocated. Charismatic leaders also act in unconventional ways to achieve their vision, and "the impact of unconventional strategies is greater when followers perceive that conventional approaches are no longer effective."[14] This is consistent with the rationale behind group leaders' decision to resort to terrorism rather than conventional means to achieve political goals. Many scholars claim that terrorism is a weapon of the weak, an element of asymmetric warfare, and used only when other forms of opposition to the status quo, like political action, are not feasible or have failed previously.[15] Finally, charismatic leaders are often very self-confident and make visible "self-sacrifices, take personal risks, and incur high costs to achieve the vision they espouse."[16] These characteristics describe numerous terrorist group leaders.

Terrorist Leaders as Clandestine Leaders

The fact that leaders of terrorist groups must operate underground has important implications for organizational learning, performance, and culture, and it often leads to poor decision making.[17]

Because of the need to maintain operational security and avoid detection by outsiders, leaders of terrorist organizations often have a disincentive to institutionalize. The reasons for this tendency are twofold. First, leaders in terrorist organizations do not want to codify how they operate because doing so makes them more susceptible to being infiltrated by the state. Bureaucratizing their organization may lead to better organizational learning, performance, and efficiency, but it may also provide the state with the knowledge necessary to destroy the organization. Although there is often a formal hierarchy within terrorist organizations, it is not likely to be understood by all members.[18] Individual cells are often kept independent and ignorant of other cells so that if an individual or entire cell is captured by state authorities, it cannot compromise the entire group because the information it holds will be insufficient to take down the group as a whole. Those who are familiar with the movie *Battle of Algiers*, an iconic historical film depicting France's counterterrorism war against the National Liberation Front in Algeria, likely remember the French commander's articulation of such a cellular structure.

The second reason leaders of terrorist groups have a disinclination to institutionalize may be more selfish and personal. They not only fear being "rolled up" by the state, but they also worry about being removed from power by their own group. As with other illicit, violent, and clandestine organizations such as gangs and drug cartels, leadership succession in terrorist groups is often based more on Hobbesian principles than on institutionalized, bureaucratic processes. Although not very common, some terrorist leaders are killed by up-and-coming group members, especially if the founders' skill sets or their ability to procure vital resources is perceived as being replaceable. As a result, terrorist group leaders not only have to keep a vigilant eye on the state's counterterrorism efforts but must also be cognizant of assassination attempts from within their own organizations, as well as from rival groups.

Terrorist group leaders are often very paranoid individuals, a personality disorder that is only worsened by a stressful clandestine lifestyle.[19]

Many living a clandestine lifestyle often suffer from what is called "burn syndrome" in the tradecraft lexicon, a "pervasive fear that other people know what they're doing."[20] Sabri al Banna, aka Abu Nidal, serves as an example of this paranoia.[21] As the head of the Abu Nidal Organization (ANO), Nidal believed his group was plotting against him, so he decided to take measures into his own hands and murdered hundreds of his followers, including 170 suspected traitors on a single night in November 1987. Those suspected of plotting against Nidal were tortured, forced to confess they were plotting against him, and sentenced to death based on these forced confessions. The victims were blindfolded and gunned down by machine guns, then pushed into a trench that was dug for the occasion.[22] Some estimates say Nidal killed more than 300 group members, a third of his group.[23] Among the victims were two of Nidal's best officers. According to one scholar, the deaths of these two leaders "destroyed the military effectiveness" of the organization.[24] Although this is an extreme example, the paranoia exhibited by Nidal is indicative of many terrorists facing similar internal and external constraints.

Abimael Guzman, the famous leader of the Shining Path in Peru, serves as another example. Guzman was apparently so paranoid about coups within his organization that he "surrounded himself with female lieutenants but readied none to command in his absence."[25] Since terrorist group leaders understand that they can both live and die by the sword, so to speak, they are naturally hesitant to provide subordinates with the knowledge and skills to run the organization in place of them.

As clandestine organizations, terrorist groups are often detached from the outside world and composed of like-minded, culturally and ideologically homogenous members. This homogeneity often works to their advantage in the sense that this environment is excellent for developing cohesiveness, trust, loyalty, and strong social bonds between members. It also allows leaders to frame reality for group members, since leaders often serve as trustworthy providers of information. Depending on how far underground the group is, it would not be unreasonable to assume that in certain cases, leaders are the *only* source of information for group members. When the Islamic State was trying to recruit a young woman from Washington State into its ranks over the Internet, her handler stopped her from asking imams at a local mosque religious questions about jihad.[26] Her Islamic State handler wanted to be her sole source of information about jihad, Islam, and the Islamic State.

However, the fact that terrorist groups are clandestine and thus detached from society, as well as the strong social bonds produced in this environment, also means they become particularly susceptible to groupthink.[27] As terrorist groups go deeper and deeper underground, the social bonds of group members intensify, and the likelihood of opposing group decisions decreases even further. This has been known to inhibit organizational learning and produce poor decision making.[28]

For these reasons, it is often difficult, yet not impossible, for terrorist group leaders to develop organizational cultures that rise above the dysfunction that plagues many clandestine organizations. Of course, terrorist group leaders vary in terms of their risk tolerance and to what extent they trust their subordinates. Variation across these two elements appears in every organization, not just terrorist groups. Terrorist leaders who are self-confident, risk seeking, and trusting of their subordinates are able to establish organizational cultures that are conducive to learning and adaptation, rather than an organizational culture like the one Abu Nidal perpetuated that was mentioned earlier.

Osama bin Laden seems to have succeeded in building such an organizational culture within al-Qaeda. He was been able to "design and implement a flexible new organizational framework and strategy incorporating multiple levels and both top-down and bottom-up approaches."[29] Hoffman suggested that bin Laden was best viewed as a terrorist CEO, who like other terrorist leaders and founders, provided his organization with a specific vision, goals, and top-down orders to accomplish those goals, but unlike most terrorist leaders, operated as "a venture capitalist, soliciting ideas from below, encouraging creative approaches, and funding proposals he [found] promising."[30] It is unlikely that al-Qaeda would have survived this long or enjoyed an institutionalized organizational learning capacity if Abu Nidal or Abimael Guzman were running the organization instead of bin Laden.

The fact that terrorist groups are clandestine is not a guaranteed death sentence. Leaders can and do succeed in overcoming the obstacles inherent to underground organizations, but it is not easy, and for reasons that will be discussed later in this chapter, overcoming these obstacles may be more difficult for successor leaders than it is for the organization's founder. This fact makes leadership decapitation an attractive tactic against clandestine organizations such as terrorist groups.

Terrorist Leaders as Values-Based Leaders

It was proposed in chapter 2 that leaders of values-based organizations, as opposed to their counterparts in profit-based organizations, are important because they help define, communicate, translate, and frame organizational goals that may not be as "specific, tangible, and calculable"[31] as goals in other organizations. For these organizations to succeed and survive, it is often not enough for their leaders to simply manage. They must motivate and inspire. For terrorist group leaders, this is especially true because not only are they often espousing ideas and values that are inconsistent with the mainstream status quo, but they also want to change the status quo through unconventional and violent means, such as killing innocent civilians. Using Burns's language, leaders of terrorist groups are transformational leaders in addition to being transactional leaders.[32] Using Weber's language, terrorist group leaders depend less on rational-legal and traditional forms of authority to accomplish organizational goals and more on charismatic authority.[33]

For example, in some terrorist organizations, followers swear allegiance not to their cause but to their leader. Take, for example, the late Abu Musab Zarqawi, a Jordanian terrorist that headed Jama'at al-Tawhid wal-Jihad, the precursor to al-Qaeda in Iraq and eventually the Islamic State. In 2004, Zarqawi publicly swore allegiance to Osama bin Laden and officially became part of the al-Qaeda enterprise. A statement by the group on an Islamic website paid homage to bin Laden and cemented Zarqawi's loyalty and the loyalty of his entire group: "When you [bin Laden] give us orders, we will obey. If you forbid aught, it will be forbidden. . . . We swear to God that should you want us to cruise the sea with you, God willing we will."[34]

Although it is difficult to measure how much loyalty and commitment buttressed this romantic rhetoric, especially considering that it was posted on a popular jihadi website, the sudden drop in beheadings in Iraq after July 2005 may serve as evidence that Zarqawi meant what he said. Once the insurgency in Iraq gained momentum following the U.S. occupation, Zarqawi's group was responsible for a slew of videotaped beheadings of coalition hostages, the first of which was American contractor Nicholas Berg on May 7, 2004. Berg's beheading not only touched off a spate of additional beheadings in Iraq by al-Qaeda and other groups but also sparked copycat beheadings in other states outside of Iraq, including the Netherlands, Haiti, and Thailand.[35] Initially, these high-profile killings seemed a perfect fit for the insurgent propaganda machine. Rime Allaf, associate fellow at the Royal Institute of International Affairs in London, commented on how effective this tactic was in November 2004: "It achieves results and it makes the headlines."[36] Jonathan Stevenson, senior fellow for counterterrorism at the International Institute for Strategic Studies, called these beheadings the "ideal terrorist tool."[37] Because the supplies needed to perform the gruesome task—a knife and a video camera—were easy to procure and the targets to choose from within Iraq were numerous, many in the West feared that beheadings would continue to be a staple of the insurgency.

However, top al-Qaeda leaders recognized that beheadings were becoming less popular with many Muslims and thought the West would eventually capitalize on the tactic's unpopularity to undermine al-Qaeda's cause in Iraq. Thus, in a letter dated July 9, 2005, then al-Qaeda's second-in-command, Ayman Zawahiri, ordered Zarqawi to stop the beheadings and the "scenes of slaughtering the hostages. . . . We don't need this."[38] At the time of the letter, Zarqawi's popularity among Islamic extremists was booming, and he was quickly becoming the face of the Iraqi insurgency. Zarqawi not only ordered these beheadings, but he is believed to have actually beheaded some of the hostages himself, including Nicholas Berg.

Somewhat remarkably, despite the fact some Western counterterrorist analysts called beheading the "ideal terrorist tool," and despite the tremendous popularity Zarqawi garnered because of these acts within the broader jihadi community, videotaped beheadings virtually disappeared in Iraq thereafter. One report estimated that at least twelve foreigners were beheaded between May and November 2004,[39] and another counted at least six more beheadings from December 2004 to July 2005.[40] A year later, after Zarqawi was killed in June 2006, insurgents from the terrorist group Ansar-al-Sunnah beheaded three Iraqi policemen in retaliation, but other than that, beheadings disappeared almost as quickly as they appeared in Iraq. They stopped after Zarqawi received Zawahiri's order.[41] What is important is not only the fact that Zarqawi complied with the order but also that other groups apparently took notice and followed suit.[42] Not coincidentally, after the Islamic State formally split with al-Qaeda in the winter of 2014, beheading hostages came back into vogue for the group.

One could argue that idolization of the group leader is more prominent in religious terrorist groups because the group leader is believed to hold special religious knowledge or powers. Shoko Asahara, the leader of Aum Shinrikyo, enjoyed this type of adulation.[43] However, the glorification of leaders occurs prominently in secular terrorist groups as well. The Liberation Tigers of Tamil Eelam (LTTE), a Sri Lankan terrorist group fighting to create their own independent state, emphasized "glorifying and idolizing the organization's leader, Velupillai Prabhakaran," during the indoctrination period for new recruits.[44] In fact, when the best trainees were singled out for selection into the Black Tigers, the LTTE's elite suicide squad, the organization did not stress the religious importance of the act (the LTTE is not a religious organization) or the monetary benefits that would be conferred to the suicide bomber's family, as was the case for other organizations like Hamas or Palestinian Islamic Jihad that also used suicide bombing as a tactic.[45] Instead, the LTTE gave the prospective suicide bomber the ultimate honor—a chance to sit next to and eat with Prabhakaran the night before the fatal mission. "During the course of the dinner, the prospective bomber receives the highest honors and his or her picture is taken standing next to the leader. Soon afterwards, and before the dinner ends, the picture is developed and hung on the wall next to the pictures of all former suicide bombers of the organization."[46] This move had an undeniable psychological effect on the would-be suicide bombers. The ceremony reduced the likelihood of members backing out at the last minute, knowing the shame and embarrassment that would befall them and their families after such an elaborate celebration with the group's leader.

The Kurdistan Worker's Party (PKK), a secular Turkish terrorist organization that espouses a Marxist-Leninist ideology and seeks to establish an independent Kurdish state, places similar emphasis on leader glorification when indoctrinating new members. Pedahzur states that "rather than committing to a religious or ideological doctrine, allegiance to the charismatic leader of the organization, Abdullah Ocalan . . . stood at the center of this indoctrination."[47]

These examples are important because they weaken the argument that jihadi terrorism should be characterized as a social movement where the masses are drawn, instead of pushed, toward certain norms and ideas. Terrorism, and jihadist terrorism in particular, does not function like an infectious disease.[48] It would seem that if Salafism and other extreme brands of militant Islamism were part of a broader social movement, such as the civil rights movement in the United States or the push to end slavery in the nineteenth century, their followers would be more interested in swearing allegiance to an idea or ideal, not to an individual leader. Swearing allegiance to a terrorist leader as opposed to a cause is a reflection of the importance these groups place on their charismatic leaders, but it may also reflect how insecure leaders of violent, clandestine organizations that are values based compensate for their shortcomings.

As leaders of values-based organizations, terrorist leaders also play an important role in information framing and interpretation. After interviewing thirty-five former Middle Eastern terrorists in prison, from groups such as Hamas, Hezbollah, Islamic Jihad, the Popular Front for the Liberation of Palestine (PFLP), and the Democratic Front for the Liberation of Palestine (DFLP), Jerrold Post was especially struck by the "stark absence of critical thinking concerning following instructions and carrying out actions."[49] One incarcerated terrorist said, "When it came to moral considerations, we believed in the justice of our cause and in our *leaders*. . . . I don't recall ever being troubled by moral questions."[50] Although Post suggests that the move by foot soldiers to transfer all of the blame and moral culpability to their leaders is common and allows foot soldiers to perform horrific acts without feeling remorse for their victims, it highlights the power leaders have in terms of information framing. According to Post, "if the group says it is required and justified, then it is required and justified. If the authority figure orders an action, then the action is justified."[51]

One of the more powerful examples of framing comes from leaders of religious terrorist groups who use religion to justify their actions. Much has been written about the hypocrisy that surrounds the religious justification given by many terrorist leaders for killing fellow Muslims and conducting suicide attacks, especially when many believe the Koran unambiguously forbids both actions.[52] The ability of some Islamic terrorist group leaders, many of whom see themselves as strict adherents to the Koran and its teachings, to alter the interpretations of the Koran's intent has been impressive and effective.[53] Hafez discusses how jihadist leaders use framing techniques to construct "martyrdom mythologies" based on ideology, religious framing, and embellished, emotional narratives to "appear as moral agents even when they are acting in immoral ways."[54] Pedahzur showed how Hezbollah paved the way for widespread social support in Iran for suicide attacks. To do so, Hezbollah's leaders marketed their first suicide bomber, Ahmad Qasir, as a "mega-celebrity" hero and found ways to make many in the Middle East "turn a deaf ear to those authoritative voices in the Muslim world which objected to the idea of suicide."[55] Pedahzur is adamant that public support for suicide attacks in the Muslim world was not a bottom-up, grassroots movement but "a highly calculated, top-down phenomenon" orchestrated by the leaders of Hezbollah and the Iranian government.[56]

Much like Hezbollah's leaders framed the religious prohibitions against suicide in the Koran to make suicide terrorism more palatable to Muslims, the leaders of al-Qaeda have found ways to frame the religious prohibitions against killing innocent civilians to include their fellow Muslims.[57] In a document released by al-Qaeda in April 2002, the organization's leadership put forth its justification for the attacks on September 11.[58] Although "the prohibitions against killing innocent civilians, in particular, are numerous" in the Koran, al-Qaeda justified killing civilians in New York and Washington on two grounds. The first argued that any civilians killed in those attacks were not "innocent" and therefore were not covered by the Prophet's prohibitions on killing noncombatants. Since the United States had a democratically elected government, the logic was that all of its citizens were partially responsible for its policies. The second grounds for justification claimed that the prohibition against killing innocent civilians was not an absolute one, and the group put forth several broad conditions where it was acceptable to do so, using several ambiguous references from the Koran as justification. Wiktorowicz and Kaltner conclude that "the sheer breadth of these conditions leaves ample theological justification for killing civilians in almost any imaginable situation."[59]

Thus Islam as a religion is certainly not to blame for jihadi terrorism or the horrific tactic of suicide terrorism; rather, the blame falls on the theological framing of a few influential terrorist leaders who have interpreted and promoted a "contorted view of what is spiritually permissible."[60] The Islamic State today continues that dangerous trend, only it has succeeded in improving on al-Qaeda's ability to manipulate Koranic references to its advantage.

Additional Organizational Features That Amplify Leader Influence in Terrorist Groups

Certain organizational characteristics of terrorist groups amplify leader influence independent of the dimensions already discussed. Terrorist leaders, and especially the founders, have powerful incentives to continue their organizations even when they fail to meet their political objectives.[61] Referencing

FrancoFerracuti's work on terrorists from Italy, Crenshaw noted that "the founders of organizations and originators of terrorist strategies are the least likely to give up."[62] In fact, some believe that terrorist group founders are incapable of repenting and rejoining mainstream society.[63]

This desire to keep the organization going is not unique to terrorist groups. It is a characteristic of more traditional organizations such as economic firms and government agencies as well. In *Permanently Failing Organizations*, Meyer and Zucker propose a theory to explain why so many organizations in the business world and in government seem to continue, "sometimes indefinitely," in spite of repeated records of poor performance, sometimes even from the time of the organization's founding.[64] They found that "those who are dependent on an organization have few alternatives to it and therefore continue to benefit from its existence independently of its performance. Moreover, the fewer the alternatives, the more dependent these actors are and thus the greater their motivation to maintain the organization regardless of its performance."[65]

The impulse for terrorist leaders to continue their organizations, even if they are deemed failures, should be demonstrably more intense than in other types of organizations where leaders have more alternatives to pursue other endeavors. For example, CEOs and leaders of bureaucratic agencies can simply leave their respective organizations for other similar organizations. They can retire or change career fields altogether. Even former gang leaders, including those who are not caught, can often meld back into society and lead constructive lives. Terrorist leaders, for the most part, are less fortunate. As one former German terrorist observed, "The only way out of the terrorist group is feet first—by way of the graveyard."[66] Terrorist leaders not only engage in terrorist activities themselves, which often includes killing innocent people and thus egregiously violating what may be the most moral taboo, but they are also responsible for creating and leading organizations that inspire others to engage in terrorist activity. Because they are ultimately responsible for these horrific acts, there are simply few alternatives to which some terrorist leaders can turn after they stop terrorist activity. Performing terrorist activity is thus analogous to crossing a moral "Rubicon" of sorts that is not associated with other illicit activity like gang warfare or drug trafficking—once the deed is done, it is difficult to shed the terrorist label, no matter how it is justified ex post.

This is a larger problem for some types of terrorist groups than it is for others. According to Post, leaders of nationalist/separatist terrorist groups find it easier to meld back into society and attain legitimate positions of authority than leaders in other types of terrorist organizations, mainly because nationalist/separatist leaders are often treated as heroes in their own microcommunities. Examples of terrorist leaders who have gone on to successful political careers include Gerry Adams and Martin McGuiness in Ireland, Nelson Mandela in South Africa,[67] and Hashim Thaci, former leader of the Kosovo Liberation Army (KLA), who eventually became prime minister. On the other hand, for leaders of terrorist groups espousing radical and extreme ideologies, such as anarchist groups, Post claims that "the decision to cross the boundary and enter an illegal underground group is an irrevocable one, what the Germans call *der Sprung* (the Leap)."[68] Not surprisingly, the skill sets that many terrorist leaders develop while in charge of an illicit, clandestine organization are not often useful in other lines of work. Thus the incentives to keep the organization alive may be more intense than in other institutional settings.

The terrorist label is hard to shed for any group member, but the costs of exit are considerably higher for leaders than they are for followers. First, the founders who start groups are often believed to have more commitment to the cause and the organization than their subordinates.[69] Without the founder, the organization may not even exist, and it is often the founder's skill set and resources that are responsible for getting the organization off the ground in the first place. These sunk costs, both material and emotional, encourage terrorist leaders to continue the organization by any means necessary.

Second, the role of terrorist leader elicits much more moral repugnance than that of a terrorist foot soldier. Proof of this fact can be seen not only in the targeting profiles of counterterrorist strategies, which often focus on terrorist group leadership, but also in the tougher sentences doled out to leaders compared to foot soldiers if they are arrested. Adel Najin Abu-Asi was the only member of the Lebanese Socialist Revolutionary Organization (or Shibbu Gang) sentenced to death because authorities simply assumed he was the leader.[70] All members of a Bolivian terrorist group that operated in the late 1980s called the Zarate Willka Armed Forces of Liberation were quickly released from prison once the group leader, Johnny Justino Peralta, was caught by police. Peralta was punished with a thirty-year sentence.[71] Although certainly not easy by any means, it stands to reason that it is *easier* for members at the bottom of the terrorist group food chain to leave the organization than it is for members at the top.

In economic firms, organizational performance is often measured in profit or market share. In legitimate political organizations, performance is often measured in the number of important pieces of legislation that get passed or the vote share a particular party receives. For terrorist group leaders, sometimes organizational performance is simply measured by staying alive and remaining politically relevant. As Crenshaw notes, " 'winning' in a conventional sense may not be the actual goal of terrorists. . . . The reward is in playing the game. Simply being able to stay in is sufficient."[72] Hoffman agrees. "For bin Laden and al Qaeda, as for guerillas and terrorists everywhere, *not losing is winning*."[73]

Crenshaw points out a psychological aspect that could be considered both an incentive and a constraint that explains why terrorist groups continue, even in the face of failure. "Terrorism is rarely abandoned as long as the organization using it continues to exist. . . . Decision makers may lack the cognitive capacity to judge the consequences of their actions. They fail to consider new information and new opportunities. In psychological terms, it is painful to reverse a decision already taken, especially if that decision was costly."[74] Thus terrorist leaders may continue to keep the group together because they cannot or do not want to admit failure, while at the same time, they may not have the cognitive abilities that are necessary to know when to quit.

Constraints

Leaders must operate under many constraints, both internal and external to the organization. In terms of external constraints, leaders in most organizations must operate under the laws of the land, the rules and restrictions that apply to their specific industry or organization, the cultural and societal norms that permeate the environment, and the limitations in technology and available resources in the system. For example, a leader hoping to start a private school will be governed by the federal, state, and local laws where the school will be located, adhere to whatever licensing restrictions and curriculum requirements pertain to teaching children, and generally comply with whatever social norms seem appropriate, such as length of the school day and appropriate school uniforms.

Internal constraints are often less formal and more malleable, but sometimes they are no less powerful than external constraints. Within their own organizations, leaders face constraints in the form of the organization's size, culture,[75] structure, and age, not to mention the quality of the members that serve in their organizations. Change in any organization is often made difficult by the inertial forces that resist it, what some organizational theorists have called "institutional stickiness."[76] The literature on the power of inertia and organizational change in both the business world and government is abundant. These internal and external constraints dilute the impact individual leaders have on performance in many of these organizations because they limit the propensity for meaningful change.

However, leaders of terrorist groups are not bound by the same constraints, and as a result, they are able to affect organizational performance to a large degree and in a more personalized manner. Their influence over all aspects of a group member's life can be pervasive. For example, members of the FARC require authorization from their leaders before they establish intimate relationships with others, especially those outside the group. Women members must get permission from their commander to give birth. Not only can their commanders order the mother to abort the baby, but commanders even separate the baby from the mother at birth so she can attend to her duties in the organization.[77] Because they head illicit and clandestine organizations, terrorist group leaders feel less bound by the laws of the land than other nonillicit organizations. In fact, with the possible exception of certain right-wing and left-wing terrorist groups, the raison d'être of terrorist leaders is often their disgust with these laws and their desire to change the status quo. They adhere to the laws of the land only to avoid attracting attention and getting caught.

Second, terrorist group leaders are less constrained by long-lasting norms or traditions that dictate how they should structure their organizations. Although many take on the traditional hierarchical structure common in many economic and political organizations,[78] they are not bound to do so. Groups have also experimented with hub-and-spoke structures, which are less hierarchical and more flattened to maximize operational security. Some groups, such as the Earth Liberation Front (ELF) and the Army of God, have been even more extreme and unconventional in structuring their groups, organizing themselves without any hierarchy whatsoever and referring to themselves as "leaderless resistances."[79]

In terms of internal constraints, leaders in all types of organizations have to contend with inertial forces that are resistant to change, such as organizational culture and age. Moreover, terrorist leaders must find ways to mitigate the principal-agent problems that plague all leaders, regardless of organizational type.[80] However, several factors unique to terrorist organizations enable terrorist leaders, particularly the group founders, to influence the structure, strategy, and function of their organizations.

Founders

Founders enjoy a privileged role in any organization and often exert more influence over the future success or failure of the organization than any other member. The decisions made at an organization's birth, both good and bad, are said to be "imprinted" into the organization for the rest of its life cycle, even after the founder is long gone.[81] Organizations do not simply arise accidentally or spontaneously,[82] and terrorist groups are no different. Organizations "are usually created because someone takes a leadership role in seeing how the concerted action of a number of people could accomplish something which individual action could not."[83] The founder is responsible for determining the group's mission, the overall strategy to accomplish the mission, core tasks, group norms, organizational culture, and the criteria for inclusion and exclusion for the group. Group founders usually have higher levels of commitment and enhanced entrepreneurial, managerial, and technical skills, and they are often solely responsible for the start-up resources required to get the group off the ground.[84] Additionally, founders are said to play a critical role in times of crisis and extreme stress.[85] Because running a terrorist group is truly a life-and-death endeavor, not to mention the fact that terrorist leaders will be punished more harshly than foot soldiers, terrorist group founders are the ultimate stakeholders, with more at risk than any other group member. As a result, they often take extreme measures when building their organizations to ensure operational security, measures that can often have debilitating effects on organizational culture and performance.[86]

Size

Group size can also help determine the influence of terrorist group leaders. The robust literature on "span of control" (the number of subordinates or entities one can effectively lead at a given time) and organizational performance shows that it is easier to control fewer subordinates than larger groups.[87] In the business world, scholars believed that the ideal span of control for bosses was 6 in the first half of the twentieth century. This number grew to between 15 and 25 later in the 1960s. In the U.S. military, the ideal span of control is usually between 3 and 5. This concept has important implications for terrorist group leaders and the types of assumptions we should make about the relationship between organizational size, the influence leaders have in these types of organizations, and what it means when those leaders are removed.

First, many terrorist groups start out as small, close-knit organizations that grow and expand over time. The leader of Aum Shinrikyo is alleged to have started in 1984 from his one-bedroom apartment with an estimated 15 followers, but the group quickly grew. A 1995 report from the U.S. Senate Government Affairs Permanent Subcommittee on Investigations of the Committee on Governmental Affairs stated that at its peak, Aum Shinrikyo boasted over 10,000 members, with some reports estimating as many as 40,000 members.[88] In 1964, Pedro Antonio Marin, one of the cofounders of the FARC, could only muster 48 group members to fight the Colombian government. Four decades later, the Colombian Ministry of Defense estimated that FARC's rolls exceeded 17,000.[89] Other terrorist groups begin as larger, nonviolent organizations such as political parties or religious groups and then cross over into terrorist activity later on.

The smaller the organization, the easier it is for the head of the group to lead in a hands-on, face-to-face manner. Leaders can directly transmit important organizational information—the group's vision, strategy, standards, and norms—without having to rely on others to articulate it for them and risk a dilution or change in the content or intent of their message. When leaders can lead directly, nothing is lost in translation.[90] Therefore, founders in small groups can align preferences much more easily than founders of large, complex organizations where they do not enjoy face-to-face leadership with most of their subordinates.

Age

Compared to other types of organizations such as economic firms or bureaucratic agencies, we can expect terrorist groups to have relatively short life spans because they operate in perpetually hostile environments.

As a result, the inertial forces that hamper organizational change in other, longer-lasting organizations have less time to solidify in terrorist organizations. Terrorist groups are not immune to organizational inertia, but these forces are less binding when the organization has been around for only a short amount of time. Groups that have been in existence for long periods of time before resorting to terrorism, including groups that began initially as political organizations or social service organizations, such as Hamas prior to 1987, are more constrained by organizational inertia than groups starting from scratch. Founders of terrorist groups that start from scratch can often build and develop their organizations as they see fit because there is most likely no precedent standing in their way. In groups that start from scratch, group members are less likely to complain to their leaders and say, "that is not the way we do it around here" because there is a high probability that the group has not been around long enough for these traditions and norms to take hold and bind their leaders.

Summary

As leaders of violent, clandestine, and values-oriented organizations, terrorist leaders are unique. These organizational factors allow terrorist leaders to affect organizational performance to a large degree. Their influence is also amplified by other organizational characteristics. These include the comparatively small size of many terrorist groups at their founding and often throughout their life span, the general lack of precedent in terms of group structure and organizational culture, and the intense desire to continue the organization at all costs because of a lack of alternatives, harsher punishments for leaders, and potential cognitive biases.

Counterterrorism: Ending Terrorist Groups, Not Terrorism

Chapter 1 discussed how researchers use three different levels of analysis to explain how terrorism ends. Like several other scholars interested in this topic, I favor the organizational approach over other levels of analysis, for several reasons.[91] Since this study focuses not on how terrorism ends per se, but on one way terrorist groups end, the organizational level is a logical place to start. Trying to find ways to end terrorism and win the so-called global war on terrorism is a pointless task. For starters, terrorism is a tactic, and many have commented on the silliness of declaring war on a tactic. We do not declare war on other tactics like amphibious landings, so why would we want to do so with the tactic of terrorism? Second, terrorism has been around for thousands of years. Laqueur claims that the first recorded terrorism attack occurred between AD 66 and 73.[92] "Terrorism, like war, never ends."[93] According to Enders and Sandler, "The one certainty is that terrorism will continue as a tactic associated with conflicts. As long as there are grievances, there will be conflict and, thus, terrorism."[94] Terrorism may never end, but terrorist groups do. Therefore, academics and policymakers should focus on ending terrorist groups as soon as possible rather than wasting limited resources in futile efforts to end terrorism.[95] But beyond this point, there are other compelling reasons for states to focus on the organization when crafting their counterterrorism strategy.

First, contrary to the views of a minority of terrorist scholars, including Marc Sageman, today's most dangerous and most likely terrorist threats come from groups, not rogue individuals. Although the Islamic State has successfully radicalized individuals to conduct several high-profile attacks in the West, including the attacks in San Bernardino, Orlando, Paris, Brussels, and Berlin, it has been relatively unsophisticated compared to the spectacular attacks of 9/11. The simple truth is the majority of terrorist attacks are still conducted by groups, groups that have the resources, skills, planning, and organizational capability to launch repeated attacks against the state in ways that no individual can. In her work on measuring counterterrorism policies, Crenshaw acknowledges that states can face different types of terrorism but that governments should "concentrate their efforts on the most threatening aspect of terrorism."[96] States will always be hard-pressed to stop the rogue "bunch of guys" or "homegrown wannabes"[97] from conducting a terrorist attack, but the empirical record suggests that the threat from the random, disorganized "bunch of guys" is not as pressing as the threat states face from organized groups.[98] As Gartenstein-Ross and Dabruzzi argued in their 2008 article about the continued relevance of al-Qaeda's top leadership, "centralized terrorist groups pose the greater threat to the United States."[99] If this is true, states should focus on defeating terrorist groups.[100] In fact, disrupting and destroying terrorist organizations has been an explicit goal of U.S. national security strategy since 2003. In the latest national strategy for combating terrorism (2011), the U.S. government explicitly moved away from the nebulous calls for defeating the tactic of terrorism or transnational movements and declared that U.S. counterterrorism would focus exclusively on one group (al-Qaeda) and its affiliates and adherents.[101] Strategies of counterterrorism should then focus on the most efficient ways to influence group behavior, not individual behavior. Organizational approaches are well suited for this task.

Second, assuming that ending terrorist groups is a worthwhile endeavor, states crafting their counterterrorism policies must consider two related concerns if they are to succeed: what state policies can realistically hope to accomplish and how much time they will take to succeed. The individual-level and macro-level approaches fare poorly in addressing both of these concerns. Counterterror policies that focus on macro-level factors such as poverty, education, and regime type are often difficult to implement and rarely yield results in the short term.[102] Altering macro-level factors can take generations and is often beyond the scope of any individual state's unilateral policies, including those of the United States. The recent attempts by the United States to democratize Iraq and Afghanistan serve as sobering reminders of how difficult this endeavor is. Likewise, the individual-level approach is equally unsatisfying because there are so many reasons why individuals choose to join terrorist groups. Stopping future people from joining terrorist organizations is an important and worthwhile task, but even if states could pinpoint the individual motivations for joining terrorist groups, which presumably are many, what could states do about those who have already joined? As mentioned earlier in this chapter, terrorist group members have powerful incentives to remain in the organization and to ensure its survival.

Instead, policymakers and scholars should focus the lion's share of their resources on understanding terrorist group dynamics, something all terrorist groups have in common and a feature that state counterterrorism policies are most capable of influencing. According to Cronin, all terrorist groups are destined to end at some point, mostly because of their dysfunctional organizational features rather than as a direct result of a state's counterterrorism efforts. Therefore, she recommends that state counterterrorism policies should concentrate on amplifying these dysfunctional aspects instead of searching in vain for "silver bullets" to end terrorism outright.[103]

Leadership Decapitation: Advantages

The benefits of decapitating the leadership of terrorist groups are rather intuitive and attractive to policymakers. The metaphor is simple: to kill the snake, simply cut off its head.[104] Unlike leaders in other organizations, it would not be uncommon for terrorist leaders to exert influence at every level in the organization—strategic, operational, and tactical. Thus killing or capturing the leader can inhibit the tactical, operational, and strategic performance of many terrorist groups. Terrorist leaders are responsible for determining the group's overall goals and the strategy it will pursue to achieve them. Unless their groups are state sponsored and function as puppets of a state leader, terrorist leaders do not have anybody above them in the hierarchy. At the operational level, terrorist leaders make the decisions necessary to achieve the organization's higher-level goals. These responsibilities include determining how the organization will function on a day-to-day basis, the criteria for entry and exit into the organization, whom the organization will target, the method of attack, and the broad timing of campaigns. Finally, it is possible that terrorist leaders are responsible for tactical planning and execution as well. Here, they not only plan missions down to the last detail but may also be instrumental in carrying them out. This is especially true in the early periods of a terrorist organization's life cycle, when the leader will likely participate in the group's attacks to demonstrate his commitment and operational competence, actions that serve to enhance the leader's credibility and trust among followers. Additionally, stories detailing their participation will often be embellished to showcase how their participation contributed to the success of these operations and will be recycled to new recruits as the group ages.

Lawrence Wright, in his book *The Looming Tower*, provides an excellent example of this kind of mythology in his description of bin Laden's military exploits in Afghanistan against the Soviets in the 1980s. Stories of bin Laden's battlefield heroism are impressive and inspiring at first blush and as told by his followers, but according to Wright, they are embellished and do not reflect the incompetence bin Laden displayed as a leader.[105] A report from the Combating Terrorism Center at West Point shares Wright's opinion, concluding that bin Laden "proved himself utterly inept as a military commander."[106] Leaders who participate in the act rather than giving orders from afar are often given the benefit of the doubt, and romanticized accounts of their battlefield heroics are important when, later in the group's life cycle, the leader is farther away from his foot soldiers, whether because of operational security reasons or because of the sheer size of the organization.

Thus, depending on the size and complexity of the organization, removing the leader can be catastrophic. To illustrate this point, picture the removal of a hypothetical top terrorist leader from a small-sized organization with less than twenty members. In addition to providing strategic guidance, imagine he is also responsible for procuring arms and intelligence for conducting their missions. Since the group is so small, the top leader not only plans missions but also is in command of their execution. If the top leader possesses a specific skill such as bomb making or paramilitary experience that no one else in the group has, he is even more important to organizational performance. Of course, over time, other group members can learn the skills and responsibilities that this hypothetical leader performs, in what Kenney refers to as *experiential metis* or what organizational theorists call "learning by doing."[107] However, this process takes not only time but also actual experience, so the timing of decapitation, in addition to the size and complexity of the organization's mission, will be important. According to Byman,

> Contrary to popular myth, the number of skilled terrorists is quite limited. Bomb makers, terrorism trainers, forgers, recruiters, and terrorist leaders are scarce; they need many months, if not years, to gain enough expertise to be effective. When these individuals are arrested or killed, their organizations are disrupted. The groups may still be able to attract recruits, but lacking expertise, these new recruits will not pose the same kind of threat.[108]

Another benefit of decapitation strategies is their ability to exacerbate the principal-agent problem that plagues all leaders.[109] Leaders want their subordinates to work hard and do what is asked of them. However, subordinates may not share these same preferences, or they may share them in different degrees than their employers. As Shapiro explained in his formal modeling of the principal-agent problem as it pertains to terrorist groups, terrorist leaders face a trade-off between control and security.[110] If they choose to exert tight control over their group followers and ensure that their orders are being carried out to their standards, they place their operational security at risk and put their entire organization in jeopardy of being compromised by the state. The other alternative is to maximize their operational security, but when they do so they risk less than efficient organizational performance because they must sacrifice some control over their subordinates.

Thus, if terrorist leaders know they are being specifically targeted by the state, this should force their hand in the trade-off just mentioned. For reasons of survival, they must take measures to maintain operational security, which in turn should lead to suboptimal planning and execution of terrorist attacks. Pedahzur provides an illustration of this trade-off during the second intifada in the Israeli-Palestinian conflict. Once the leaders of Hamas and Palestinian Islamic Jihad "became targets for the Israeli army, much of the responsibility for suicide missions fell on the shoulders of the lower-ranking local activists. The selection process became irrelevant and almost anyone who volunteered for a suicide mission was immediately accepted."[111] Because these prospective suicide bombers were of a lower caliber than the leadership preferred, they had to be escorted by other members of the group into Israeli territory, a move that significantly increased their chances of being detected and foiling the mission. Although this trade-off often results in poorer efficiency and organizational performance for the terrorist group, as this example shows, it may result in more attacks than would be the case if the leadership were calling the shots. The upside is that if the group conducts more attacks because of poor decision making by incompetent, lower-level leaders, it is more likely that the group will lose public support. This is especially true if the lower-level leaders lack the political acumen of their top leaders, as was the case in Iraq in the mid-2000s over the beheading of hostages. Al-Qaeda's top leaders were able to see the winds of public support changing before their field commanders did and made moves to solve the problem.

One of the responses terrorist groups use to counter decapitation strategies is to keep the identity of the group's leader a secret or leak multiple identities to the press about who is running their organization. For example, a spokesman for the Movement for the Emancipation of the Niger Delta (MEND), a Nigerian terrorist group fighting to gain control of that country's lucrative oil supply, once said the group's leaders must remain anonymous to protect them from being targeted by the government.[112] While this move is effective for maintaining operational security and protecting the lives of the group's leadership, it is less than optimal for running an organization. After the Israelis decapitated Hamas's top leader, Sheikh Ahmed Yasin, and his successor, Dr. Abd al-Aziz al-Rantisi, within a three-week span in 2004, the group decided not to name Rantisi's successor publicly.[113]

As Byman noted, this may have been necessary to protect the new leader of Hamas, but it "was hardly a way to inspire the group's followers or win new converts with a show of bravery."[114] Not only is this likely to confuse group members about who is giving the orders in critical situations, but it creates attractive opportunities for lower-level leaders in the organization to exploit this confusion, especially if, as Shapiro argues, they have different preferences than higher-level leaders.[115] For example, one can easily imagine a lower-level leader invoking the name of a higher-level leader in the organization who may not even exist just to get things done because it would be impossible to verify.

Concealing the names of an organization's leadership is related to a broader trend in terrorist groups to structure their organizations as networks rather than hierarchies. Many scholars suggest that this move is advantageous for the survival and resiliency of terrorist groups.[116] However, recent work has challenged this claim. In their 2008 article in *International Security*, Eilstrup-Sangiovanni and Jones argue that decentralization often makes information sharing more difficult and leads to decision making that is poor and slow.[117] When extreme measures are taken to decentralize and hide the identities of a terrorist group's leader or leaders, problems are bound to emerge:

> In a network, as in a hierarchy, complex decisions have to be made regarding resource allocation, tactics, whether and when to use violence, what social and political levers to manipulate, and so on. Because these decisions will not flow from centralized leadership, decision-making is likely to be a complicated, protracted process as all members try to have a say—or go their own way. Decisions also may not be respected as readily due to the lack of an authoritative stamp.[118]

Eilstrup-Sangiovanni and Jones argue that while networks have certain advantages over hierarchies, terrorist groups cannot enjoy many of them because they must operate as illicit, clandestine organizations.

Policymakers who advocate decapitation strategies against terrorist groups often enjoy domestic support for taking what is perceived to be an active, aggressive approach rather than a passive, reactive approach.[119] When the state successfully decapitates a terrorist leader, it is not only decreasing the organizational effectiveness of the terrorist group but is also showing off its competence and power to its citizenry.

Finally, if decapitation strategies succeed in killing or capturing the group leader, this event can act as a credible deterrent. When states advocate decapitation strategies, they send a message to the current members of the group as well as future recruits about the competency of the leadership and the relative power of the state. As has been mentioned, leadership glorification is common in many terrorist groups. Often leaders in these organizations appear larger than life. When these leaders are killed or captured by the state, it is commonly believed that group members become angry and seek to avenge their fallen leaders.[120] This is especially the case when leaders are killed and the group glorifies the leader as a martyr.

It is also reasonable, however, to assume that group members see the death or arrest of their leaders in another light. Group members might question their allegiance to the organization once they recognize that their all-powerful leader was killed or arrested by the state. If the state can reach out and kill my leader, the thinking goes, than what does it say about its ability to come after me? In fact, states often taken explicit measures to knock terrorist leaders from their pedestals, especially after they are arrested.[121] When the leader of the Shining Path, Abimael Guzman, was finally captured by the Peruvian government in 1992, the government put him on display for all to see. According to García, "Guzman was displayed in a cage outdoors, first without a shirt, later in a striped prison outfit. Peruvians saw a fat, defeated lunatic, not the elusive, godlike leader of a movement that had managed to bring civil war to the country."[122] It was a clear move to humiliate Guzman and show the supremacy of the state. In another example, Israeli Prison Services released a video in 2004 showing Marwan Barghouti, a leader in Fatah and the al-Aqsa Martyrs Brigade, secretly eating in prison while he and his fellow terrorist group members were three days into a much-publicized hunger strike that he himself coordinated. Barghouti apparently did not know he was being videotaped, and the state exploited the video as propaganda.[123]

Beyond the rank and file's reaction, successor leaders may reconsider donning the mantle of leadership if they know they will instantly become a target of decapitation themselves. Additionally, those considering membership may think twice about joining an organization whose competence in leadership is in question. It must also be difficult for groups who make new members swear allegiance to a particular leader to deal with that leader's death or incarceration. Fractionalization is likely to occur if there is disagreement about who is the legitimate successor.

Leadership Decapitation: Disadvantages

The benefits of leadership decapitation may not always outweigh the disadvantages.[124] Some even say it is counterproductive in combating terrorism.[125] The most common critique of decapitation strategies is that killing or capturing the group's head leader only makes him a martyr in the eyes of the group. Critics argue that instead of breaking the group's will and esprit de corps, decapitation makes the group more resolute, encourages more members to join its ranks, and intensifies the group's desire to inflict more violence against the state in vengeful retaliation.[126]

Other detractors emphasize the legal and moral problems associated with decapitation strategies.[127] As the debate over targeted killings by the United States in Pakistan's northwest provinces will attest, questions of sovereignty arise when states kill terrorist leaders in other states.[128] Additionally, some argue that terrorists should be treated as regular citizens and not combatants by international standards because they cannot officially declare war.[129] Decapitation also raises moral questions because some feel that states, especially those that do not feature the death penalty in their judicial system, lose legitimacy when they assassinate terrorist leaders. These critics also couple this argument with one that suggests that there is more to be gained by arresting and interrogating leaders than by killing them.[130] Since, as they say, dead men tell no tales, killing terrorist leaders decreases the state's chances of learning about and ultimately destroying the group.

Of course, another criticism of decapitation strategies is the inherent difficulty in actually killing and capturing top leaders.[131] Terrorist leaders have obvious incentives to avoid being killed or captured, and they will often go to extreme measures to ensure their own security. Therefore, a lot of resources may be expended before the state even gets the opportunity to decapitate a terrorist leader, and even then, the state may not succeed in decapitating the leader at all. Consider the resources it took for the United States to track down and kill bin Laden. Additionally, if a state publicly announces its goal to kill or capture the terrorist group leader and cannot make good on its promise, the state loses face, and terrorist groups can exploit this failure as propaganda. Worse, when the state attempts to decapitate a leader and fails, it appears incompetent and weak, a perception that only serves to embolden the terrorist group.[132]

This discussion has explored the arguments for and against using decapitation strategies to defeat terrorist groups. So far there have been major disagreements in academia and the policy community over the effectiveness of this option. It is an issue ripe for empirical testing.

Hypothesis Generation

Much of the previous discussion suggests that decapitation strategies should contribute to the organizational decline of terrorist groups. Because of the organizational features of terrorist groups, leaders play an important role in all aspects of these organizations. Removing them should disrupt and dissolve terrorist groups. Since group leaders generally have more commitment and more at stake than group followers, and since "founders play a special role in times of stress and in reassuring the organization that it will survive,"[133] decapitation events should convince some group members with less commitment and less at stake to leave the organization. Additionally, unless the decapitated leader was very self-confident and trusted his subordinates to the point where he felt comfortable training a successor and communicating this plan of succession to the group, there is likely to be disagreement over who will succeed after a decapitation event. Decapitation can also lead to fractionalization inside the group, as members debate who should be the legitimate successor. If the group receives resources from a third party outside the group, such as in the case of state sponsorship, those resources may be contingent on who leads the terrorist group, and external donors may no longer be willing to contribute once the founder is gone.[134]

Thus, assuming that leadership succession crises are negatively correlated with organizational performance and resiliency,[135] and assuming that terrorist leaders are more influential than leaders in other types of organizations, inducing these leadership succession crises (decapitation events) should lead to organizational decline in terrorist groups. Thus,

Hypothesis 1: Terrorist groups that experience a decapitation event will have higher mortality rates than groups that do not experience a decapitation event.

In accordance with Carroll, assuming that leadership crises are more traumatic for organizations the earlier they occur during the organizations' life cycles, and leadership crises involving founders are more traumatic than subsequent successions,

Hypothesis 2: Terrorist groups that experience a decapitation event earlier in their organizational life cycle will have a higher mortality rate than groups that experience a decapitation event later in their organizational life cycle.

Hypothesis 3: Decapitation events should result in an immediate increase in the group's mortality rate, but this effect should decrease over time as successor leaders become more comfortable in their role.

Hypothesis 4: The magnitude of the effect that decapitation events have on mortality rates will be negatively correlated with the number of subsequent decapitation events.

Since leadership effectiveness may also be determined by group size in terrorist organizations, we should expect the following:

Hypothesis 5: Smaller groups experiencing a decapitation event will have higher mortality rates than larger groups that experience a decapitation event.

It is important to note that the hypotheses just proposed are aimed at understanding variation in terrorist group duration, not in other dependent variables, such as the number or frequency of terrorism attacks. Other works have examined the effects of leadership decapitation on the frequency of attacks[136] and whether removing the leader radicalizes the group.[137] Mannes could not conclude that the frequency of attacks was any different in the five years before and after a decapitation event, but he did find evidence that was marginally statistically significant suggesting that religious groups conducted more lethal attacks in the five years after losing their leader.[138] Langdon and her team concluded that groups that lose a leader are not likely to become more radical. No work, to my knowledge, has investigated the effect leadership decapitation has on terrorist group duration, and other than Jordan, nobody has empirically tested which groups are more susceptible than others.[139] I attempt to do both in the next chapter.

CHAPTER 4

Quantitative Analysis of Leadership Decapitation in Terrorist Groups

As a child growing up, I was told by my parents that there were two topics to avoid when attending a dinner party and conversing with people I did not know very well—religion and politics. Unfortunately for terrorism scholars, contemporary terrorism often includes both of these topics, so arguing about the nuances within each is one of the occupational hazards in the field. Religious terrorism has affected our lives in very meaningful ways since 9/11, and as a result, it is a contentious topic that provides a seemingly endless array of debates about the threat and the best ways to mitigate it. Should we pay ransoms to terrorist groups after they kidnap hostages and threaten to kill them unless they get paid? How far should we go in extracting intelligence from interrogated terrorists after they have been arrested? Should we shut down encrypted social media platforms to inhibit terrorist communication? Should we treat captured terrorists as enemy combatants or as common criminals in the eyes of the law?

These hotly contested debates occur not only in academic circles but also with practitioners, policymakers, and the public. Regrettably, these debates are often emotional and include a great deal of anecdotal evidence that is cherry-picked to support a particular side, but they rarely include a comprehensive analysis of the empirical record. The debates about leadership decapitation and its effectiveness as a counterterrorism tactic are no exception. Critics and proponents of the tactic have generated a lot of heat in the debate about how to evaluate its efficacy, but not a lot of understanding.

This chapter is a modest attempt to bridge the gap in our understanding of leadership decapitation and put forth one way of evaluating its effectiveness. It is not the *only* way to evaluate decapitation's efficacy, but I argue that it is a useful way of understanding the effects of decapitation, particularly in the long term.

In that vein, this chapter presents an empirical test of leadership decapitation's effects on the survival rate and organizational decline of 207 terrorist groups from 1970 to 2008. This test differs from previous quantitative analyses in that it evaluates the effects of decapitation events on the duration of terrorist groups rather than on the number, frequency, or lethality of attacks following a decapitation event.[1] Because of the large number of terrorist groups that are still active, I use a model capable of accommodating right-censored data and one that is commonly used in organizational ecology to study the mortality rates of populations of organizations; it is also used in biomedicine to study mortality rates in populations of patients after receiving particular treatments.

The chapter is structured as follows. First, I describe the issues in terrorism research that warrant the development of an original data set for examining leadership decapitation, including a discussion of the time period covered in this study. Second, I present some descriptive statistics pertaining to the terrorist groups that populate my data set as well as some information about the counterterrorism capacity of the states they target. Third, I describe the model and explain how it is useful for understanding terrorist group duration. Finally, I summarize my findings and discuss their implications for counterterrorism.

Data on Terrorist Groups

One of the more frustrating aspects of terrorism research is the lack of available and reliable data on terrorist groups and their behavior.[2] Since terrorist groups are clandestine organizations that operate underground, organizational characteristics like size, resources, and structure are inherently difficult to determine.[3] In 1991, terrorist scholar Ariel Merari remarked that "the clandestine nature of terrorist organizations and the ways and means by which intelligence can be obtained will rarely enable data collection which meets commonly accepted academic standards."[4] That claim still holds true to this day. Even when terrorist groups release this information, they have incentives to inflate their capability. It is in their best interests for their supporters and enemies to have an overinflated estimation of the group and its resources.

On the other hand, the information on terrorist groups that *is* available often comes from the state, the validity of which is often questioned because of the politicization and calculated efforts to downplay the threat.[5] Additionally, states are often hesitant to publicize much of what they know about terrorist groups for operational security reasons. Terrorist groups already know more about the state than the state knows about them, at least initially in their life cycle. Releasing what information is known about the group to the public shows the state's hand and may improve the terrorist group's ability to survive.[6] For example, Osama bin Laden reportedly cut back on the use of his satellite phone communications after published media reports indicated that the United States was conducting surveillance on his calls.[7]

To explain variation in terrorist group behavior, including studies of decapitation effects on terrorist groups, researchers have often focused on dependent variables such as the number and frequency of terrorist attacks,[8] as well as the lethality of these attacks.[9] The problems associated with each of these dependent variables have been frequently cited in the literature.[10] For example, many scholars explaining variation in the number and frequency of terrorist incidents use the Global Terrorism Database (GTD).[11] In 2009, 29,293 of the 80,000 plus incidents recorded in the GTD1 (1970–1997) and GTD2 (1998–2004) were attributed to what the database labeled "unknown groups." These "unknown groups" accounted for over 36 percent of all the incidents recorded in the database. Moreover, for a period of time the GTD had incomplete records for attacks from the year 1993 because of a filing error when the information was moved to the University of Maryland.[12]

Determining the number of fatalities from terrorist attacks may be even more problematic. Using data from another widely used source, the Memorial Institute for the Prevention of Terrorism's (MIPT) Terrorism Knowledge Base (TKB), Asal and Rethemeyer were "only able to account for slightly more than half of all fatalities" in their study of terrorist group lethality from 1997 to 2005.[13] Assuming that the time period between 1997 and 2005 is generally considered to contain more accurate data than those obtained during the 1970s and 1980s, accurately determining the number of fatalities across the entire spectrum of this study from 1970 to 2008 may even fall short of Asal and Rethemeyer's 50 percent success rate.

In light of these data limitations, an alternative approach to examining the effects of decapitation is to focus on the mortality rate of terrorist groups themselves instead of the number of incidents or fatalities they produce. Other organizational theorists have selected organizational mortality rate over other dependent variables because "organizational death is a fundamental standard of organizational performance" and "has the advantage of relatively unambiguous measurements and interpretation, which is often not the case with performance variables."[14] Since it is difficult to capture these performance variables when it comes to terrorist attacks, organizational death in terrorist groups is a worthwhile dependent variable to examine.

One important consideration when referencing the most widely used data sets in terrorism research, such as the Terrorist Organization Profiles (TOPs) database and the GTD, is their inclusiveness.[15] For example, the platform for the GTD was the Pinkerton Global Intelligence Services (PGIS), whose database was initially constructed to provide risk assessment to corporate customers, and thus it "was designed to err on the side of inclusiveness. As a result, the PGIS data includes many acts that likely would not be included in other terrorism open source databases."[16] Examples of these acts include attacks on property that result in no casualties or injuries and purely criminal acts such as robberies and bank heists with no political purpose. Because of this inclusiveness in the GTD and TOPs databases, even the casual observer would be hard-pressed to describe many of the 856 groups in the TOPs database as terrorist organizations. Many of the groups in these databases have performed only a single act of violence, and only a few of these single attacks included fatalities. Other groups in these databases have not even carried out a single act of violence, such as in cases when the group was compromised and rolled up before it could attack or when the group only issued rhetorical threats without following through with action.

For researchers, it is preferable to weed out groups and incidents that do not belong for a particular study rather than take a database that is too restrictive and look to outside sources to supplement it. However, taking these databases at face value can be dangerous because they can lead to misleading conclusions about terrorism and terrorist group behavior. For example, while on the 2008 campaign trail, the Republican presidential candidate and former Massachusetts governor Mitt Romney gave a speech in June 2007 about global terrorism threats. The theme of the speech was "The War on Terrorism Is Not a Bumper Sticker," and Romney specifically referenced the GTD to show the number of European countries on a heat-density map that had experienced ten or more terrorist acts since 1990. It was unsurprising, given the inclusiveness of the database, that most of the European countries on the map were displayed in red, which indicated rampant terrorism. However, a closer review of the actual attacks involved showed that some of the incidents and groups were much less threatening than the slide indicated, and several blogs subsequently ridiculed Romney for inflating the terrorist threat.[17] Many of these attacks were sophomoric and could have easily been the work of pranksters. For example, in Germany, a group called the Autonomous Decorators conducted its first and only "terrorist" attack on January 4, 2001, when group "operatives lobbed bags of paint at Germany's Interior Ministry Building" to protest the imprisonment of another group's members.[18] Many "terrorist" activities in Greece during this time period are equally dubious. A Greek group called the Knights of the Torched Bank attempted its only "attack" in May 2003, when it tried to set a small fire outside a local bank, but the fire went out by itself and caused zero damage.[19] Similarly, the Solidarity Gas Canisters took out its frustrations against a Greek bank ATM on one occasion in November 2003, resulting in "minor damage to the ATM and no casualties."[20]

These are only a few examples of the terrorist groups and attacks that populate these databases. And politicians like Romney are not the only ones who reference these groups and attacks when making assertions about trends in terrorism; these groups also show up in many academic data sets. For instance, all of the groups previously described appear in numerous academic studies that examine the lethality of terrorist attacks.[21] Although it is unlikely that there will ever be a consensus definition of terrorism, the "attacks" described here were performed by trivial and transient groups that should not be included with a list of consequential terrorist groups. Their attacks bore more resemblance to minor protests than to violent acts intending to cause psychological fear or physically harm someone.

The data set in this study consists of 207 terrorist groups from 65 countries that were active from 1970 to 2008.[22] Compared to other quantitative analyses that have examined decapitation effectiveness and terrorist groups, it is the largest data set of its kind. Langdon and her team examined 19 groups, not all of which were terrorist groups, and 35 decapitation events for their article.[23] Mannes included 71 terrorist groups in his study,[24] omitting groups that had less than 100 members, and examined 60 cases where groups lost their leaders.[25] Jordan's data set is the most comprehensive.

It includes 169 terrorist organizations as well as 290 observations of decapitation, but these observations include the removal of lower-level leaders she classifies as the "upper-echelon" as well as the top leaders. For decapitations involving only the removal of the head leader or leaders, Jordan coded 124 observations.[26] To compare, my data set lists 207 groups, including 204 observations where the head leader or leaders were either killed or captured. Additionally, I recorded 95 other incidents where the head leader or leaders were removed for other reasons. These included leaders who were thrown out or expelled from their own groups, leaders who died of natural causes or accidents, leaders who voluntarily stepped down or quit their organization, and instances where the leader entered the political process or accepted a cease-fire agreement with the government. In total, 299 observations of leadership change are included. In short, this data set not only features more groups than previous data sets but also includes more observations of leadership decapitation as well as instances where the leader was removed by other means.

Since the dependent variable of interest is the duration of terrorist group survival, the data set needed to include only those groups posing a legitimate threat to the target state. Terrorist groups that committed only a few (if any) minor attacks that resulted in superficial damage may not ever make it onto the state's "radar" and could conceivably remain active for decades. Or more likely, these groups ended soon after committing one or two attacks, never to be heard from again. Thus using the TOPs database without vetting each group would bias the study by including groups that are, for all intents and purposes, politically irrelevant. As a result, groups were screened so that only those committing at least four attacks, including at least one resulting in a fatality, were included in the data set. Since this study is interested exclusively in the organizational decline of consequential terrorist groups, this seemed like a reasonable criterion that would ensure that only groups that we could genuinely define as terrorist organizations pursuing a systematic campaign of violence would be included.[27] To borrow a phrase from Michael Kenney's Israeli handlers, who were giving him a tour of the Gilboa maximum security prison, which houses only the most hardened terrorist suspects, "there are no stone throwers here."[28]

Additionally, this study purposefully did not include the killing or capture of high-ranking or upper-echelon leaders who were not the primary leader or coleader. It only included instances where the primary leader or leaders were removed. Groups that were created by states to counter oppositional groups within their borders were also excluded. Including such groups established by the state would bias the results because the state, not the state's counterterrorism efforts, would determine when the group ceased activity. It is highly unlikely that the state would decapitate an organization it created, unless of course the group leader went rogue and tried to escape the state's control.

To account for groups that joined umbrella organizations, I only included the umbrella organization if it conducted attacks under the umbrella organization's name. Individual groups that joined umbrella organizations were not coded as ending after they joined the group. Instead, I coded these individual organizations as surviving as long as the umbrella organization. For example, the Armed Forces of National Liberation (FALN) was one of several terrorist groups in El Salvador that joined forces to form the Farabundo Marti National Liberation Front (FMLN) in 1980. Since the FMLN conducted attacks under its umbrella name, it was included as a separate group in the data set with a start date of 1980 and an end date of 1992, when it signed a peace agreement with the government. Instead of coding the FALN's end date at the time of the merger in 1980, I gave it the same end date as the FMLN in 1992. Three groups—the Breton Liberation Front (France), the People's Liberation Army (Bangladesh and India), and the Free Aceh Movement (Indonesia)—appear twice in the data set because of lengthy periods between attacks and multiple sources indicating that there was an identifiable break in group activity. If these groups were coded as operating continuously, it would bias the results, making them appear more durable than they actually were.[29]

Groups that appear on the terrorism lists of the major state powers were also considered as possibilities. These include the U.S. Foreign Terrorist Organization (FTO) list and comparable lists from the United Kingdom, Russia, the European Union, Australia, and Canada. If a group appeared on these lists but did not meet my coding criterion, I included them anyway, because most of these groups were relatively recent and had not yet conducted four attacks, or because their attacks had not been logged into the GTD2 by the time the coding ended in 2008. Two examples of these groups are the Libyan Islamic Fighting Group (LIFG) and the Moroccan Islamic Combatant Group (MICG). Both groups appeared on the U.S. FTO list as well as the United Kingdom's Proscribed List of terrorist organizations, but they did not have at least four attacks recorded in the GTD or TKB when coding for this study ended.

The number of attacks was verified using the GTD, which includes domestic and international terrorist incidents from 1970 to 1997 and 1997 to 2004, and the MIPT's TKB, which includes international terrorist incidents from 1968 to 2007 (and which is no longer maintained). Open source research served as a supplement as well as additional validation of the information found in these data sets. Websites operated by the South Asia Terrorism Portal (www.satp.org) and the Northern Ireland Conflict Archive on the Internet (CAIN) (http://cain.ulst.ac.uk), as well as the data set created by RAND scholars Jones and Libicki,[30] were also consulted and cross-checked for accuracy.

This study covers leadership decapitation events that occurred between 1970 and 2008. It begins in 1970 mainly because 1970 was the first year that the National Consortium for the Study of Terrorism and Responses to Terrorism (START) at the University of Maryland started the GTD. In 2008, START stopped updating the TOPs database. Both served as primary sources for vetting the groups in this study. This time period is important, however, for other reasons. The fact that the study goes through 2008 allows researchers to analyze arguably the most important period for leadership decapitation tactics in U.S. counterterrorism history. Initially made famous by a deck of playing cards printed by the Department of Defense that featured the fifty-two "most wanted" leaders in Iraq, leadership decapitation was one of the most highly touted counterterrorism tactics of President George W. Bush's two administrations. The majority of these leaders were killed or captured between 2001 and 2008.[31] One could argue that these successes touted by the Bush administration between 2001 and 2008 subsequently led the Obama administration to double down on the tactic in the next eight years. Initial indications suggest that the tactic enjoys similar prominence in the early days of the Trump administration.

Terrorist group mortality, the dependent variable, is measured in years. To determine the start time of each group, I used the date of the group's first attack, not its purported founding date.[32] For example, Peru's most infamous terrorist group, Sendero Luminoso or Shining Path, was allegedly formed under Abimael Guzman in the late 1960s but did not perform its first terrorist attack until a decade later.[33] Since all of the groups in the TOPs database are clandestine organizations, reliable and accurate information about when each group officially formed is often unavailable or unverifiable. Thus it made practical sense to use the group's first attack as the start date. Determining when a group "dies" was equally problematic. Groups can exist for months and years without committing any violence, as the case of Sendero Luminoso demonstrates. This lack of activity can be due to extended planning cycles, reconsolidation efforts, effective counterterrorism campaigns by the state, and of course, patience, as a group bides its time until the perfect opportunity presents itself. I considered a group inactive if two years passed without it conducting any attributable violent attacks, with the year of its last attack serving as the end date. A list of all groups and dates is presented in Appendix A.

Other covariates that may help explain terrorist group mortality include the presence of allied groups, rival groups, and hierarchical versus decentralized organizational structures. The *ally* and *rival* groups were coded using information from the TOPs database. These are coded as dichotomous variables in the data set, where 1 indicates the presence of at least one ally or rival terrorist group, and 0 otherwise. Having allied groups should theoretically increase the longevity of terrorist groups because they can pool resources and information and coordinate attacks against the state, all of which may improve their chances of achieving their political goals. If these allied groups operate within the same state, they may force the state to divide its counterterrorism resources to combat multiple threats. Recent research on terrorist group cooperation supports this line of thinking. In his study of terrorist groups between 1987 and 2005, Phillips showed that a group's longevity increased in accordance with the number of terror group allies it had, even in states with highly capable counterterrorism capabilities and those that are less democratic.[34]

The presence of rival groups, however, raises some interesting questions about this factor's influence on a terrorist group's longevity. Even if rival groups espouse different ideologies, they may play a similar role in distracting the state from focusing on one particular group. If the state is forced to divide its counterterrorism resources to combat multiple groups, this should hypothetically decrease the mortality rate of terrorist groups. On the other hand, rival groups sometimes present a legitimate decapitation threat to each other. Although targeting other terrorist group leaders is sometimes considered taboo, as was the case during the 1970s when Abu Nidal broke an unwritten rule with his assassination attempt on the leader of the Palestinian Liberation Organization (PLO), Yassir Arafat, it is a common occurrence in some parts of the world.[35] For example, terrorist groups in Ireland routinely targeted and killed the leaders of rival groups. Rival groups must also compete with others for limited resources, especially when it comes to replenishing their ranks. Thus groups that do not have a rival to contend with may, on average, last longer. A potential counterargument comes from the literature on organizational ecology, particularly the "Red Queen" theory, which claims that groups facing intense competition from other groups are better equipped to learn, adapt, and thus survive than groups without this competition.[36] Findings from more recent works show mixed results. Young and Dugan found that the existence of rivals increases the mortality rate of terrorist groups,[37] while Phillips found the exact opposite to be true in his study.[38] Therefore, while we should expect groups with allies to generally last longer than groups without allies, the predicted relationship between longevity and the presence of rival groups is less obvious.

The variable *coleader* was coded as 0 for groups with only one identifiable primary leader, and 1 if the group had multiple leaders occupying the top position. It was also coded as 1 if the group's leaders were identified as being cofounders or coleaders in open sources, or if the group was governed by a ruling council. Numerous scholars claim that decapitation is more successful against groups that are more hierarchical and less decentralized.[39] Since "looking under the hood" and verifying the organizational structure of a particular terrorist groups is an inexact science and often impossible, determining the degree to which a group is hierarchical versus decentralized is difficult.[40] Thus this variable is an admittedly rough measure.

The data set also includes information about each group's ideology and estimated size. Some scholars believe these are important factors for explaining group strategy, resiliency, and longevity.[41] Cronin argues that terrorist groups with a predominantly religious ideology are more dangerous because these groups attack to please a certain deity and are seemingly unconstrained by secular laws and norms.[42] This commitment may lead religious terrorist groups to frame their goals in terms of a longer time horizon, thus increasing the group's longevity. Hoffman disagrees and argues that ethno-nationalist/separatist terrorist groups are more resilient and ultimately more successful because they can "draw sustenance and support from an already existing constituency" and because they benefit from "the clarity and tangibility" of their stated goals.[43] In other words, ethno-nationalist/separatist groups will continue to fight because they feel they are on the right side of history. Richardson believes that ethno-nationalist terrorist groups survive longer because they have closer ties to their communities than other types of groups.[44] Hutchinson and O'Malley also claim that "groups inspired by ethno-nationalist or separatist causes [have] generally lasted the longest."[45]

Pinning down a group's ideology, however, is often problematic, and some scholars put more stock in an ideology's usefulness in explaining terrorist behavior than others. Post often quips that "the cause is not the cause" when discussing the relationship between ideology and the motivation behind terrorist group behavior.[46] Crenshaw believes that cultural influences can be as strong, if not stronger, than ideological influences. Instead of blindly following ideological ambitions, she suggests that terrorist leaders may first develop a set of beliefs and "then seek justification for them through the selection of fragments of compatible theories."[47] To muddy the waters further, groups are not necessarily beholden to one specific ideology. For example, one could argue that the Popular Front for the Liberation of Palestine (PFLP) advocates both nationalist/separatist and Marxist-Leninist ideologies. Hamas is both nationalist and Islamist. Moreover, ideologies may change over the course of a group's life cycle; so too can the degree to which ideology is important to the organization and its goals. This was particularly the case for terrorist groups like the Revolutionary Armed Forces of Colombia (FARC) or Sendero Luminoso. These groups were once considered deeply ideological organizations, but over time ideology became less important as both groups became more heavily involved in the drug-trafficking business.

Therefore, because several scholars think that it could play an important role in explaining longevity in certain types of terrorist groups, I included *ideology* as a variable in the data set. Although several of these groups could actually be considered hybrids, I used the same ideological types as coded by RAND in the Jones and Libicki study, which coincidentally also runs through 2008.[48] The authors classified ideology into a common set of four types: right wing, left wing, nationalist, and religious.[49] The groups in my data set contain 74 left-wing (*LW*), 6 right-wing (*RW*), 74 nationalist/separatist (*nationalist*), and 53 religious (*religious*) groups.

The size of the group is another variable often used to explain mortality rates in organizational ecology studies. As groups age, they have a tendency to grow and increase in size. Additionally, several large-N terrorism studies use the size of the group as a proxy for group capability.[50] This convention is based on the idea that larger groups are able to draw upon more resources than smaller groups, and thus they are better able to conduct attacks and withstand a state's counterterrorism efforts. Some scholars estimate a group's exact size down to the individual member; however, these estimates are rather unreliable. Since terrorist groups are clandestine organizations, they have a vested interest in concealing the names and numbers of those filling their ranks. Furthermore, even if terrorist groups make the size of their organization public, they have incentives to inflate their numbers to appear more formidable in the eyes of the state and other target audiences. To claim exact numbers of terrorist group membership is a questionable act, and audiences should be skeptical of studies drawing conclusions based on such estimates. Thus I used the less ambitious but probably more accurate estimates from the RAND study of how terrorism ends.[51] These estimates placed terrorist group size in one of four "buckets": 1–99, 100–1,000, 1,000–10,000, and greater than 10,000 members. This type of bracketing is a common feature in several academic studies on terrorism.[52] The breakdown of groups by size in this data set is as follows: 48 groups under 100 members (23 percent), 87 groups between 100 and 1,000 members (42 percent), 52 groups between 1,000 and 10,000 members (25 percent), and 20 groups with more than 10,000 members (10 percent).

Because states are by no means passive actors in determining the longevity of terrorist groups, it is necessary to include control variables that might influence the state's ability to combat such groups. To do so, I needed a measure of state counterterrorism capacity and regime type. States, like terrorist groups, are naturally hesitant to show all their cards and make their exact capabilities part of the public record, mainly because doing so would tip their hand to terrorist groups and reveal sources and methods of intelligence gathering. Reliable data on a particular state's counterterrorism budget and the size of its counterterrorism bureaucracy are not readily available. However, we can approximate a state's counterterrorism capability by using the same logic used to measure a terrorist group's capacity to attack—the larger the resources available, the more robust a state's capability should be to wage its counterterrorism campaign. The argument that wealthier states are better equipped to create, resource, and maintain counterterrorism efforts than poorer states should not be controversial.

To capture this measure, I obtained an estimate of GDP per capita for the target state or states from the Penn World Tables. Using this measure as a proxy of state capacity is consistent with other works in political science.[53] However, this variable becomes tricky to measure when international terrorist groups are involved. When a terrorist group targets and launches attacks from multiple states, as the Islamic State and al-Qaeda do (al-Qaeda is said to operate in as many as sixty states),[54] it is necessary to measure the counterterrorism capacity of more than one state.[55] To account for the counterterrorism capacity in these circumstances, I used an average GDP per capita of the top three targeted states. This is an admittedly imperfect measure, but since no other studies of leadership decapitation have made any attempt to control for a state's counterterrorism capability, it seems that an imperfect measure is better than no measure at all.[56] Fortunately, averages were only needed for 37 groups in my data set (17 percent), 11 of which include the averages of Ireland and the United Kingdom for many of the terrorist groups operating in Northern Ireland.

Regime type also served as a control variable because many scholars believe that democracies are at a greater disadvantage than autocracies when battling terrorism within their borders.[57] According to this line of thought, democracies are constrained by commitment to civil liberties and accountability to electorates, and thus they cannot use the heavy-handed tactics and tools that many authoritarian regimes rely on to fight terrorism. Thus one could argue that terrorist groups are more likely to have shorter life spans in autocratic states than in democracies. Another argument for using regime type as an explanatory variable has to do with the motivation for terrorism in the first place. The logic here is that terrorist organizations in democratic governments may not last as long because they have more options to achieve their political ends than they do in authoritarian governments.[58] As a result, Polity IV scores for each group-year were included in the analysis.

The following tables present descriptive statistics about the 207 terrorist groups in this data set. Table 4.1 shows the status of these groups in this data set and whether they have experienced a decapitation event, which is defined as when the primary leader is either killed or captured by the state. Seventy percent of the groups in this data set that experienced a decapitation event ended between 1970 and 2008. Table 4.2 shows the descriptive statistics of the groups according to the study's variables, and table 4.3 shows the breakdown according to the size and ideology of groups in this data set.[59]

TABLE 4.1
Status of the Group Versus Whether the Group Has Experienced Decapitation

		Group ended	
		No	Yes
Experienced decapitation	No	32	44
	Yes	38	93

TABLE 4.2
Descriptive Statistics of Group Variables

Variable	Mean	Standard Deviation	Minimum	Maximum
Years of survival	15.26	11.91	1	50
Experienced decapitation	0.63	0.48	0	1
Size	1,262	2,892	10	10,000
Log(size)	5.09	2.10	2.30	9.21
Time since decap	4.49	7.58	0	35
Ideology—LW	0.36	0.48	0	1
Ideology—nationalist	0.36	0.48	0	1
Ideology—RW	0.03	0.17	0	1
Ideology—religious	0.26	0.44	0	1
Rival	0.26	0.44	0	1
Ally	0.77	0.42	0	1
Coleader	0.21	0.41	0	1

Note: 207 groups in data set.

TABLE 4.3
Group Descriptive Statistics and Decapitation

	N	Decap	Not decap	Decapitated		Not decapitated	
				Alive	Dead	Alive	Dead
Size							
Under 100	48	37	11	1	36	3	8
100–1,000	87	63	24	24	39	11	13
1,000–10,000	52	25	27	11	14	14	13
Over 10,000	20	6	14	2	4	4	10
Ideology							
LW	74	55	19	6	49	4	15
Nationalist	74	36	38	13	23	15	23
RW	6	4	2	0	4	0	2
Religious	53	36	17	19	17	13	4
Total	207	131	76	38	93	32	44

The Model

In order to properly evaluate the effects of decapitation events on terrorist group survival, it is important to (a) accurately measure the survival times of all groups and not just those that experience decapitation events, (b) allow for long-term effects of decapitation on groups rather than focus on short-term effects with arbitrary time horizons, (c) account for right-censoring to include those groups that are still active but may experience a decapitation event in the future, and (d) account for groups that have experienced a decapitation event but whose effects may not have materialized by the end of the observation period in the study. Dropping groups in this fashion is problematic. For example, Mannes chose to remove almost 10 percent of his observations because the decapitated groups in his data set had only recently lost their leader.[60] Omitting this type of data, referred to as right-censored data in methodological circles, can lead to case selection bias and an unrepresentative sample, which ultimately leads to biased findings.[61]

Survival analysis is a potential solution to these methodological problems. Although not as widely used as regression models in many of the social sciences, survival analysis and event history models are regularly used in the fields of biostatistics, medicine, and engineering.[62] These models are used to understand the causes and consequences of change over time in a particular population, such as in evaluating the medical treatment effects on different patient populations or understanding the failure rates of machine components. One of the more attractive features of these models is their ability to account for censored data, something that is more difficult to do with linear regression models.

The Cox proportional hazards model is the most widely used model in survival analysis, not only because it can accommodate censored data and time-varying covariates (e.g., variables like size and age), but also because it is a semiparametric model that allows researchers to use event history analysis without knowing the exact distribution function of failure times.[63] For example, if a researcher knew that the risk a terrorist group endures from a decapitation event was going to always increase or decrease with time, then other models such as the Weibull model or the exponential model, both parametric models, would be preferable. However, if there is ever any doubt as to what the distribution function of failure times is, as is the case with terrorist groups and decapitation events, the Cox model is considered the better model to use.[64]

Central to all survival analysis models is the hazard rate. This is defined as the "rate at which units fail (or durations end) by t (a predetermined period of time) given that the unit has survived until t."[65] For Cox models, "the hazard rate for the ith individual [or terrorist group in the case of this study] is:

$$h_t(t) = h_0(t)\exp(\beta'x),$$

where $h_0(t)$ is the baseline hazard function and $\beta'x$ are the covariates and regression parameters."[66]

In this case, my model seeks to explain how certain covariates affect the duration times or longevity of terrorist groups. The model can tell us which variables increase or decrease the risk of failure for terrorist groups, or whether the variable has no effect on mortality rate at all. The right-censored data—those groups that were still active in 2008 when the observation period for this study ended—still contribute information to the baseline hazard rate, but they do not provide any information about the failure rate because the terrorist groups were still active.

To best interpret the results of the model, it is easier to analyze the hazard ratios than the individual coefficients. In fact, the hazard ratios are derived from the exponentiated coefficients. Although it sounds complicated, interpreting the hazard ratio is quite simple and should be done as follows:

- If the hazard ratio is greater than 1, then that variable increases the hazard rate for terrorist groups and places them more at risk of "dying."
- A hazard ratio less than 1 means that the variable decreases the hazard rate for the terrorist group and makes it more resilient and longer lasting.
- If a hazard ratio is exactly 1, then the variable neither increases nor decreases the risk to the terrorist group. For example, if the hazard ratio for the dummy variable *ally* (1 indicated the presence of an ally, 0 otherwise) is 0.5, then this should be interpreted as a 50 percent decrease in the mortality rate for terrorist groups that call other terrorist groups allies. Another way of saying this is that terrorist groups with allies are 50 percent less likely to end than terrorist groups without allies.[67]

Results

The null model, one in which all of the terrorist groups are treated as a single population without including any of the covariates, can be graphically depicted by plotting the Kaplan-Meier (K-M) estimates. The plotted curve in figure 4.1 is the K-M curve along with its 95 percent confidence intervals. The confidence intervals widen out at the longer periods simply because there are fewer observations of terrorist groups that have been around for this amount of time. In other words, fewer groups make it to forty and fifty years of age, so the confidence intervals are much larger. The dotted vertical line that intersects the K-M curve represents the estimated mean survival time for all 207 groups in the sample. It is estimated because 76 of these groups are still active. The estimated mean group survival time is 16.2 years. Looking at only the 131 groups that have ended between 1970 and 2008, the actual mean survival time for these defunct groups is 13.9 years.

These mean survival times differ quite drastically from Rapoport's widely cited claim that 90 percent of all terrorist groups survive less than a year, with nearly half of the remaining groups unable to survive more than a decade.[68] This figure is routinely cited by many high-profile terrorism scholars, all of whom attribute the finding to Rapoport when discussing

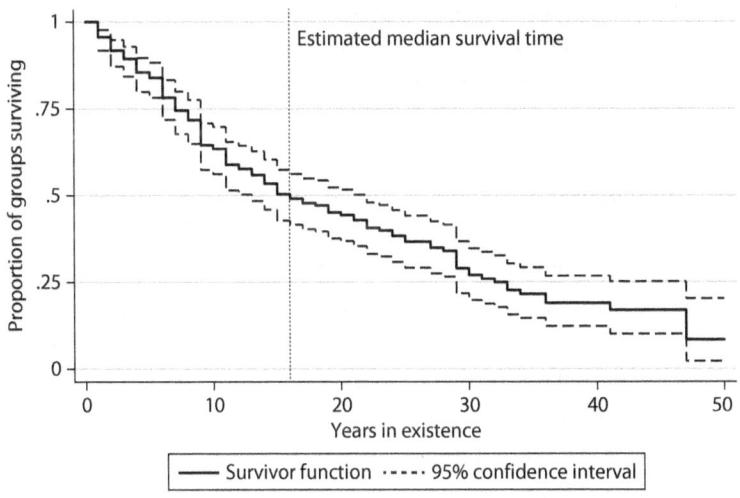

Figure 4.1 Terrorist group survivorship, 1970–2008

the longevity of terrorist groups.[69] Closer review, however, indicates that the basis for this claim may not be as strong as currently believed. The Rapoport claim appears in a general chapter on terrorism in Volume 2 of the *Encyclopedia of Government and Politics*.[70] Rapoport's chapter is a very short and broad survey of terrorism, including its history and a summary of prominent groups, as well as a brief discussion of counterterrorism. In fact, the section describing the longevity of terrorist groups takes up just four sentences. Additionally, Rapoport does not provide any evidence to support his claim, although in his defense, the sentence actually reads, "*Perhaps* as many as 90 percent last less than a year."[71] Thus it appears that Rapoport was merely offering an estimate instead of a bold empirical fact. Since then, however, scholars have dropped the qualification of "perhaps" from the sentence and have treated it as though it were an actual finding.[72] As a result, this estimate routinely appears as conventional wisdom in the terrorism literature. For a comprehensive look at terrorist group longevity and a comparative analysis of various terrorist group databases that largely debunks this oft-cited statistic, read Brian Phillips's 2017 article in *Terrorism and Political Violence*.[73]

An estimate of average terrorist group duration, of course, depends largely on how one defines a terrorist group. Including groups from data sets like the TOPs database at face value may lead to shorter mean and median duration times because many of these so-called groups only performed one attack, if they performed any violent attacks at all. For example, in their 2008 article Asal and Rethemeyer tested hypotheses against 499 organizations from the TOPs database that had conducted at least one attack from January 1, 1998, to December 31, 2005. After dropping groups for which there was little or no information, as well as groups that were front names for other groups, Asal and Rethemeyer were left with 395 groups, but 240 of these groups, or over 60 percent of terrorist groups within their data set, never killed a single person.[74] Although the authors do not divulge how many of these groups committed only one alleged attack, my experience with this data set suggests that the majority of these groups did just that. The authors are careful to offer a caveat to their findings, but other scholars sometimes are not. Thus scholarly works relying on data sets that are overly inclusive may run the risk of giving policymakers an unwarranted sense of security, especially if they lead governments to think that most terrorist groups, on average, never kill anybody, conduct only one nonlethal attack, and dissolve in a short period of time.

Conversely, results obtained from data sets that are more selective, like the data set presented in this analysis, suggest that terrorist groups last longer than previously believed.[75] Thus, compared to Rapoport's much-quoted claim, I show that terrorist groups from 1970 to 2008 that conducted at least four attacks and killed at least one person were rather durable, with half of the groups surviving longer than sixteen years, and the longest-lasting group surviving over fifty years.

As a warning to the reader, the next section explains in relatively significant detail the various models used to conduct the empirical analysis. It may be too deep "into the weeds" for readers who do not really care how the quantitative sausage was made. If that is you, feel free to jump to the section on policy implications, where the findings from this analysis are synthesized.

Base Models

Since we know very little about how decapitation events might affect the longevity of terrorist groups, I specified the main explanatory variable, *exp decap*, in a number of ways. In Model 1 (M1), I allowed the effect of a decapitation event to linger in the organization forever. In this case, once the group's leadership was decapitated, the effect was "left on" as long as the group was active. This may or may not be a valid assumption. Specifying the variable in this way suggests that groups are permanently affected by a decapitation event and thus have a different survival rate than groups that have never experienced decapitation. In Model 2 (M2), I "turned off" the effect after two years. This model assumes that the effect of a decapitation event is short and temporary. In other words, it assumes there will be a period of organizational chaos and turmoil for the first two years while the group deals with the loss of its leader, but once a successor has settled into the leadership role, the group's hazard rate is no different from that of any other group. I specifically chose this two-year time horizon because I wanted to compare it to Jordan's empirical tests, which examined the probability of a group ending within two years after a decapitation event.[76] Model 3 (M3) is even more restrictive and assumes the group is able to quickly recover from a decapitation event. The effect of a decapitation event in this model is "turned on" for only one year. After a momentary shock to their hazard rate in the year of decapitation, the group is assumed to have the same hazard rate in subsequent years as any other group.

Each model also controlled for group-specific characteristics such as group size, the existence of coleaders, and whether the group had at least one ally or rival group. To control for *ideology*, a variable with four factors in my model, I had to omit one type of ideology to serve as a comparison group.[77] In Cox models, it is often customary to drop the most prevalent factor and use it for comparison. However, the choice is ultimately up to the researcher. I chose nationalist/separatist groups as my comparison group for two reasons. These groups were the most prevalent in my data set (along with left-wing groups, which also had 74 entries), and I specifically wanted to see how they compared to religious groups. As previously mentioned, there is currently a debate in the field about which type of group is more resilient, and I wanted to see if there was a statistically significant difference between the two. Each model also contains target state specific control variables such as states' regime type (measured by their Polity IV score) and counterterrorism capacity (measured in GDP per capita).

Table 4.4 displays the results of this analysis. Regardless of how the decapitation effect was conceptualized, groups that experienced a decapitation event were much more at risk than groups that did not. In other words, depending on how one chooses to model the duration of a decapitation's effects, groups are 3.6 to 6.7 times more likely to end than groups that are not decapitated. The effect on the hazard ratio is more conservative when one permits the effects of decapitation to linger in the organization over time because organizational collapse is not always imminent. Although some groups survive longer than others following a decapitation event, groups have a mean life span of seven years after experiencing their first decapitation event. Some groups last even longer. The Turkish Communist Party/Marxist-Leninist group, for example, lost its founder a year after its first attack, yet still endured for over four decades.[78] The results show that groups are especially vulnerable to organizational death in the early years following a decapitation.

The effect of the variable for the log of group size is in the right direction (less than 1), indicating that an increase in group size leads to a decrease in the hazard rate, but it is not quite statistically significant at the 10 percent level (p-value = .11). This holds true for all three base models and is consistent with findings that suggest that an increase in size translates into an increase in group longevity.[79]

In terms of group ideology, right-wing groups are the only ones that are different from nationalist/separatist groups (the comparison group) based on

TABLE 4.4
Cox Prop Hazards Model: Base Models of Terrorist Group Duration

Comparison group: nationalist/separatist	Left on	Turned off > 2 yrs	On for 1 yr only	Decap × time	Multi decaps	1 vs 2+ decaps
	M1	M2	M3	M4	M5	M6
	Haz ratio	Haz ratio	Haz ratio	Haz ratio	Haz ratio	Haz ratio
Variable	(coef s.e)	(coef s.e)	(coef s.e)	(coef s.e)	(coef s.e)	(coef s.e)
Exp decap left on	3.686***					
	(0.814)					
Exp decap turned off after 2 years		5.449***				
		(1.148)				
Exp decap year only			6.769***			
			(1.507)			
ED left on × time				0.930***	0.930***	0.931***
				(0.021)	(0.021)	(0.021)
Exp decap 1×					8.275***	8.199***
					(3.001)	(2.971)
				8.757***		
				(3.109)		

TABLE 4.4 (*Continued*)

Comparison group: nationalist/separatist	Left on	Turned off > 2 yrs	On for 1 yr only	Decap × time	Multi decaps	1 vs 2+ decaps
	M1	M2	M3	M4	M5	M6
	Haz ratio	Haz ratio	Haz ratio	Haz ratio	Haz ratio	Haz ratio
Variable	(coef s.e)	(coef s.e)	(coef s.e)	(coef s.e)	(coef s.e)	(coef s.e)
Exp decap 2×					11.438***	
					(5.207)	
Exp decap 3×					8.351***	
					(4.324)	
Exp decap 4×					32.470***	
					(23.829)	
Exp decap 2+						10.843***
						(4.438)
Log(group size)	0.912	0.940	0.945	0.923	0.933	0.933
	(0.052)	(0.055)	(0.055)	(0.052)	(0.054)	(0.054)
Ideology—LW	1.180	1.415	1.404	1.230	1.270	1.277
	(0.290)	(0.340)	(0.336)	(0.307)	(0.322)	(0.321)

Ideology—RW	4.298***	4.447***	3.735**	4.259***	4.498***	4.262***
	(2.204)	(2.274)	(1.940)	(2.203)	(2.359)	(2.209)
Ideology—religious	0.625	0.549*	0.546*	0.636	0.661	0.659
	(0.219)	(0.191)	(0.190)	(0.223)	(0.232)	(0.231)
Rival	0.652*	0.614*	0.612*	0.583**	0.588**	0.578**
	(0.169)	(0.161)	(0.162)	(0.155)	(0.159)	(0.153)
Ally	0.502***	0.484***	0.503***	0.483***	0.463***	0.469***
	(0.112)	(0.110)	(0.114)	(0.109)	(0.107)	(0.107)
Coleader	0.863	0.938	1.008	0.880	0.815	0.839
	(0.200)	(0.221)	(0.240)	(0.205)	(0.198)	(0.201)
Average target state Log(GDP/capita)	1.490***	1.530***	1.466***	1.449**	1.444*	1.462***
	(0.221)	(0.225)	(0.214)	(0.212)	(0.216)	(0.215)
Polity	0.975	0.973	0.976	0.982	0.983	0.982
	(0.018)	(0.018)	(0.019)	(0.018)	(0.018)	(0.018)
N	2,637	2,637	2,637	2,637	2,637	2,637
N fail	111	111	111	111	111	111
LogLikelihood	−435.62	−426.43	−424.72	−430.37	−428.36	−429.85

conventional standards of statistical significance (p-value $< .05$). However, considering there are only six right-wing groups in the data set, and the fact that all four of the right-wing groups that have been decapitated have ended, this is not really surprising. In Models 2 and 3, where the effect of decapitation is "turned off" after two years and one year, respectively, religious groups appear to be slightly more than 45 percent less likely to end than nationalist/separatist groups. This finding is only statistically significant at the 10 percent level, but it does provide some support for the argument that religious groups are more resilient than nationalist/separatist groups. This finding is consistent with Jones and Libicki's claim that "religious terrorist groups take longer to eliminate than other groups."[80]

The presence of a rival group is statistically significant at the 10 percent level (p-value $< .10$) for Models 1 through 3, indicating that having a rival reduces the hazard rate by up to 39 percent. Having an ally is also significant and reduces the hazard rate by up to 52 percent. These results indicate that multiple groups force the state to spread its counterterrorism resources, reducing the amount of resources it can focus on defeating just one group. Additionally, having a rival group may remove the debilitating effects of complacency and force groups to evolve more quickly, learn faster, and adapt more efficiently. This is consistent with Phillips's findings.[81] Interestingly, the effect of the variable measuring the presence of a coleader never approaches statistical significance.

For the target state control variables, regime type does not seem to matter in explaining terrorist group mortality. The descriptive statistics for regime type, however, are telling. Although the data set contains groups that have targeted states with Polity IV scores from either extreme (i.e., −10, indicating highly autocratic, to 10, indicating highly democratic) and the mean score for all targeted states is 4.5 (indicative of a middle-of-the road democracy), the median score is 8. This fact lends support to claims made by several scholars that democracies are targeted more often than autocracies.[82]

The one state-level characteristic that *was* highly statistically significant throughout several models was GDP per capita, a proxy for state counterterrorism capacity. An increase in the log of GDP per capita results in a 47 to 53 percent increase in the mortality rates for terrorist groups. Wealthier states simply have more money to allocate to counterterrorism efforts than poorer states, which may improve the effectiveness of their counterterrorism campaigns. This measure may also suggest that citizens within wealthier states may be dissuaded from joining terrorist organizations because they have weaker grounds for economic grievances.[83]

In comparing the fit of all three models, Model 3 fits the data best, although it is only slightly better than Model 2. Thus limiting the effect of decapitation in the year the leader is removed, as opposed to allowing it to linger on forever, is the preferred method. However, to check the robustness of my findings, I used the more conservative "left-on" method of specifying decapitation effects for future tests.

The base models did not account for the timing of leadership decapitation events, which is important if one believes that the timing of a decapitation matters in influencing group longevity. Imagine losing an influential and charismatic leader of a small organization in the first year of existence and compare it to losing a group founder in the thirtieth year of the group's existence. The former's loss should, theoretically speaking, be more detrimental to the group than the latter's loss.

Therefore, to account for the timing of decapitation events, I included an interaction term in Model 4 that conditioned decapitation with when it occurred in the group's life cycle.[84] Indeed, the results show that timing really matters. The interaction variable is highly significant (p-value = .001). In the first year of a group's existence, t or year 0, the group is 8.757 times more likely to end if its leader is killed or captured. The following year, $t + 1$, the group's risk of death is now reduced by the interaction effect, which is .07 percent ($1.00 - 0.93 = .07$).[85] Thus, looking solely at the explanatory variable, a decapitated group is now at less risk than it was the year before. Compared to its first year of activity, when its hazard ratio was 8.757, the following year its hazard ratio decreases to 8.166.

Figure 4.2 depicts how the hazard rates for terrorist groups decrease as a function of time as specified in Model 4. As the figure shows, the effect of decapitation is cut approximately in half after 10 years of group existence. At approximately 20 years it is possible that a decapitation will not have any effect on the group's mortality rate. Looking at the upper bound of the confidence interval, this is very unlikely, but the possibility does exist. However, the most important takeaway from this graph is that time matters when decapitating a terrorist group leader. The longer it takes for the state to remove a terrorist leader, the less impact it will have on the group's mortality rate.

What happens when some groups suffer multiple decapitation events? To test whether successive decapitations increase a group's hazard rate,

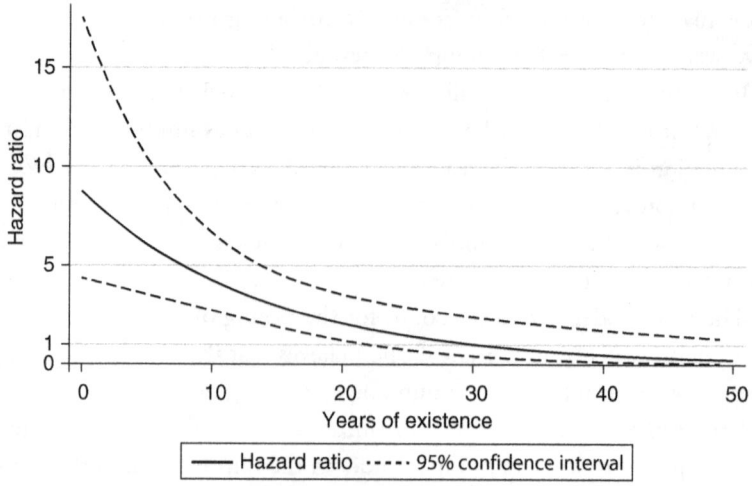

Figure 4.2 Effect of decapitation over time on the hazard ratio of group survival

Model 5 includes dummy variables for every decapitation event. Although it is not uncommon for groups to have many leaders arrested or killed, I only included decapitation events that removed the primary leader or leaders. In this data set, 131 out of 207 groups experienced at least one decapitation of their primary leader. While 87 groups experienced only one decapitation event, 30 had two events, 15 had three events, and 3 groups experienced four decapitations.

The results from Model 5 indicate that groups are more than three times as likely to end when they experience a second decapitation. Going from two decapitation events to three seems to decrease a group's hazard rate, but one must consider the small number of observations that this result is derived from. In fact, after conducting chi-squared tests on each factor, I found that none of these dummy variables are statistically significant from each other, so it is impossible to accurately determine what the magic number of decapitations is that leads to organizational decline the fastest.

Since the number of groups experiencing three and four decapitations is relatively small compared to the number of groups experiencing one or two, I tested to see whether experiencing one decapitation was different from multiple decapitations in Model 6. Here, all groups that experienced multiple decapitation events were collapsed into one category and compared to groups experiencing only one decapitation. The results show that groups experiencing multiple decapitation events were almost 2.6 times more likely to end than groups experiencing only one decapitation, but again, these two groups are not statistically significant from each other based on chi-square tests.

Size Models

Does the size of the group matter in influencing group longevity after the loss of a leader? Earlier I hypothesized that removing the leader of a smaller group would be more detrimental than removing the leader of a larger group. I estimated three models to test this. The first model is a slightly modified version of the base model using the log of size (the only difference being the addition of *decaptime*, a running counter of time since the last decapitation event). The second features dummy variables for the four "buckets" of size, and the third model uses an interaction term to test how groups of different sizes react after leader decapitation. In order to test the differences between different sizes of groups, I had to omit one of the size ranges. Similar to the logic I used to select the omitted ideological type, I selected groups with 100–1,000 members as the comparison group because they were the most prevalent group size in my data set. The results from these three models are in table 4.5.

In Model 7, the effect of the variable measuring the log of group size is not statistically significant, but it is in the hypothesized direction and decreases the hazard rate, as we would expect. The inclusion of *decaptime*, a variable that acts as a counter for each year since the organization's last decapitation event, brings the *rival* variable into statistical significance at the 5 percent level, but it does little to improve the fit of the overall model. There is no substantive change to any of the other variables in the model from the base model.

The results from Model 8 indicate that none of the other group sizes differ from the comparison group size of 100–1,000 members. Statistically speaking, small groups are no different than large groups when it comes to explaining the hazard rates of terrorist organizations.

Model 9 tests whether groups of varying sizes are at greater risk when they are decapitated. There are no statistically significant differences between groups with 100–1,000 members that have experienced a decapitation event

TABLE 4.5
Cox Proportional Hazards Model: Size Models

Comparison group: nationalist/separatist, 100–1,000 members Variable	Log size M7 Haz ratio (coef s.e)	Size dummies M8 Haz ratio (coef s.e)	Decap × size M9 Haz ratio (coef s.e)
Exp decap left on	8.658***	8.688***	9.163***
	(3.077)	(3.100)	(4.172)
Exp decap left on × time	0.945**	0.945**	0.949**
	(0.024)	(0.024)	(0.024)
Log(group size)	0.933		
	(0.053)		
Size under 100		1.287	1.040
		(0.324)	(0.519)
Size 1,000–10,000		0.909	1.144
		(0.273)	(0.528)
Size over 10,000		0.812	1.363
		(0.318)	(0.676)
Exp decap left on × size under 100			1.280
			(0.718)
Exp decap left on × size 1,000–10,000			0.687
			(0.419)
Exp decap left on × size over 10,000			0.292
			(0.240)
Decaptime	0.971	0.971	0.977
	(0.023)	(0.023)	(0.023)
Ideology—LW	1.261	1.255	1.167
	(0.314)	(0.313)	(0.295)

TABLE 4.5 *(Continued)*

Comparison group: nationalist/separatist, 100–1,000 members Variable	Log size M7 Haz ratio (coef s.e)	Size dummies M8 Haz ratio (coef s.e)	Decap × size M9 Haz ratio (coef s.e)
Ideology—RW	4.239***	4.264***	3.931***
	(2.189)	(2.206)	(2.040)
Ideology—religious	0.608	0.608	0.627
	(0.214)	(0.214)	(0.224)
Rival	0.572**	0.571**	0.557**
	(0.151)	(0.151)	(0.153)
Ally	0.489***	0.500***	0.468***
	(0.111)	(0.118)	(0.112)
Coleader	0.888	0.898	0.874
	(0.207)	(0.211)	(0.208)
Average target state Log(GDP/capita)	1.484***	1.468**	1.497***
	(0.219)	(0.219)	(0.225)
Polity	0.980	0.981	0.980
	(0.018)	(0.019)	(0.019)
N	2,637	2,637	2,637
N fail	111	111	111
LogLikelihood	−429.59	−429.5	−427.63

and groups of both larger and smaller sizes. The only groups that come close to statistical significance are groups boasting over 10,000 members (p-value = .119). Large groups that lose their leaders have higher mortality rates than smaller groups, a somewhat surprising and counterintuitive finding. However, since only 6 of the 20 groups numbering more than 10,000 members in this data set were decapitated, the number of observations this finding is based on is relatively tiny.

Thus size does not seem to be an important variable in explaining organizational decline in terrorist groups. There are no statistical differences between groups of varying sizes. More importantly, smaller groups seem to behave no differently than larger groups when their leaders are killed or captured.

Ideology Models

Taking stock of the findings thus far, the timing of decapitations matters, the size of the group does not matter, but what about ideology? Does a religious terrorist group suffer differently after a decapitation than an ethno-nationalist terrorist group? To find out, I employed a similar progression, and again, groups that experience a decapitation event are more at risk than those that do not, and group survival is enhanced by the presence of both allies and rivals. Model 10 is the base model. For Models 11 and 12, I included dummy variables for each ideological type (e.g., LW, RW, religious, and ethno-nationalist) and interactions between ideological type and *exp decap*, omitting nationalist groups the first time and right-wing groups the second time. The results from these models can be found in table 4.6.

Interacting ideological type and *exp decap* in Model 11 leads to a marginal increase in the overall fit of the data. Unlike the base model, where right-wing groups were the only ideological type to be statistically different from nationalist groups, this time religious groups are statistically different. Compared to nationalist groups, religious groups are almost 77 percent less likely than nationalist groups to suffer organizational death. However, the interaction between religion and decapitation tells a different and interesting story. When religious groups suffer the loss of their leader, they are almost five times more likely to die than nationalist groups that lose theirs. This finding is statistically significant by conventional standards (p-value < .05). Of the 19 religious groups that have died in this data set, 16 lost their leaders to kill or capture. Of the 34 religious groups that are still active, 20 have been decapitated.

When right-wing groups are omitted and serve as the comparison group, as is the case in Model 12, none of the interaction terms are statistically significant, indicating that groups with other ideologies do not act differently when decapitated. Here religious groups are very resilient when compared to right-wing groups, with right-wing groups 90 percent more at risk.

TABLE 4.6

Cox Proportional Hazards Model: Ideology Models

Comparison group: Models 10, 11—nationalist Model 12—RW Variable	Base model M10 Haz ratio (coef s.e)	Ideology dummies omit (nat'l) M11 Haz ratio (coef s.e)	Ideology dummies omit (RW) M12 Haz ratio (coef s.e)
Exp decap left on	8.658***	5.443***	14.152**
	(3.077)	(2.550)	(16.112)
Exp decap left on × time	0.945**	0.945**	0.945**
	(0.024)	(0.024)	(0.024)
Log(group size)	0.933	0.937	0.937
	(0.053)	(0.055)	(0.055)
Decaptime (years since)	0.971	0.976	0.976
	(0.023)	(0.024)	(0.024)
Ideology—LW	1.261	0.980	0.439
	(0.314)	(0.384)	(0.469)
Ideology—RW	4.239***	2.232	
	(2.189)	(2.378)	
Ideology—religious	0.608	0.237**	0.106*
	(0.214)	(0.151)	(0.127)
Ideology—nationalist			0.448
			(0.477)
Exp decap left on × LW		1.568	0.603
		(0.765)	(0.721)
Exp decap left on × RW		2.600	
		(3.164)	
Exp decap left on × religious		4.908**	1.888
		(3.760)	(2.540)
Exp decap left on × nationalist			0.385
			(0.468)

(continued)

TABLE 4.6 (Continued)

Comparison group: Models 10, 11—nationalist Model 12—RW Variable	Base model M10 Haz ratio (coef s.e)	Ideology dummies omit (nat'l) M11 Haz ratio (coef s.e)	Ideology dummies omit (RW) M12 Haz ratio (coef s.e)
Rival	0.572**	0.534**	0.534**
	(0.151)	(0.145)	(0.145)
Ally	0.489***	0.458***	0.458***
	(0.111)	(0.105)	(0.105)
Coleader	0.888	0.881	0.881
	(0.207)	(0.207)	(0.207)
Average target state Log(GDP/capita)	1.484***	1.528***	1.528***
	(0.219)	(0.227)	(0.227)
Polity	0.980	0.981	0.981
	(0.018)	(0.018)	(0.018)
N	2,637	2,637	2,637
N fail	111	111	111
LogLikelihood	−429.59	−427.07	−427.07

Founder Models

Since founders play an important role in any organization, losing the founder is often a chaotic event in an organization's life cycle. In my data set, 131 out of 207 groups have experienced at least one decapitation event. Of these 131 groups, 121 of them have lost at least one of their founders to decapitation. Groups, of course, can also lose their founders to circumstances other than decapitation. For example, founders can voluntarily leave the organization, be expelled by their own group, die of natural causes, or step down for other reasons. In this data set, founders left the organization for reasons other than decapitation a total of 14 times. Some groups are fortunate enough to never experience the loss of their founders, which is the case for 64 groups in this data set.[86]

Model 13 tests whether the decapitation of a founder has an effect on the hazard rate for a terrorist group that is different than the rate when a nonfounder is killed or captured. In previous models, the variable *exp decap* has measured the effect of all decapitation events involving the primary leader or leaders. This included the decapitation events of the founders. Model 13, however, includes the variable *founder decap*, which is measured similarly to *exp decap* in that the effect is "left on" for the duration of the group's existence, except that it only involves the killing or capture of the organizations' founders. The variable *nonfounder decap* is measured the same way, only it includes decapitations exclusively involving nonfounders. Finally, I included a variable called *founder in control* to account for groups that have their original leader or leaders in control of the organization. Since the group founder is so influential in determining organizational culture and performance, I hypothesized that the effect of this variable would decrease the hazard rate for terrorist groups.

As the results show in table 4.7, when a group's founder is in control of the organization, the group is almost 70 percent less likely to end than groups run by follow-on leaders. This holds true no matter how long the effect of decapitation is allowed to linger (e.g., one year, two years, or indefinitely). In Model 13, where the effect of decapitation is "left on" and allowed to linger indefinitely, it appears that decapitation events involving nonfounders place the group at more risk than when the founder is decapitated. Although this is a somewhat surprising finding considering the importance usually attributed to removing the founder, chi-square tests performed on *founder decap* and *nonfounder decap* reveal that the two are statistically indistinguishable from each other (chi-sq = .35, p-value = .55).

Model 14 is the same as the previous model except it includes a dummy variable *all founders gone* that changes from 0 to 1 when the founder or founders of the organization are no longer in power, regardless of how they left. This model also limits the effect of decapitation to the year in which decapitation occurs. In this model, removing the founder appears to put the group at more risk than removing the nonfounder, but again, chi-square tests confirm that these are statistically indistinguishable from each other. Since the dummy variable for *all founders gone* is statistically insignificant, we cannot conclude that groups face any more (or less) risk in the year their founders are removed from the organization.

TABLE 4.7

Cox Proportional Hazards Model: Founder Models

Comparison group: nationalist/separatist Variable	Founder vs nonfounder left on M13 Haz ratio (coef s.e)	All founders gone year only M14 Haz ratio (coef s.e)
Founder in control	0.328***	0.310***
	(0.088)	(0.085)
Founder decap	3.875***	6.747***
	(1.140)	(4.554)
Nonfounder decap	4.041***	4.220***
	(1.511)	(1.590)
All founders gone—year only		0.538
		(0.370)
Decaptime	0.991	0.989
	(0.019)	(0.019)
Log(group size)	0.945	0.945
	(0.055)	(0.055)
Ideology—LW	1.218	1.218
	(0.291)	(0.291)
Ideology—RW	2.911**	3.058**
	(1.518)	(1.598)
Ideology—religious	0.569	0.565
	(0.199)	(0.198)
Rival	0.692	0.698
	(0.181)	(0.183)
Ally	0.447***	0.445***
	(0.104)	(0.104)
Coleader	1.166	1.145
	(0.281)	(0.277)
Average target state Log(GDP/capita)	1.445**	1.437**
	(0.212)	(0.211)

TABLE 4.7 (Continued)

Comparison group: nationalist/separatist	Founder vs nonfounder left on	All founders gone year only
	M13	M14
Variable	Haz ratio (coef s.e)	Haz ratio (coef s.e)
Polity	0.978	0.979
	(0.018)	(0.018)
N	2,637	2,637
N fail	111	111
LogLikelihood	−414.85	−414.43

In sum, although removing both founders and follow-on leaders increases the hazard rate of terrorist groups, we cannot say with any certainty that killing or capturing the founder affects the hazard rate any differently than decapitating successor leaders. But we can conclude that groups with their founders still in control of the organization are significantly less likely to end than groups without their founders at the helm.

Method of Decapitation Models

Proponents and critics of decapitation strategies debate the merits of certain decapitation methods, namely, whether it is better to kill or arrest the leaders of terrorist groups. Some scholars believe that arresting the leader is more beneficial than killing the leader, and they support this claim using several arguments.[87] First, as mentioned in the previous chapter, there are more moral and legal issues involved with targeted killings than there are with capturing and incarcerating terrorist leaders.[88] Second, by arresting instead of killing the group leader, the state can interrogate the leader and obtain useful information about the organization. Better to arrest and interrogate than to bury the leader, because dead men tell no tales. Third, having a leader in state custody also damages the psyche of the group and reduces morale. According to Cronin, the incarceration of the group's leader is "an implicit answer to the illegitimacy of terrorism, and demonstrates the authority of the rule of law."[89] Hutchinson and O'Malley believe that "the demoralization that accompanies seeing a leader captive and under control of the enemy appears highly relevant to group perseverance."[90]

On the other side of the debate are those who argue that killing terrorist leaders is more beneficial than arresting them. Proponents of targeted killing contend that the tactic serves as a more effective deterrent. It sends a message to the group that future leaders will be next in line.[91] When the terrorist group leader is killed, the operational routine of the organization is interrupted, and the group must invest resources into finding a suitable successor. Moreover, knowing that the state is specifically targeting the leadership means the organization will probably invest its resources in protecting future leaders, which ultimately detracts from their ability to conduct terrorist attacks. These interruptions in the organizational routine are "liable to have ongoing consequences, rather than merely a short-term effect."[92] In other words, decapitation is the proverbial gift that (theoretically) keeps on giving.

Which side is correct? In order to provide some empirical evidence in this unsettled debate, I coded each decapitation event according to method. As previously mentioned, decapitation events included leaders who were either killed or captured, but I also coded a dummy variable (*both*) for when the leader is first captured and then killed by the state at a later date. When I was initially coding decapitations according to the two methods of "kill" or "capture," I was struck by the number of instances where leaders were arrested, only to die several days later in custody, ostensibly at the hands of their state captors. The logic here is that by capturing the leader first, the state has an opportunity to interrogate the leader and obtain information about how the organization functions in hopes of destroying it completely. Killing the leader afterward may provide the deterrent that Ganor and others describe.[93] Therefore, the decapitation method of *both* includes cases where death was a result of execution after receiving the death penalty or when the leader died from wounds suffered at the hands of the state, often during brutal interrogation sessions.

I examined the effect each method had on the hazard rate in several different ways. The results from these models are found in table 4.8. In Model 15, only the first decapitation event was included. If killing a leader does indeed have a deterrent effect, we should be able to see it clearly here. Additionally, looking at only the first decapitation removes all of the noise from this test to include additional decapitations and leadership

TABLE 4.8

Cox Proportional Hazards Model: Decap Method Models

Comparison group: nationalist/separatist Variable	1st decap method M15 Haz ratio (coef s.e)	All decaps left on M16 Haz ratio (coef s.e)	All decaps on for 2 years M17 Haz ratio (coef s.e)
Exp decap left on × time	0.948**	0.944**	
	(0.024)	(0.024)	
Exp decap left on × both	13.594***		
	(8.026)		
Exp decap left on × capture	8.859***		
	(3.308)		
Exp decap left on × kill	7.297***		
	(2.876)		
Decap method—capture		9.189***	2.171**
		(3.436)	(0.841)
Decap method—kill		8.100***	1.738
		(3.106)	(0.708)
Decap method—both (capture + kill)		8.451***	1.645
		(5.396)	(1.456)
Exp decap turned off × time			0.971
			(0.023)
Decap method turned off × capture			4.319***
			(2.054)
Decap method turned off × kill			5.625***
			(2.672)

(*continued*)

TABLE 4.8 (Continued)

Comparison group: nationalist/separatist Variable	1st decap method M15 Haz ratio (coef s.e)	All decaps left on M16 Haz ratio (coef s.e)	All decaps on for 2 years M17 Haz ratio (coef s.e)
Decap method turned off × both			8.345*
			(9.806)
Log(group size)	0.949	0.932	0.940
	(0.057)	(0.055)	(0.056)
Decaptime (years since)	0.971	0.972	0.993
	(0.023)	(0.023)	(0.023)
Ideology—LW	1.369	1.271	1.339
	(0.356)	(0.323)	(0.334)
Ideology—RW	4.711***	4.462***	4.317***
	(2.467)	(2.359)	(2.278)
Ideology—religious	0.644	0.604	0.603
	(0.231)	(0.214)	(0.213)
Rival	0.566**	0.565**	0.599*
	(0.150)	(0.150)	(0.158)
Ally	0.488***	0.483***	0.490***
	(0.112)	(0.111)	(0.113)
Coleader	0.890	0.890	0.894
	(0.208)	(0.208)	(0.211)
Average target state Log(GDP/capita)	1.536***	1.483***	1.491***
	(0.233)	(0.221)	(0.226)
Polity	0.981	0.980	0.978
	(0.019)	(0.019)	(0.019)
N	2,637	2,637	2,637
LogLikelihood	−428.86	−429.47	−422.03

removal via other means. Follow-on decapitation events will be included in later models.

When I interact the decapitation variable with each method of decapitation (e.g., kill, capture, or both) for the first decapitation only, the results show that all three methods significantly increase the hazard rate. Speaking in relative terms, killing the leader leads to the lowest relative increase in the hazard rate, while the state enjoys larger increases in the hazard rate by capturing the leader, and the largest increase when it both captures and kills the leader. However, none of these interaction terms are statistically different from each other.[94] All we can tell is that they all significantly increase the hazard rate.

But what happens when we include all decapitation events and not just the first decapitation of the group's leader? Model 15 only included the first decapitation, but Model 16 includes all decapitation events. Additionally, the effects of these decapitation events are allowed to linger until the next decapitation event and exist independent of previous decapitations. In other words, a group will continue to experience the decapitation effects of *kill* as long as no other decapitation events take place. If this group were to lose its next leader to arrest, the effect of *kill* would be "turned off" and the effect of *capture* would be "turned on." The results from this model reflect a change in the relative ordering of the three methods. According to Model 16, capturing a terrorist leader now appears to be the preferred method of bringing the organization down, but the two other methods are close behind. Interestingly, when the effect of decapitation method is conceptualized this way, capturing leaders first and then killing them results in the lowest increases in the hazard rate.

Model 17 is similar to Model 16, except that it limits the effect of decapitation to the first two years. After two years, the model assumes that the group's hazard rate is no different from that of a group that has never experienced a decapitation event. The interactions including capturing and killing a leader are both highly statistically significant, while the interaction involving cases where the leader is both captured and killed is only statistically significant out to 10 percent, and larger in magnitude than the other two hazard ratios. These relative differences are less important, however, considering that none of the effects from these methods are statistically different from each other based on chi-square tests. Model 17, though, does boast a modest increase in the overall fit of the data.

Since none of the methods differ in terms of statistical significance, it is impossible to determine which method results in the highest increase in a terrorist group's hazard rate. We can only conclude that each method significantly increases the hazard rate.

Leadership Turnover Models

Models 18 and 19 assess whether the effects of leadership decapitation differ from the effects of leadership turnover via alternative means. In Model 20, I collapse all forms of leadership removal to include decapitation into a single variable, *T/O all* (*T/O* is an abbreviation for *turnover*). This variable includes not only the killing or capture of a terrorist group leader but also all other forms of leadership turnover. Examples of alternative forms of leadership turnover include when leaders resign from the organization (*T/O mutual*), when they are thrown out by the group (*T/O thrown out*), and when they die as a result of illnesses and accidents.

Table 4.9 displays the results from these models. In Model 18, we see that removing the leader from any terrorist group increases the hazard rate significantly, over 6.5 times more than for groups that do not experience any leadership turnover. When leadership turnover is collapsed into this one variable, the difference between the hazard ratios of right-wing groups and nationalist groups is less than it was in previous models, but right-wing groups still face greater risk of extinction. The statistical significance of the variable measuring state counterterrorism capacity is reduced from previous models, and its effect on the hazard rate decreases, although wealthier states still appear more effective in causing the organizational decline of terrorist groups than poorer states. In short, Model 18 suggests that any type of leadership turnover seems to increase the hazard rate of terrorist groups.

But what happens when we compare leadership turnover due to decapitation to other means? Model 19 addresses this question. To answer it, I limited the effect of leadership turnover to the year in which it occurs.[95] The results from Model 19 show that leadership turnover via decapitation has the largest effect on the hazard rate compared to instances where leaders are thrown out of the group or when they leave under their own volition. The hazard rate is larger when a leader is thrown out of the organization than when it is a mutual decision, but the former is only statistically

TABLE 4.9

Cox Proportional Hazards Model: Leader Turnover Models

Comparison group: nationalist/separatist	All turnover (yr only) M18 Haz ratio (coef s.e)	Decap vs other (yr only) M19 Haz ratio (coef s.e)	All turnover (left on) M20 Haz ratio (coef s.e)	Decap vs other (left on) M21 Haz ratio (coef s.e)
Turnover (T/O) all	6.526*** (1.413)			
Exp decap—year only		7.235*** (1.634)		
T/O thrown out—year only		5.842* (6.027)		
T/O mutual—year only		4.727** (3.670)		
T/O all—left on			3.496*** (0.660)	
Exp decap—left on				5.328*** (1.329)
T/O thrown out—left on				1.724 (0.923)
T/O mutual—left on				1.984 (1.052)
T/O natural causes—left on				2.514* (1.286)
Log(group size)	0.921 (0.053)	0.932 (0.055)	0.881** (0.051)	0.917 (0.055)
Decaptime (years since)	1.023 (0.017)	1.025 (0.017)	0.972 (0.018)	0.952** (0.020)
Ideology—LW	1.381 (0.333)	1.362 (0.330)	1.260 (0.307)	1.218 (0.302)
Ideology—RW	3.036**	3.161**	3.426**	3.801**

(continued)

TABLE 4.9 (*Continued*)

Comparison group: nationalist/separatist Variable	All turnover (yr only) M18 Haz ratio (coef s.e)	Decap vs other (yr only) M19 Haz ratio (coef s.e)	All turnover (left on) M20 Haz ratio (coef s.e)	Decap vs other (left on) M21 Haz ratio (coef s.e)
	(1.593)	(1.698)	(1.757)	(1.980)
Ideology—religious	0.571	0.573	0.510*	0.547*
	(0.199)	(0.200)	(0.180)	(0.196)
Rival	0.647	0.640*	0.647*	0.618*
	(0.172)	(0.169)	(0.168)	(0.161)
Ally	0.506***	0.507***	0.464***	0.487***
	(0.114)	(0.114)	(0.106)	(0.112)
Coleader	0.935	0.972	0.870	0.860
	(0.222)	(0.232)	(0.204)	(0.205)
Average target state Log(GDP/capita)	1.437**	1.420**	1.531***	1.520***
	(0.213)	(0.210)	(0.230)	(0.228)
Polity	0.975	0.977	0.970	0.976
	(0.019)	(0.019)	(0.018)	(0.018)
N	2,637	2,637	2,637	2,637
N fail	111	111	111	111
LogLikelihood	−423.23	−421.44	−433.41	−429.63

significant at the 10 percent level. However, yet again, chi-square tests confirm that the effects of decapitation are no different from the other forms of leadership turnover.

Policy Implications

There is a robust literature on Israel's targeted killings of terrorist leaders and whether they are an effective tactic in stemming the tide of terrorism.[96] Decapitating terrorist leaders has been called "a misguided strategy" and "an ineffective means of reducing terrorist activity."[97] Decapitation strategies have even been characterized as "counter-productive."[98] However, the findings in this study cast doubt on the conclusion that decapitation strategies are ineffective in ending terrorist groups.

Of course, much depends on how one chooses to measure effectiveness. For example, one of Jordan's criteria for evaluating decapitation in her study was whether the group ceased any activity within two years of experiencing the loss of its leader. When the primary leaders were removed in the 124 cases that Jordan analyzed, the organization collapsed 24 percent of the time. To compare our results, I counted how many organizations in my data set ceased activity within two years of experiencing their first decapitation event. Of the 131 groups that were decapitated at least once, 40 met Jordan's criteria of organizational collapse within two years. Thus, compared to Jordan's conclusion that 24 percent of the groups collapsed, my finding is that 30 percent groups collapsed, which is not startlingly different. However, the two-year time frame is relatively short and fails to consider the long-term consequences that a decapitation event inflicts on a terrorist group. Although the two-year time frame is certainly a legitimate criterion for evaluating the success of a certain counterterrorism strategy, it flies in the face of many scholars and policymakers who state ad nauseum that there are no silver bullets in ending terrorism.[99] Thus one of the central arguments in this book is that the long-term effects of decapitation should be considered in conjunction with the short-term effects when policy decisions about counterterrorism strategies are made.

My analysis shows that decapitated groups experience a higher risk of organizational death than nondecapitated groups. Leadership decapitation has a disproportionate effect on the survival of groups early in their life cycle, and the magnitude of this effect decreases over time.

Therefore, in order to increase the chances that a terrorist group will end, policymakers should consider devoting more resources to decapitating a terrorist group as early in the group's life cycle as possible. Waiting does not necessarily negate the effects that decapitation will have on the organization's hazard rate, but the effects appear to diminish by half in the first 10 years, and it is statistically possible that decapitation may fail to have any effect on the organization's mortality rate after 20 years. A prudent counterterrorism strategy, therefore, may seek to identify terrorist groups and their respective leaders as early as possible and increase the allocation of resources to kill or capture the leader before the group ages and grows in experience.

One can also make an institutional argument to explain why the effects of decapitation appear to be more important in the early years of an organization's life cycle. This is because groups during the early years are likely more dependent and reliant on a terrorist group leader's charisma, resources, and individual organizational skills than in later years. Since terrorist organizations operate clandestinely, they have a natural disinclination to institutionalize. This is an often an impediment to organizational learning, but as others have pointed out, terrorist groups also learn by doing and through increased exposure to members with experiential *metis*.[100] Over time, group norms, procedures, tactics, and techniques, not to mention the social bonds between group members, may begin to assume a certain "taken for granted" quality that makes groups better equipped to cope and be more resilient in the face of a decapitation event. As Crenshaw stated, there may be "a threshold point, beyond which the extremist organization becomes self-sustaining."[101] Jordan argues that a terrorist group's level of bureaucracy also makes it less susceptible to organizational death following a leadership decapitation event.[102] Because leaders have unique organizational talents, their loss should increase the group's hazard rate, but the timing of decapitation determines how large the increase will be.

Another important finding concerns the effect of multiple decapitation events on an organization. Almost half of the groups that experienced decapitation in this data set (48 of 131) lost more than one of their leaders. However, notwithstanding the relative difference between the hazard rates of groups that have experienced different numbers of decapitation events, the results from Models 4 and 5 provide evidence that precludes one from saying, statistically speaking, that more decapitation events are better than one at bringing down a terrorist group. Supporting this point are the results from the models examining founders and leadership turnover, which suggest that any type of leadership turnover, not just decapitation, will increase the hazard rate. This is important because states may not have to kill or capture a leader in order to hasten the demise of terrorist groups. States that are uncomfortable with decapitation strategies, whether for moral or legal reasons or fear of the retaliatory "boomerang effect,"[103] may choose instead to exploit the intra-organizational rifts that exist in many terrorist groups and remove the leader through shaming or by pitting one side against the other.[104] It is unclear, however, how long it would take for these internal processes to succeed in destabilizing the leader, not to mention how difficult it is to implement this type of strategy in the first place. Ultimately it is up to individual states to weigh the costs and benefits associated with the employment of decapitation tactics.

Killing the groups' founders increases the hazard rate for terrorist groups, but so does removing their successors. It is impossible to statistically determine which subset increases the hazard rate more. The same goes for the different methods used in decapitating the group's leadership. It does not matter which of the three methods the state employs—kill, capture, or capture and then kill the leader of a terrorist group—all counterterrorism responses significantly increase the terrorist group's hazard rate. The relative ranking of each method differs according to how one specifies the duration of the decapitation effect, but even then, each method's effect is statistically no different from that of the other methods.

Finally, the results from the statistical analysis provide support—albeit relatively weak support—for the claim that religious terrorist groups are more resilient and tougher to destroy than nationalist groups. More often than not, the hazard rates of these groups are statistically indistinguishable. The most interesting finding regarding this debate comes from Model 11. Here, religious groups appear to be 80 percent less likely to end than nationalist groups based on ideology alone, but after including an interaction term of decapitation and ideological type, religious groups were almost five times as likely to die than nationalist groups (see table 4.6 Model 11). This runs counter to Jordan's finding that "religious organizations are the least likely to fall apart after decapitation, followed by separatist [analogous to nationalist groups in my data set] and ideological organizations [analogous to LW and RW groups in my data set]."[105] As Model 11 shows, compared to nationalist groups, religious groups were the most likely to end following a decapitation event.

Controlling for Endogeneity and Omitted Variable Bias

Some may argue that instead of measuring the effect that leadership decapitation has on terrorist group mortality, this variable is instead measuring "bad" groups or "bad" leaders who are incompetent or who needlessly put themselves in jeopardy. In other words, one could argue that of course "bad" groups and "bad" leaders get selected out of the system, but this does not have anything to do with leadership removal in particular. To control for this endogeneity problem and problems associated with selection bias, I included a dummy variable for groups whose leaders die while in command for reasons that have nothing to do with the state's counterterrorism efforts. These include leaders who have died of natural causes or were killed in some other random way, such as in a car or plane accident. If the hazard ratio for this variable is statistically significant and greater than 1, then this reduces the chances that my analysis suffers from an omitted variable bias or an endogeneity problem.

In Model 19, the variable for natural causes drops out of the model because the effect of decapitation is only "turned on" for the year in which decapitation occurred. Since there are no instances where a group ended in the same year that a leader died (16 observations), the variable is dropped from the model. However, in Model 21 I changed the specification for the effect of decapitation so that the effect is "left on" for the duration of the terrorist group's life cycle; the variable for natural causes is statistically significant at the 10 percent level (p-value = .07) and positive, indicating that groups that lose their leaders because of illness and accident are 2.5 times more likely to end than groups that do not. Considering the fact that several of these cases include leaders who lost long battles with chronic diseases such as terminal cancer, cases that allow the group to prepare and plan for the day when their leader died, this is an impressive finding. It points to the notion that this is a story about leadership and the loss of leadership, not a story about incompetent or inept groups.

Others could argue that intelligence is the driving force behind the effects derived from leadership decapitation. Do these terrorist groups end because the state happened upon good intelligence that gave away the leader's position? This is obviously very difficult to control for, but I can make a weak argument that the GDP per capita variable that serves as a proxy for state counterterrorism capacity may be controlling for this as well. Although some intelligence is certainly obtained through luck and happenstance, wealthier states may be more likely to have better and more robust means of obtaining intelligence than poorer states. Moreover, obtaining intelligence is one thing, but acting on it appropriately is another.

Conclusion

The quantitative analysis in this chapter provides strong evidence that leaders play an important role in determining the ultimate fate of terrorist groups. Removing them from power significantly increases the mortality rate, no matter how the effect of leadership decapitation is specified. It does not matter whether the effect is "turned on" indefinitely throughout the group's life cycle or is limited only to the year the decapitation took place. Controlling for time dependence, terrorist groups that are decapitated are more than eight times as likely to end than groups that are never decapitated. Additionally, any leadership changes, including changes that occur independently of the state's efforts, such as accidents or terminal illnesses, increase the mortality rate of terrorist groups. Decapitating the founder has the potential to net higher increases in the mortality rate, but it is not statistically different from killing successor leaders. The timing of decapitation matters as well. As terrorist groups age, they become more resilient to decapitation, a finding that has important implications for how states allocate their counterterrorism resources.

Group ideology and size are of marginal importance to a group's survival. More often than not, religious groups survive at a rate that is no different than nationalist/separatist groups, although the former appear especially susceptible when their leaders are decapitated. Groups that have allies and rivals are more resilient than groups that have neither.

For the variables measuring state characteristics, the analysis suggests that wealthier states increase the mortality rate of terrorist groups by approximately 50 percent, the argument being that they can devote more resources to counterterrorism than poorer states. On the other hand, the argument that democracies are at a distinct disadvantage compared to authoritarian regimes, who can use more heavy-handed counterterrorism tactics, is not supported by the results.

CHAPTER 5

The Effects of Leadership Decapitation on Hamas

The quantitative analysis from chapter 4 suggested that removing the leader of a terrorist group significantly contributes to organizational decline. It also identified several key variables that affect a terrorist group's mortality rate, the most important of which were the target state's GDP per capita, the existence of allies and rivals, the timing of the decapitation event in the organization's life cycle, and to a lesser degree, the ideology the group espoused.

These correlations may be statistically significant and substantive findings, but they tell us little about the causal process. It is difficult to see from the statistical analysis what micro-level processes are occurring at the group level that link leadership removal with the demise of the organization. Terrorist leaders were hypothesized to be important in determining organizational performance and capable of influencing all aspects of their organizations. Depending on the size and complexity of their organizations and the security environment in which they operate, their influence permeates all levels of command and control—tactical, operational, and strategic.[1] Yet what are the observable implications of removing a terrorist leader from power? How can we infer causality? After all, the relationship between leadership removal and organizational decline may be a spurious one. Maybe some omitted variable is actually causing both.

This chapter attempts to specify some of the micro-level effects that leadership decapitation can have on a terrorist organization. Although decapitation does not always result in organizational decline, decapitation often degrades organizational capability and sets the conditions for organizational decline. The large-N analysis in the previous chapter examined the systematic effects that leadership decapitation had on the duration of terrorist groups, but the most effective way to examine the micro-level processes that affect duration is through detailed case studies.

In that spirit, this chapter presents a case study of Hamas and its experiences coping with multiple leadership decapitation events. First, I explain why I chose Hamas as an in-depth case study. Second, I outline the history of Hamas, highlighting critical junctures that threatened the group's survival and affected its ability to conduct terrorist attacks, such as decapitation events and significant changes in Israel's counterterrorism strategy. Third, I provide evidence suggesting that leadership decapitation decreased the operational capability of Hamas, especially the group's ability to kill and injure Israeli citizens, even though the loss of several leaders did not succeed in ending the group.

Case Selection

Hamas is an interesting in-depth case study even though it did not suffer organizational collapse immediately following a decapitation event. There are certainly cases in which groups collapse after losing their leader, but Hamas is not one of them.[2] Hamas might seem like an odd case to study considering that the group has endured the loss of several leaders due to decapitation since its founding and yet is still active today. However, as the quantitative analysis showed, decapitation does not always lead to organizational death. Decapitation by itself does not predict any particular group's fate; it only increases the chances that groups will not, on average, survive. When oncologists diagnose a patient with cancer, they cannot predict with complete accuracy whether the patient is going to die, nor can they pinpoint how long the patient has to live. Based on the data available, doctors can, however, give patients an estimate on how their particular type of cancer has affected most patients in their demographic. Similarly, the quantitative analysis in chapter 4 showed that decapitation makes groups more likely to end and highlights the factors that make group dissolution more likely.

Hamas is an illustrative case study because it provides a test of the theory as a "least likely" and a "crucial case."[3] It also includes some interesting in-case variation. The group not only suffered the loss of its leader to arrest early in the organization's life cycle but also lost the same leader fifteen years later to assassination. This unique situation allows us to examine the evolution of the organization through four distinct phases. These phases coincide with the timing of Hamas's decapitation events. The first phase traces the group's history from its early days as an offshoot of the Muslim Brotherhood up to the arrest and incarceration of the group's founder, Sheikh Ahmed Yasin, in 1989. The second phase starts here and lasts until Yasin reassumes control of the organization in 1997. The period from 1997 until Yasin is killed in 2004 represents the third phase. The fourth phase starts after Yasin's death and continues to the present day. This case also presents an opportunity to see how important policy shifts in Israeli counterterrorism strategy affected the group. For the first fourteen years that Hamas was in existence, Israel purposefully excluded top political leaders from its targeted killings campaign. When it removed this constraint in 2003, Israel killed Hamas's founder and his successor in a span of one month. Researchers can therefore compare the effects of the targeted killing campaign before and after this policy shift.

Hamas represents a "least likely" case because its organizational characteristics, many of which were detailed in the quantitative analysis in chapter 4, should make it more resilient and, for lack of a better term, more decapitation proof than other groups.[4] First, Hamas operated as a nonillicit, aboveground organization for a decade before using terrorism as a tactic. The group was built around al-Mujamma' al-Islami (the Islamic Center), an institution that has provided social, medical, and educational services in and around Gaza City since 1976.[5] In fact, the Islamic Center was officially licensed by the Israeli government and run by Yasin. Providing social services made the group and its leader extremely popular among Palestinians, and the organization quickly developed a fundraising capability that would serve it well when it turned to terrorism. The ideology espoused by Hamas was a combination of nationalist/separatist sentiment and Islamic fundamentalism, which are the two ideologies in the terrorist literature thought to be the most resilient and dangerous.[6] Although estimates of Hamas's size differ, the group is thought to have more than one thousand regular members today, and possibly tens of thousands of supporters, according to the Council on Foreign Relations, making it a formidable adversary and capable of absorbing losses. The group has had both allies and rivals to contend with, two characteristics in the statistical analysis that were shown to increase a group's likelihood of survival. Hamas also faces a state whose experience with countering terrorism is relatively unmatched. Unlike groups like Fatah that featured a heterogeneous membership, Hamas was more selective in its recruitment, a characteristic that led to a more homogeneous membership and thus eliminated many sources of preference divergence within its ranks.[7] Finally, much has been written about the external support Hamas has received in terms of money and weapons, not only from states such as Syria and Iran, but also from its vast web of charitable donors across the globe, including in the United States.[8]

Hamas also qualifies as a "crucial case."[9] Although several states, including the United States, employ decapitation strategies for counterterrorism purposes, Israel is probably the first state that people think of when it comes to this method.[10] I think many scholars would look down upon a serious analysis of decapitation effectiveness without an in-depth analysis of at least one terrorist group waging war against Israel. It would be difficult to avoid talking about Israel in any discussion of decapitation strategies. Israel's policy of targeted killings is also highly controversial, and the debate over its effectiveness is well documented. As previously mentioned in chapter 3, the debate on decapitation effectiveness centers around the arguments made by two camps of academics and policymakers. Proponents believe that targeted killings are not only morally justified and a perfectly ethical method to protect Israeli citizens but are also effective in preventing terrorist attacks.[11] Critics argue that the targeted killings are immoral and unethical.[12] They say that instead of reducing violence, targeted killings incite revenge attacks and drive individuals into joining terrorist groups.[13]

No works, to my knowledge, have examined Hamas's organizational behavior and operational effectiveness purely through the lens of leadership change. By breaking the evolution of Hamas into four phases, it is possible to better analyze the effects of decapitation on organizational performance. This approach allows us to see how decapitation affected the group's internal dynamics and how it responded to the loss of its leader, and also to examine how losing its leader affected Hamas's ability to successfully execute terrorist attacks. Although the group did not catastrophically collapse, a closer look at Hamas during each phase reveals that decapitation made the group noticeably weaker, something that other counterterrorism policies, including those that targeted the group's lower-level leadership, failed to do previously.

Hamas is also an interesting case study because it has been cited by other researchers such as Jordan to support a general argument *against* the effectiveness of leadership decapitation.[14] A second look at the data is warranted in order to understand how the removal of top leaders affected Hamas's organizational performance and its chances of survival.[15]

In examining the state of the organization in each phase, I attempt to answer the following questions. How did leadership decapitation affect organizational performance, if at all? What changes did the group make following decapitation, and how did these changes affect organizational performance? And finally, since Hamas was able to endure multiple decapitation events, what made Hamas so resilient?

Phase I: The Beginnings of Hamas (1976–1989)

This phase begins with the start of Yasin's Islamic Center in 1976 and continues until he was arrested by Israeli authorities in 1989, two years after the official formation of Hamas. During these early years, Yasin's organization melded as a team and built strong ties that would serve it well when it became a terrorist organization. The Islamic Center was closely affiliated with the Muslim Brotherhood, a fundamentalist Islamic movement that started in 1928. The Brotherhood opposed the Egyptian regime and called for reinstatement of the Caliphate. It was not until 1987 that Yasin formally created the organization known today as Hamas, although almost all of its early members came directly from his Islamic Center.[16]

Background

When one thinks of the archetypal terrorist leader, the image of Sheikh Ahmed Yasin probably does not come to mind. Yasin was a quadriplegic, bound to a wheelchair because of a wrestling accident with a boyhood friend.[17] Yasin's hate for the Israelis was forged at an early age. After his father died when Yasin was three years old, he and his mother were forced to flee their village of al-Jurah in 1948, when the Jewish state was established. He spent the rest of his childhood in a poverty-stricken refugee camp in the Gaza Strip, close enough to see Jewish settlers move into his old neighborhood.[18]

Restricted by his lack of mobility, Yasin pursued a teaching career and tried to attend university in Cairo, Egypt, in the mid-1960s. Traveling back and forth between Cairo and Gaza, Yasin was arrested by Egyptian officials on suspicion that he was involved with the Muslim Brotherhood. Although Yasin was not a formal member of the organization, he received a month in solitary confinement in a Gaza prison (the Egyptians were then in control of Gaza).[19] Ironically but not surprisingly, the experience encouraged Yasin to become a full-fledged member of the Muslim Brotherhood in 1966 or 1967. He became a gifted orator, giving speeches in schools and mosques across the Palestinian territories, and was so popular that he became "the most famous voice in the Gaza Strip" during the outbreak of the Six-Day War.[20]

It was during this time that Palestinians began to refer to Yasin as Sheikh Yasin, despite the fact that he did not have any formal theological training. "The young sheikh's charisma, Islamic scholarship, and organizational mastery proved particularly influential among the youth of the refugee camps."[21] It was also around this time that Yasin was approached by Fatah, but Yasin refused to join because he felt the timing of armed resistance was not right.[22] Despite the nationalist fervor created by the Six-Day War, violent struggle was not in accordance with the Muslim Brotherhood's emphasis on reform through peaceful da'wah or preaching.[23] As a result, Yasin put all of his energy into expanding the influence of his Islamic Center in mosques, kindergartens, schools, and medical clinics throughout Gaza.[24] Yasin was instrumental in the establishment of the first university in Gaza, the Islamic University, which became a primary source for recruits years later when the group turned to terrorism.

Sparked by the success of the Iranian Revolution in 1979, several Palestinian groups split from the Muslim Brotherhood to join the fight against Israel. Still hesitant to militarize his organization, Yasin established several smaller armed wings that conducted terrorist attacks as early as 1983.[25] These armed wings conducted several small-scale attacks, and their initial success encouraged Yasin to militarize his main group. He then began procuring weapons in the mid-1980s from what he thought were sympathetic arms dealers, who turned out to be Israeli intelligence agents.[26] They arrested Yasin in 1984 and found him guilty of plotting to destroy the state of Israel, sentencing him to thirteen years in prison.

Yasin's incarceration was a mixed blessing for him and the future of Hamas. The botched arms delivery served as a relatively cheap wake-up call to Yasin about the skill and scope of Israeli intelligence. It was cheap because Yasin was not considered a major security threat at the time; otherwise he would have likely received a harsher sentence. Moreover, it was rumored that the weapons Yasin intended to buy for Hamas may have been meant to combat the Palestinian Liberation Organization (PLO), a move that many Israeli authorities tacitly encouraged. Thus, when Israel wanted to make a prisoner exchange with another Palestinian faction, the Popular Front for the Liberation of Palestine—General Command (PFLP-GC), a group that had taken three Israeli soldiers hostage, Israel saw Yasin as a small-time player. Israeli officials released him a year later on May 20, 1985, as part of the deal.[27] In the end, it was a relatively inexpensive lesson for Yasin to learn what he was up against in terms of Israeli intelligence, and as a result he took immediate measures to improve security within his organization.[28]

Less than two years later, on December 9, 1987, Yasin assembled his closest colleagues from the Islamic Center, and together they created a new organization named Hamas.[29] The outbreak of a violent uprising in the Palestinian territories against the Israeli government, known as the first intifada, was instrumental in Hamas's popularity and provided it with a target-rich environment from which to practice and perfect violent acts, including both terrorist attacks and guerrilla warfare against the Israeli military.[30] During the first intifada, Hamas would distinguish itself as the most militant group among a sea of violent competitors.

The First Intifada: 1987

Yasin structured his organization into several different wings, each headed by founding members of the Islamic Center whom Yasin knew well and trusted. Hamas had a separate wing for political decisions, communications, internal security, youth protests, and, of course, an armed wing.[31] As the first intifada gained momentum in 1988, Israeli authorities cracked down on Hamas, and at one point, they arrested more than 120 senior officials in less than two months, including each wing's leader. Strangely enough, despite several confessions that confirmed Yasin as the ringleader, Israeli intelligence officials never arrested Yasin, preferring to monitor him with twenty-four-hour surveillance instead.

With all of his primary leaders in prison, Yasin assumed an even more influential role in the organization. Already the head of the group's political wing, Yasin found himself coordinating other branches of the group, including the tactical decision making of the military wing. His "involvement in every aspect of Hamas activities" made him more powerful not only within the organization but also within the Palestinian movement overall, since the leadership of the PLO was headquartered outside of the Palestinian territories.[32] While Hamas had offices in other countries, including Amman, the fact that Yasin was not afraid to "get his hands dirty" and risk being killed or captured endeared him to throngs of Palestinians. One Hamas scholar said it best: "The Fatah-backed PLO leadership recognized that because it was in exile, and not side by side with the rock-throwing masses, it was losing organic support on the Palestinian street to Hamas."[33] This feeling of desertion was intensified when Yasser Arafat, leader of the PLO, announced in December 1988 that his organization recognized Israel's right to exist and rejected all forms of terrorism. This move was highly celebrated by the West, but to the millions of Palestinian refugees who dreamed of returning to their homes, it was a bitter pill to swallow.[34]

However, Yasin's micromanagement of his organization had a downside, and he repeated the same mistake he made in 1984. After one of his cells kidnapped and killed two Israeli soldiers in a three-month span in early 1989, the perpetrators failed to cover their steps and were quickly rolled up by Israeli intelligence officials. Israeli authorities were able to move up the organizational ladder after several interrogations until one member fingered Yasin with personally providing him with the money and specific instructions to conduct the attacks.[35] Israeli officials arrested Yasin in May 1989 and subsequently tortured him. When he would not disclose enough information to satisfy the interrogators about his organization, which by now was considered a serious security threat, Israeli officials allegedly brought in Yasin's son and tortured the boy in front of his father. Yasin still refused to confess. Yasin's interrogators brought the boy back in a couple hours later and tortured him again, and according to Yasin, the torture was so severe the boy almost died. Again Yasin refused to give up any more information. It was not until Israeli authorities marched in each Hamas member implicated in the plot and had them confess to Yasin's face what they had already told authorities that Yasin relented and gave up the information they wanted to hear. As a result, Israeli officials rounded up an estimated fifteen hundred members, including the entire first and second tiers of his leadership structure.[36] The lesson for Yasin was much costlier this time around. According to Barsky, "Yasin's involvement in every aspect of Hamas activities and his centralized control over a small, tightly-knit organization were nearly the cause of its downfall."[37]

Phase I: Discussion of Key Variables

Yasin's arrest and the subsequent crackdown on what remained of Hamas reflected a critical juncture in the organization's history.[38] Israeli security officials had arrested the group's most influential leader and almost every other leader in the organization. "The arrests effectively paralyzed Hamas and created a vacuum at the top level of leadership."[39] How was Hamas able to survive? The next section discusses the group's response to this mass decapitation as well as the blunders committed by the Israeli side that ensured the group's survival. But first there are several factors to consider that help explain why decapitation was not effective in causing an immediate collapse of Hamas.

One of the major findings in the statistical analysis was that timing matters when removing a group's leader. The earlier a leader is removed in an organization's life cycle, the more likely the group will end. If we use the same coding criteria from the statistical analysis and start the clock for Hamas in 1987, when it formally turned to terrorism and conducted its first attack under this name, then it appears that Yasin was in charge for only eighteen months before he was arrested. Thus the effect of decapitation on the group's chances of survival should have been relatively large. However, Yasin, his leaders, and many group members had already been in the same organization for over a decade before Hamas came into existence. Thus Hamas was not an organization built from scratch in the late 1980s. It was a group that had meticulously prepared for years until the opportunity to strike was right. If the group had followed other offshoots from the Muslim Brotherhood in the late 1960s and early 1970s, and Yasin had been decapitated two years in, the outcome might have been different. Hamas may not have survived the loss of its leader. The fact that Hamas could already rely upon a robust and mature organizational network, including many leaders who were intimately familiar with how the organization was run, helped it weather the storm of Yasin's arrest.

This anomaly suggests that coding the first attack of an organization as the organization's start date, as was done in the statistical analysis in chapter 4, deserves more scrutiny. If there are other groups that had similarly long periods of organizational history prior to turning to terrorism, then the effect of a decapitation's timing on the mortality rate will be different. In fact, if this is true, then the effect is severely underestimated in my statistical analysis.[40] The effect that decapitation timing has on group mortality may be even larger than it appears to be in the current models.

Additionally, the psychological effect of the mass decapitation may not have been as discouraging for the group as it could have been if it were not for the mood of the times. This factor is not accounted for in any statistical analysis. During the years of the first intifada, from 1987 to 1991, the Palestinian uprising galvanized the region and touched a sensitive nerve throughout the Middle East. Massive demonstrations, strikes, and protests consumed Palestinian society. And what was perceived as the heavy-handed and disproportionate response of the Israeli government only exacerbated the tensions.

In the statistical analysis, the presence of rivals and allies made groups less susceptible to organizational death. At this time in the organization's life cycle, Hamas viewed Fatah as a rival, but Fatah did not consider Hamas to be a serious threat to its influence in the Palestinian territories.[41] Hamas had a relationship with Palestinian Islamic Jihad and other factions, but it would not collaborate with them in joint attacks until later. In addition, Hamas was heavily financed and supported by external donors during this period. Although Hamas did not have a close and reliable ally at this moment in its life cycle, the group was not hurting for resources. According to Mishal and Sela, Hamas had "a marked financial dependence on the outside," including many international ties it established through the Islamic Center.[42]

Hamas's size at this time may have also made it more susceptible to organizational collapse after suffering the loss of its leader. Although there are no reliable estimates of Hamas's size during these early years, the fact that Yasin was heading up several wings at the same time, not to mention he allegedly handed over the funds in person to the cell leaders responsible for the 1992 kidnappings, leads one to believe that the organization was relatively small during this stage.

There is no doubt that Hamas was critically wounded during this episode in its organizational history. The next section will discuss how it was able to survive and how decapitation affected its operational capability.

Phase II: Yasin in Prison (1989–1997)

Phase II begins with Yasin's incarceration in 1989 and ends with his release in October 1997. During this time, Hamas had to function without its founder and most of its top-level leadership. The group was vehemently opposed to the Oslo peace accords in 1993 and waged many violent attacks, including its first use of suicide bombings, to spoil the process. As a result, Hamas and the PLO became bitter rivals and competed for influence among Palestinians.

There are four major reasons that Hamas was able to survive after the mass decapitation in 1989, one of which was internal to the organization. The other reasons were due to policy decisions made by the Israeli government.

The first reason Hamas was able to survive had to do with its strong roots as a social service provider and its deep base of what is called "leadership capital."[43] Before Hamas was formed, Yasin's Islamic Center depended on international donations to provide education, health care, and other public services to its constituency in the Palestinian territories. As the size and scope of the organization grew, it needed group members to work outside of the Gaza Strip and manage its expanding network of international contacts. When Yasin and most of the leadership were arrested in the mass decapitation of 1989, the organization turned to one of these leaders to come back and run the organization.

The group turned to Abu Marzuq, a close confidant of Yasin and a fellow member of the Muslim Brotherhood who had been studying for his doctorate in the United States during the first intifada. Marzuq was intimately familiar with the organization and had previously coordinated the group's international activities before moving to the United States.[44] Marzuq succeeded in doing what Yasin failed to do twice before—restructure the organization in a way that would make it more resilient in the face of Israeli pressure. Instead of controlling the organization from within Gaza, a move that made the organization more vulnerable to Israeli pressure, Marzuq decentralized activities within Gaza and the West Bank and controlled these entities from a safe haven in Amman, Jordan. Gaza was divided up into five areas, and Marzuq hand-picked each sector's leadership.[45]

Marzuq also streamlined the organization from Yasin's many wings into three distinct categories—security, activities, and propaganda.[46] This arrangement compartmentalized the cells so that if one was compromised, it did not compromise the entire division. Additionally, while the group slowly received its lower-level members back from prison, the activities section of Hamas (Jihaz al-Ahadith) was busy keeping the organization relevant in the eyes of the public by holding demonstrations, painting graffiti, harassing Israeli soldiers during protests, and carrying out other nonkinetic tactics.[47] These activities were not lethal, nor were they particularly effective against

Israeli forces, but they kept the group together and bought time for the group to recuperate. Moreover, Marzuq made it a priority to continue providing the social services that made Hamas so popular in the Palestinian territories. Thus, even though the group was not functioning at its maximum operational capacity during this time, its effective and consistent provision of public goods ensured that it maintained a strong base of support and a stable crop of recruits.[48]

Several events that took place external to Hamas also enhanced its chances of survival, including miscalculations by the Israeli government. First Israel made Yasin a household name by nationally televising his trial in 1989 (Yasin was sentenced to life and fifteen years in prison) and giving him national television exposure again in 1992, a move that allowed him to speak directly to Israel, Palestine, and the world. The second television appearance in 1992 was a move by the Israeli government to save one of its own. Hamas had kidnapped an Israeli soldier in December 1992 and demanded Yasin's release within twenty-four hours along with a televised public apology by the government. In an attempt to buy time and ascertain the hostage's location, Israeli officials interviewed Yasin on national television in the hope that he would order his group to release the hostage. However, because of the frail and wheelchair-stricken body of Yasin, not to mention his calm, measured, and charismatic articulation of the situation (Yasin favored saving the soldier's life but clearly spun every question so that it put the plight of the Palestinian struggle in the most favorable and sympathetic light), Yasin won over external audiences outside Palestine and put Israel and its actions during the first intifada in a negative light.[49]

Israel immediately followed up this public affairs propaganda loss with an even greater one. Once the deadline for negotiating the hostage crisis expired, Hamas executed the soldier and dumped the body. In response, Israel rounded up approximately 2,000 Palestinians suspected of being terrorists, and after determining that 415 of them were full-fledged members of Hamas and PIJ, they deported them on buses to the Israel-Lebanon border.[50] The highly televised event caught the attention of Lebanese officials, who refused to accept the deportees at the border. With seemingly no good options, the Israelis made the deportees disembark from the buses and left them standing in a snow-covered field, all of which was being broadcast to millions around the world. As reporters flocked to interview the deportees and told their story, the public learned that many turned out to be well-respected and upper-class Palestinians, including many university professors, graduate students, doctors, engineers, businessmen, and imams. The move was internationally condemned by both the United Nations and Israel's closest ally, the United States.[51]

One of the deportees was Hamas's second-in-command, Dr. Abd al-Aziz al-Rantisi, who shrewdly took advantage of the media exposure and ordered his contingent to stand fast instead of moving into Lebanon. The situation quickly became a media circus. Here the "outside" members of Hamas were able to meet up with the former "inside" members with ease, and key members were able to coordinate the group's next moves.[52] Mishal and Sela also believe that Hamas officials met with Hezbollah and learned about suicide attacks and the construction of car bombs. They say that "it was no coincidence that Hamas's first suicide operation was carried out shortly after the deportees had returned to the occupied territories."[53] Thus, in a span of a few days, Israel handed Hamas two badly needed propaganda victories that likely saved the group from what looked like certain defeat. As Tamimi noted,

> Before this crisis, which had begun with the kidnapping of the two Israeli soldiers, the name of Hamas had rarely been mentioned anywhere in the international media. There had been little interest in what it stood for or what it sought to achieve. . . . For the first time, Hamas was able to get its message across to individuals, organizations, and governments all over the world. In the Palestinian context, the movement forged fresh links with various Palestinian organization and factions. At the Arab level, it established contacts throughout the Arab world, both at governmental and nongovernmental levels. And in the international sphere, it was able to communicate with individuals and institutions within or associated with the United Nations and the European Union.[54]

The situation put Hamas not only in the international spotlight but also in a relatively favorable light. It kept the group politically relevant when its militant capability was at an all-time low.

After Yasin was arrested, the group experienced a steep learning curve in terms of operational effectiveness. Figure 5.1 graphs Hamas's operational effectiveness in terms of fatalities and injuries per attack.[55] Data for these measures were obtained from the GTD. Although some scholars focus on the number of attacks performed by a group, this measure can sometimes

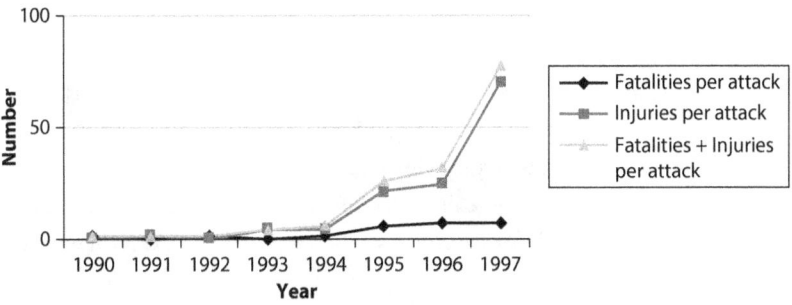

Figure 5.1 Organizational performance of Hamas (1990–1997)

be deceiving. Since terrorist groups use violence as a means to a political end, violence may be used more in some years than others, according to the political situation and the decisions made by group leaders. Therefore, when groups like Hamas sign cease-fires with the government and rival factions such as the PLO, as they have done several times, a reduction in the number of attacks does not necessarily indicate a lack of operational capability or a dip in organizational performance. On the contrary, it is a measure of the group's discipline. While Yasin was alive, Hamas was considered the most disciplined Palestinian terrorist group, not only in terms of its controlled use of violence but also in how it managed its finances.[56] However, once a group decides to attack, I assume it intends to kill or injure as many victims as possible for maximum effect.[57] Thus the ratio of fatalities or injuries per attack, not the number of attacks, may be more useful in measuring an organization's operational capability.[58]

According to the GTD, the group could only muster a few attacks in the immediate years after Yasin's arrest, and many were ineffective in causing large numbers of fatalities or casualties. On April 16, 1993, Hamas became the first Palestinian group to perform a suicide attack on Israel.[59] The popularity of this method grew, and Hamas quickly became more lethal. In 1991, Hamas killed one victim in three attacks (.33 fatalities/attack). After the group began its suicide bombing campaign, the ratio of fatalities per attack rose to 5.33 in 1995, 6.63 in 1996, and 7.67 in 1997. The noticeable increase in violence is also a reflection of Hamas's attempts to derail the Oslo peace process in late 1993, as well as a series of purported revenge suicide bombings sparked by the assassination of Hamas's top bomb maker, Yahya Ayyash, in early January 1996. Although "the Engineer," as Ayyash was called, was by far the most talented bomb expert in Hamas, he had already taken others under his wing and taught them what he knew about bomb making. His apprentice, Adnan al Ghoul, wasted no time in demonstrating his capability, masterminding five devastating attacks following Ayyash's death in February and March of that year. Since Ayyash's assassination interrupted a six-month period of relative calm between Hamas and Israel, the reprisal attacks sparked intense debate among Israeli policymakers about the efficacy of leadership decapitation.

During this period, it is important to emphasize that Israel's decapitation strategy was focused on killing suicide bombers before they attacked and the operational commanders on the military side who coordinated them.[60] It specifically did not target the top political leaders for assassination, although it did not hesitate to arrest top leaders when the evidence warranted it.[61]

According to the data, it took some time for the group to recover from Yasin's arrest. During this period, the armed wing of Hamas, the al-Qassam Brigades, operated with more autonomy than Yasin had allowed prior to his incarceration. The armed wing received even more autonomy when Marzuq was arrested at JFK airport in New York on July 25, 1995. Prior to his arrest, Marzuq was instrumental in a deal with the Jordanian government to permanently house a Hamas office on its soil. This deal provided a permanent and safe home to Hamas and facilitated command and control over its operations in the Palestinian territories.

It was in Jordan that Israel committed its final miscalculation of this phase, a blunder that would breathe new life into the organization and enhance the group's military capability. In September 1997, an attempt by two Mossad agents to kill Khalid Mishal, a rising star in Hamas and thought to have temporarily taken over the organization after Marzuq's arrest in the United States, went awry in Amman, Jordan, the new headquarters of Hamas.[62] The Mossad agents were apprehended and confessed to Jordanian authorities their intent to kill Mishal with a lethal injection of poison. The incident received international attention when the king of Jordan became involved and after it was discovered that the two Mossad agents had used Canadian passports that were illegally obtained. Israel immediately tried to minimize the damage caused by the embarrassing affair and not only agreed to deliver an antidote for the poison that threatened Mishal's life but also released Yasin from prison in return for the release of the Mossad agents.[63]

Hamas got its charismatic leader back in October 1997. It was a fortuitous event for Hamas since it was relatively rudderless after Marzuq's arrest.

When Yasin was released, tensions were already high between the "outside" leadership in Jordan and the "inside" leadership based in Gaza and the West Bank.[64] According to one report, the tension between these two camps was so great that a Hamas military wing in Gaza issued death threats to some of the political leaders such as Mahmoud al-Zahar and Jamal Salim.[65] Yasin's release occurred just in time to prevent "the Amman-Gaza rift from getting out of hand."[66] Without Yasin at the helm, a Hamas leader in the West Bank said there "was no centralized leadership in the West Bank and no decision common to the West Bank and Gaza. Here, it's a case of everyone deciding for himself."[67]

This lack of centralized control was especially apparent after the Ayyash assassination a year earlier. While Hamas leaders within the territories were trying to prevent a violent rampage in response to the targeted killing of "the Engineer," unbeknownst to them a small cell within Hamas conducted three suicide attacks in a span of two weeks. This rogue element allegedly received orders from the "outside" leadership in Jordan, but the "inside" leaders were completely unaware of such an order, and certainly would not have sanctioned it if they had been aware. As another illustration of how disorganized Hamas was prior to Yasin's release, several of the "inside" leaders held a press conference in early March 1996 calling for an end to all retaliatory attacks against Israel, while a few days later the "outside" leaders warned of continued bombings.[68] These sorts of mishaps did not happen when Yasin was in charge.[69] Not only did Yasin excel at mitigating the principal-agent problem between the "inside" and "outside" leadership of Hamas, but he also consistently smoothed over relations with the PLO and other factions.[70]

After his release from prison, Yasin went on a tour of the Middle East and was treated as a guest of honor and a hero of the Palestinian movement in Saudi Arabia, Qatar, Yemen, Sudan, United Arab Emirates, and Kuwait. Yasin had become so popular that Israeli officials even allowed him entry back into Israel in the hopes of confining his influence to the Gaza Strip instead of serving as a lightning rod for the Palestinian movement all over the world.[71] Yasin's tour not only raised awareness for the Palestinian cause but also netted the organization millions in donations, and he was able to expand the number of financial contacts the group would call upon in the future. Much has been written about Hamas's ability to raise funds for its cause, but what is even more impressive is the disciplined way in which Yasin made use of these financial windfalls.[72] Unlike the PLO under Arafat, an organization where corruption was rampant, there have been no public allegations accusing Hamas of misappropriating funds.[73] Yasin definitely diverted some of these donations to beef up the group's military capability, but he also made it a priority to fund the social services and programs that made his organization so popular among Palestinians.[74] When Hamas's leaders under Yasin wanted him to increase his monthly stipend to $1,000, Yasin would only accept $600, saying he did not need any more to maintain his standard of living. According to Tamimi, "Sheikh Yasin's example was followed throughout the ranks of the movement. No one joins Hamas to make money or has become rich by virtue of their position within it."[75]

Phase II: Discussion of Key Variables

When Yasin was removed from power and arrested in 1989, it took several years for the organization to regain its bearings. According to one scholar, "the removal of Sheikh Yasin created a vacuum that temporarily destroyed Hamas's ability to function."[76] The resiliency of the organization and the successful reorganization of the group by Marzuq after Yasin's arrest are testaments to the deep "leadership capital" Hamas had developed as an aboveground organization in the previous decade.[77] This resiliency mitigated the effects of the decapitation event so early in the organization's life cycle. However, if it had not been for several decisions made by the Israeli government—the national and international media exposure Yasin received while in prison, the deportation episode along the Israel-Lebanon border, and the botched assassination attempt on Mishal's life, which resulted in the release of Yasin—the effects of decapitation would have been much more debilitating.

Some scholars argue that political provocations such as the deportation fiasco are more important in explaining Palestinian terrorist behavior than targeted killings.[78] In their study of suicide bombings by Hamas, the PLO, and PIJ from 1991 to 2003, Gupta and Mundra found that military provocations in the form of targeted killings could not predict the number of suicide attacks committed by Hamas in any significant way. Moreover, they found that targeted killings had a highly significant *negative* effect on the number of attacks committed by the PLO.[79] In contrast, Gupta and Mundra found that political provocations by the Israeli government increased the expected number of suicide bombings from Hamas and PIJ and shooting incidents from the PLO.[80] These findings conflict with the widely held belief that targeted killings automatically incite immediate retaliation from terrorist groups.[81]

In addition to the debate regarding decapitation's effectiveness as a counterterrorism tactic, there is also a current debate surrounding which method of decapitation is more likely to end the group with the least amount of negative consequences. Some counterterrorism scholars and policymakers believe that arrests are better than assassinations.[82] There are several reasons for this argument. First, there are more legal and moral issues associated with killing a terrorist leader than there are with an arrest.[83] Second, the state believes it can obtain valuable information from interrogations that can help take down the entire group. Israeli officials certainly learned more about Hamas through Yasin's confession than they would have if he had been assassinated in 1989. Third, policymakers are afraid of inciting more terrorist violence because of the "boomerang effect" or the "martyr effect" after a leader is killed.[84] The logic here is that arresting a leader will not lead to such violent retaliatory attacks.

In the case of Hamas, however, the arrest of Yasin served as a rallying cry for the organization. Sometimes arresting a leader can provoke similar types of violence that killing incites, except that the former often produces violence in the hopes of rescuing a leader from incarceration whereas the latter is more retaliatory in nature and intended solely to inflict as much damage as possible. For example, the sole demand made by the Hamas cell that kidnapped and executed the Israeli soldier in December 1992 was for Yasin's immediate release.

Hamas's relationship with PIJ and other smaller Palestinian factions, not to mention its collaboration with Hezbollah, was important for the group's survival during this time. Some claim that the first joint attack between Hamas and PIJ occurred on January 22, 1995, when two suicide bombings took place at an Israeli bus stop.[85] It is unclear whether the deportation event was the culminating factor in linking the leadership of Hezbollah and Hamas, but sharing information about suicide tactics and car bombing definitely made Hamas a more lethal terrorist group.[86]

Phase III: Yasin's Return (1997–March 22, 2004)

Phase III begins with Yasin's release from prison in 1997 and continues until he was killed by Israeli forces in March 2004. With its founder back in power, Hamas was more active and lethal than it had ever been. This phase is telling because we can observe the effects of Israel's decision to remove its previous targeting constraint against top political and ideological leaders.

Israel released Yasin in October 1997, but he was placed under house arrest in Gaza by the PLO upon returning from his travels in 1998.[87] The house arrest did not stop Yasin from running the organization and solving problems that had festered during his incarceration.[88] Reacting to pressure from the United States to crack down on extremist groups, Jordan closed the offices of Hamas in its country in 1999, forcing the "outside" leaders to set up shop elsewhere. Hamas would eventually open new offices in Qatar, Syria, and Lebanon.[89]

Violence escalated in the fall of 2000 when the second intifada broke out, and it was during this time that Israel ramped up its employment of targeted killings. According to one scholar, the campaign of targeted killings that Israel embarked on during the second intifada had "never been implemented in such a systematic, continuous, large-scale, and overt manner elsewhere."[90] From September 2000 to April 2004, the Israeli government attempted 159 targeted killings and had an 85 percent success rate. Half of those targeted were Hamas leaders. Approximately 75 percent of these 159 attempts, however, targeted low-level military leaders and local operatives. Only 8 percent (13 targeted killings) involved senior political-ideological leaders.[91]

Despite the targeted killing of many of its low-level military leaders, with Yasin back in charge, Hamas was attacking at "full capacity" by mid-2002.[92] Figure 5.2 illustrates the operational effectiveness of Hamas during these years before Yasin was assassinated in March 2004. The effectiveness of this targeted killing campaign was hotly debated in Israeli policymaking circles. On one

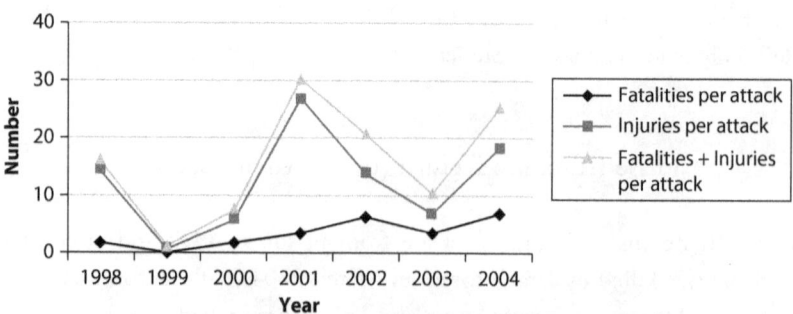

Figure 5.2 Organizational performance of Hamas (October 1998–April 2004)

hand, there were "signs of more than the usual poor planning, inadequate preparation, and sloppy execution" of attacks by Hamas and other groups as a result of the targeted killing campaign.[93] Pedahzur noticed the same trend. The targeted killings put terrorist leaders under intense pressure and "loosened their control over recruitment and training processes."[94] Whereas training for many of these attacks took weeks to coordinate and execute before 2000, some attacks during the second intifada were planned and executed in only a few hours.[95] On the other hand, there was also an increase in the number and lethality of attacks. According to the GTD database, there were only six attacks from Hamas in 1999 and 2000. The number of attacks increased to 21 in 2001, 37 in 2002, and 35 in 2004.[96] Hamas was credited with causing 474 fatalities and injuring 1,462 others from 2000 to 2004. Compared to the years when Yasin was in prison, Hamas was more lethal than ever, killing and injuring at a higher rate than ever before.

Hamas bore the brunt of Israel's targeted killing campaign during the second intifada. Although Hamas continued to carry out attacks against Israel in spite of the targeted killings, the offensive campaign took a toll on the organization. Both Hamas and PIJ agreed to stop launching attacks from the pre-1967 Israeli borders in December 2001 if Israel agreed to stop the targeted killings.[97] When Israeli prime minister Ariel Sharon approached the Palestinian leaders in February 2002 about a potential truce to end the fighting, he asked them point-blank for their demands. Sharon said the Palestinians' top priority was "to stop the targeted killings of the terrorist leaders."[98] Rantisi, Yasin's right-hand man and the primary spokesman for the group, uncharacteristically told a Danish newspaper how difficult it was to cope with the constant stream of lost leaders due to targeted killings: "The IDF has succeeded in hurting us. . . . I cannot help but admit it, there is an impact from the killing and arrest of Hamas leaders on our operational capability."[99]

Sensing that the campaign of targeted killings was showing increasingly positive returns, Israeli policymakers expanded the program.[100] Since the number of Israeli deaths had reached new heights in 2002, the government was desperately searching for better ways to protect its citizens. In 2001, 88 Israeli civilians were killed because of the fighting caused by the second intifada. In 2002, this number jumped to 188, including 66 deaths in the month of March (B'Tselem). In a major policy shift, Israel lifted the ban on targeting the highest-ranking political and ideological leaders. On July 22, 2002, an Israeli F-16 dropped a 2,000-pound bomb on the apartment building that was home to Hamas senior leader Salah Shehada.[101] The bomb killed not only Shehada but also fourteen civilians, including his daughter.[102] Senior Hamas leader Abu Shanab was next. He was assassinated on August 21, 2003. Two weeks later, the Israelis went after Yasin, dropping a 500-pound bomb on a residential building in Gaza City. Yasin was superficially wounded but survived the incident.[103]

It was only a matter of time before the Israelis killed Yasin. Unlike other Palestinian leaders, Yasin had a stable of bodyguards, but he "refused to take even the most basic security measures," even after the 2003 assassination attempt.[104] Six months later, on March 22, 2004, as Yasin was being wheeled out of the mosque he regularly attended every Friday, an Israeli Apache helicopter fired three 100-pound laser-guided Hellfire missiles that killed him and his entourage.[105] Rantisi, Yasin's successor, was assassinated in a similar fashion less than a month later.

Phase III: Discussion of Key Variables

Yasin's return to Hamas after his release from prison led to several observable improvements in the organization. First, Yasin had a unique ability to relate to many different subgroups within the organization. This skill helped maintain group cohesion, especially during trying times. As a longtime member of the Muslim Brotherhood, he had the respect and admiration of the older generation, including rival leader Yasser Arafat.[106] However, he also could relate to the younger, more activist generation that grew up as children of the first intifada and knew little about the Muslim Brotherhood and its earlier struggles. Thus Yasin served as a bridge between these different generations within his organization, a difficult task for any long-lasting leader in any organization. Although Hamas often battled with the PLO, Yasin is often credited with minimizing the friction between the two groups and keeping Hamas focused on the common cause of expelling Israel.[107]

Second, Yasin personally eased the tensions between the "inside" leadership and the "outside" leadership in Jordan that had developed while he was in prison. The divergence in preferences between these two groups led to confusion, resentment, and what one scholar called "Hamas's darkest hours."[108] The friction between these two parts of the organization was a serious problem when Yasin was in prison, and it would resurface after Yasin's death.

Third, Yasin's charisma was an undeniable source of organizational strength, regardless of the audience. Unlike Arafat, who was shunned by several Middle East leaders, Yasin was welcomed with open arms and treated like a hero throughout the region.[109] When he was interviewed by the media, he never failed to put his organization in the most sympathetic light and often refrained from the firebrand rhetoric that typified many other terrorist leaders. People were drawn to him. In an interview with an Israeli television station in the 1990s, the prison officer in charge of Yasin while he was in jail later stated that he was simply awestruck by Yasin's charisma, despite the fact that he was a terrorist leader.[110]

Thus Yasin's return to power in Hamas led to immediate improvements within the organization. He deftly handled intra-organizational conflicts, served as the bridge between different generations and competing groups, and seemed to make all the right military and political decisions to keep his group relevant. As Kristiansen aptly noted, "Ten years of imprisonment and multiple physical handicaps had not dimmed Shaykh Yasin's ability to seize the moment."[111]

Phase IV: Hamas After Yasin (2004–2008)

This fourth and final phase of the organization begins immediately following Yasin's death on March 22, 2004, and ends just before the 2009 Israeli-Gaza conflict. Rantisi was announced as the successor. During this period, Hamas endured yet another loss of its top leader, but the death of Arafat in November 2004 provided an opening for Hamas to become even more influential in Palestinian politics, which it exploited in the 2006 elections. Even with its newfound political power, however, without Yasin's leadership the group became more susceptible to fractionalization. The same rifts that emerged between the "outside" and "inside" leadership when Yasin was in prison resurfaced. So too did the friction between the political and military wings of the organization.[112]

While Israeli policymakers anxiously waited to see what the group's response would be after Yasin's assassination, many feared the worst. While Israel security forces had successfully killed numerous senior Hamas leaders, none were as senior or beloved as Yasin. Soon after the assassination, Hamas declared that Israel had "opened the gates of hell" and promised to kill "hundreds of Zionists."[113] Despite the thousands of protestors that came out to mourn Yasin and condemn the attacks, however, Hamas's response was meager at best, and weak at worst. Why?

First, it was reported that Rantisi, Yasin's immediate successor, "spent most of his time in hiding during the four weeks he served as Hamas's leader" and was killed by Israeli officials when he broke from his security routine to make an impromptu visit to see his family.[114] After losing two of its top leaders in a span of one month, the group then refused to name Rantisi's successor for fear of losing another leader. As Byman noted, although this was a necessary step to protect the new leader's security, it was "hardly a way to inspire [the group's] followers (let alone win converts) with [its] bravery."[115] Many believed Mishal was the next in line to assume the mantle of Hamas's leadership. He literally "phoned in" his speech for Yasin's funeral from his safe perch in Damascus, Syria.[116]

Hamas attempted two unsuccessful attacks in the wake of the assassinations against Yasin and Rantisi. The first occurred three days after Yasin's death. Two Hamas members emerged from the Mediterranean Sea on the beaches of the Gaza Strip, complete with wet suits and flippers, and began firing at Israeli settlements and a nearby army post. No Israeli citizens were injured, and the two militants were quickly shot and killed by Israeli soldiers. Hamas took responsibility for the unsuccessful attack but warned of more "earthshaking operations to come."[117] The second occurred over a month later on April 28, 2004, near a settlement in the Gaza Strip called Kfar Darom. A Hamas suicide bomber tried to drive a jeep loaded with explosives into an Israeli checkpoint, but the Israeli soldiers shot the man before he could reach his target. The jeep exploded prematurely, only slightly wounding four soldiers in the process.[118]

Hamas was unable to make good on its promise to deliver more "earthshaking operations" for the rest of 2004. According to the GTD, Hamas conducted only five more attacks after the botched suicide bombing in April. More importantly, the group was significantly less efficient in its attacks after Yasin's death. The number of fatalities and injuries Hamas caused per attack returned to pre-1997 levels, when Yasin was in prison. The average fatalities per attack, injuries per attack, and a measure combining both fatalities and injuries per attack appear in table 5.1. Hamas was almost twice as lethal when Yasin was coordinating attacks than when other leaders were at the helm.

Some may question whether it is justified to give so much credit for Hamas's tactical success to Yasin's leadership. After all, Yasin was officially the

TABLE 5.1
Summary of Operational Effectiveness (1989–2004)

	Yasin in prison May 1989–Oct 1997	Yasin out of prison Oct 1997–Mar 2004	After Yasin's death Mar 2004–Dec 2004
Fatalities per attack	2.24	4.28	2.33
Injuries per attack	9.00	13.87	3.83
Fatalities + injuries per attack	11.24	18.15	6.17
Number of attacks	75	109	6
Number of fatalities	168	466	14
Number of injuries	675	1,512	23

head of Hamas's political wing in the Gaza region. However, despite the organization's best efforts to separate the political wing from the militant wings, the latter were subservient to the former. Yasin was once quoted as saying, "We cannot separate the wing from the body. If we do so, the body will not be able to fly. Hamas is one body."[119] Several accounts point out that Yasin was "the authorizing and initiating authority for all Hamas terrorist attacks emanating from the West Bank and Gaza Strip" and "the decision-maker of last resort, managing most tactical and strategic issues."[120]

B'Tselem, the Israeli Information Center for Human Rights in the Occupied Territories, maintains a database of fatalities and injuries from the second intifada that includes separate statistics for Israeli citizens and Palestinians living in the territories. Its database starts in 2000 and extends to 2008, and it has been used by other scholars to make inferences about the effectiveness of Israeli counterterrorism.[121] According to B'Tselem, Palestinian militants killed 53 Israeli citizens in 2004 (more than half of which occurred prior to Yasin's assassination), and after cross-checking with the GTD database,[122] it seems that Hamas was responsible for 43 of these fatalities. In the years following Yasin's death, the number of Israeli citizens killed by Palestinian militants plummeted. B'Tselem lists 24 Israeli deaths in 2005, 10 in 2006, 5 in 2007, and 18 in 2008.[123] This is compared to 184 Israeli deaths in 2002 and 104 in 2003. Byman believes that attacks from

Hamas have actually increased over the years, but these attacks have not been effective in terms of fatalities.[124]

Hamas did not collapse following Yasin's death, but its operational capability was seriously weakened. What can explain these differences in the operational capability of Hamas? Was the loss of Yasin the determining factor in Hamas's declining operational capability? While it would be foolish to give all of the credit to Israel's decapitation of Yasin, additional evidence points to how important he really was to the organization.

In June 2004, three months after losing Yasin and two months after losing Rantisi, Hamas agreed to unilaterally accept a " 'period of calm' because of the losses it had suffered among its senior cadre."[125] It was at this time that some scholars think the group reevaluated its military capability and decided to enter the political system to further its goals, something it was hesitant to do in the past based on its commitment to armed struggle.[126]

When Israel disengaged from the Gaza Strip in August 2005, Hamas quickly built up its military capability, bringing arms and equipment into the area, allegedly with help from Iran and Syria.[127] Artillery and mortar fire from the Gaza Strip into Israeli settlements became a frequent method of attack. Although these attacks were not very effective in killing Israeli citizens, they created tremendous fear and anxiety in the population. It was difficult for Israel to respond militarily because these attacks were often launched from residential areas where retaliation risked civilian lives, not to mention the culprits were often long gone before the retaliatory rounds impacted. However, after the Israeli defense minister Shaul Mofaz gave Mahmoud al-Zahar and Isma'il Haniyya, two of Hamas's top leaders, an ominous warning about their own personal security should these attacks continue, Hamas quickly announced its decision to stop the rocket attacks.[128] When asked why Hamas agreed to the 2005 cease-fire, Avi Dichter, then head of Israel's internal security agency Shin Bet, said it was because "senior Hamas leaders decided they were tired of seeing the sun only in pictures."[129]

There are other plausible reasons for Hamas's inability to successfully execute terrorist attacks during this time. At the top of the list was Israel's increasing ability to protect its citizens. Although not popular with Palestinians, the expansion of security checkpoints and the construction of the security fence in 2003 made it much more difficult to attack Israel. As Byman notes, while Hamas and other groups continuously voice their objections over targeted killings and want Israel to abolish the practice, they have yet to make tearing down the barrier a primary demand at the negotiating table.[130] However, since Israeli casualties from terrorist attacks fell in areas of the West Bank that are unprotected by the border fence, these defensive measures do not deserve all of the credit either.[131]

In fact, it is surprising that Hamas did not become *more* lethal in the years following Yasin's death. After winning a majority of the votes in the Palestinian Authority's 2006 election, Hamas inherited much of the PLO's military equipment, including artillery pieces, rockets, ammunition, and even its small naval fleet. Its weapons were more powerful and accurate and had longer maximum effective ranges than the weapons used when Yasin was in power.[132] Additionally, during Yasin's reign, Hamas had to worry not only about Israeli intelligence infiltrating its organization but also about the PLO's security services. In 2008, as the majority party, Hamas was in control of these security services and did not need to be nearly as concerned with infiltration by PLO operatives as in the past. Thus the change in operational effectiveness after Yasin died cannot be attributed to inferior weapons or a more restrictive security environment.

Finally, there is much evidence to indicate that Hamas was haunted by the same organizational ghosts that plagued it during Yasin's incarceration, namely, the dysfunctional relationship between the "inside" and "outside" leadership. Even when Yasin was alive, the "outside" leaders were known to be more extremist and militant in their approach to the conflict with Israel, while the "inside" leaders were thought to be more pragmatic.[133] Safe from retaliation from both the PLO and the Israeli government, Hamas leaders in Jordan and Syria pushed a hard-line approach, but Yasin often ensured that cooler heads prevailed because he believed that such an approach would invite internecine warfare with the PLO and attract more pressure from the Israeli military.[134] After Yasin's death, there was significantly more friction between the Gaza and Damascus leaders.

There was also friction between the political and military wings of Hamas after Yasin's death. As Gleis and Berti put it, "Internal control of Hamas would never be the same."[135] Hamas's militant wings were unhappy with the focus on shoring up domestic support for the Hamas-led Palestinian government, and although Haniyya was serving as the prime minister, many believe that Mashal was directing operations from Damascus.[136] This friction was particularly evident during the conflict between Israeli forces and Hamas at the end of December 2008. Reports indicated that there was mass confusion between the Gaza leaders, who seemed to vanish from the public eye when the conflict erupted, and Hamas leaders in Syria, leading some analysts to question whether there was anyone really in charge of the organization during the crisis.[137] A telling example of this confusion was when two senior Hamas envoys were sent from the political bureau's headquarters in Damascus to Cairo to negotiate a cease-fire with the Israeli government. When reporters asked the leaders on the ground in Gaza what they thought of the potential cease-fire, the Gaza leaders had no idea Hamas was even considering a cease-fire.[138]

Conclusion

This chapter examined the organizational effects of losing a leader to arrest and assassination. The case of Hamas provides over three decades of organizational history, with important changes in leadership and organizational stability over time. Hamas experienced multiple decapitation events, but it was able to weather the storm and remains active today.

So what does this case say about the policy implications for a strategy based on leadership decapitation? First and foremost, this case study reinforces the fact that decapitation does not guarantee organizational collapse. The statistical analysis in chapter 4 showed that decapitation only increases a group's probability of collapse. The qualitative analysis shows that Hamas was definitely affected by the loss of Yasin, including the period when he was incarcerated and the period following his death. That said, the group went on to score a major political victory in 2006 and captured a majority of the seats in the parliamentary elections. The fact that the organization suffered three incidents of losing its top leader, including two in the span of a month, should warn policymakers that decapitation does not always succeed in dissolving the group.

The second point illustrated in this case study is that decapitation events do not occur in a vacuum. On paper, Hamas featured many characteristics that suggested it could withstand a decapitation event. It had important allies in PIJ and Hezbollah and a rival in the PLO, including Fatah and the al-Aqsa Martyrs Brigade. It had a relatively long history of organizational experience, albeit nonviolent experience, from its days as the Islamic Center and prior to becoming a terrorist organization. It enjoyed a broad base of domestic support[139] and had lucrative international connections that funded its social services program and its terrorist attacks against Israel. The state it targeted had to distribute its counterterrorism resources to counter multiple threats, which made it difficult to focus all of its resources against Hamas or any one group.

On the other hand, Hamas's reliance on Yasin should have made it especially susceptible to decapitation. The best evidence for this point comes from the significant fluctuations in the group's operational capability during his incarceration and after he died. Yasin not only was the group's spiritual leader but also exercised tactical and operational control and prevented internal rivalries from tearing the group apart. This fact should have made the group more likely to collapse after his death, but it obviously did not.

As this case study shows, several key factors weakened the effect that decapitation had on the organization, and most of these were decisions made by the Israeli government and external to Hamas. This point suggests that scholars should focus on taking a more cautious approach when evaluating the effectiveness of counterterrorism policies, especially when large-N statistical analyses are used as the only evidence for success or failure. There is a tendency for studies of decapitation effectiveness to focus primarily on the organizational features of the terrorist group—its size, ideology, organizational structure, bases of support—rather than on characteristics of the state and its policies. For example, in Jordan's 2009 statistical analysis of the connection between leadership decapitation and organizational collapse, she only includes variables that describe group characteristics; she does not include any measures of the state.[140] This case shows that other state counterterrorism policies in addition to leadership decapitation have substantive effects on the survivability of terrorist groups.

Finally, this case also speaks to the difference in effects between the targeted killings aimed at military operational leaders before 2003 and the targeted killings of top political and ideological leaders after 2003. When Israel targeted the former, the leaders of these organizations were able to turn the victims of targeted killings into propaganda tools, and they channeled the anger caused by the killings into vengeful action. After Ayyash was killed in 1996, Hamas conducted nine attacks in the next two months, including three attacks that all together killed 57 and wounded 164.[141] After Shehada was killed on July 24, 2002, Hamas responded less than a week later, killing 8 and wounding 80 at the Hebrew University in Jerusalem.[142] Yet despite warnings about "opening the gates of hell" after Yasin was assassinated, Hamas did not launch similar retaliatory attacks.[143] Neither did Hamas retaliate after Rantisi's death a month later.[144] The difference in how Hamas responded to the loss of lower-level operational commanders and how it responded to losing its top leadership has puzzled scholars and policymakers alike. Many thought that targeting military leaders would destabilize groups, bring down morale, and increase tension and group infighting.[145] The conventional wisdom was to avoid targeting the political leaders for fear this would create a martyr effect and an unending supply of terrorist recruits.[146] Although this case study is only one example, it suggests that killing the top political leader does not always provoke massive bloodshed, nor does it automatically harden the group's resolve.[147] To the contrary, the evidence suggests that the deaths of Yasin and his successor Rantisi have made Hamas a weaker organization that is more susceptible to fractionalization than it was before and much less proficient at carrying out terrorist attacks.

CHAPTER 6

Conclusion

Policy Implications and Future Research

Compared to other research topics in the field of terrorism, the question of how leaders affect terrorist group behavior is understudied. Terrorist group leaders have a unique incentive structure and face different constraints than leaders in other organizations. Although we know relatively little about how leadership succession ultimately affects terrorist groups and their behavior, several states have made decapitation strategies a central part of their counterterrorism strategy. The debate surrounding the efficacy of leadership decapitation as a tactic in the so-called war on terror is a heated one. Arguments on both sides of the debate, made by both scholars and policymakers, are not often grounded in the empirical record, and if they are, they tend to be overly reliant on a few case studies that exclusively support a specific viewpoint. The topic is only now being studied in a systematic fashion.[1] Not only is the issue ripe for empirical testing, but it is also in need of theoretical justification to explain why leadership decapitation might succeed against terrorist groups when it has failed against other types of organizations such as drug cartels and state leaders.[2]

This book was an attempt to fill in some of these gaps and understand how leadership decapitation affects terrorist group duration. This chapter summarizes the major findings from my analysis, provides insight into the current policy implications surrounding leadership decapitation, and concludes by recommending useful extensions to this project, the most important of which is bringing better data to bear on the problem.

The Argument

Chapter 1 illuminated the gaps in the terrorism literature that deal with leadership and its effects on organizational performance. Leaders are important in every organization, but they are especially important in terrorist groups. Studies that examine the causes of terrorism focus primarily on large-scale, systemic factors such as the political and economic grievances that motivate groups to resort to terrorism. Other studies focus on the individual-level factors that cause people to join terrorist organizations. Both levels of analysis are important for developing a coherent and comprehensive counterterrorism strategy, but they downplay the organizational approach and the crucial role that leaders play in determining terrorist group behavior. More importantly, numerous U.S. national security documents state that disrupting and destroying terrorist groups are important counterterrorism goals. The first core task in the *National Strategy for Combating Terrorism* of 2003 declares that "the United States and its partners will defeat terrorist organizations of global reach."[3] The 2011 *National Strategy for Counterterrorism* specifically targets one terrorist enterprise, al-Qaeda. Finding effective ways to affect the macro-level factors that promote fertile environments for terrorism and understanding how to prevent future generations from joining terrorist groups are vital to our long-term counterterrorism strategy, but they do little to address the problem of disrupting and destroying active terrorist groups in the short term. Therefore, it is imperative that we learn the most effective ways to end terrorist organizations.

Decapitating the group's top leader is one of the ways in which states have tried to destroy and dissolve terrorist groups in the past, but there is much disagreement about the efficacy of this tactic. Some even argue that it is counterproductive and allows groups to survive longer than they would have otherwise.[4] Kaplan and his team argue that decapitations increase the "terror stock" and inspire more individuals to join terrorist groups.[5] Additionally, some scholars examine the effectiveness of decapitation strategies by aggregating across vastly different types of organizations, including states, religious organizations, and cults.[6] This approach is problematic because different organizational types feature different leader-follower dynamics. These dynamics are important in explaining variation in the effectiveness of decapitation strategies. They are the reason why leadership decapitation is ineffective against some organizations but not others.

Chapter 2 attempted to disentangle the organizational dimensions that affect a leader's influence on organizational performance. It presented a typology that depicts how organizational types differ across three dimensions that are important in explaining not only how important leaders are to each organization but also where and when leadership succession should create the most instability. The typology illustrates why leadership succession is more difficult in some organizations than others. For example, the sudden death of CEOs seems to have little impact on the organizational performance of the economic firms they led, while capturing or killing a prominent terrorist leader has often been credited with causing decline in the terrorist organization. Why do some fanatical cults collapse shortly after losing their leader, yet drug cartels and street gangs are seemingly unaffected after losing their top leaders, time and time again? Chapter 2 proposes a theoretical justification that answers these questions. In short, leaders of violent, clandestine, and values-oriented organizations are influential in determining organizational performance. Replacing leaders in these types of organizations is often more difficult than replacing leaders in nonviolent, aboveground organizations that are primarily driven by profit maximization.

Chapter 3 provided an in-depth look at the influence leaders wield in terrorist organizations based on the three dimensions outlined in chapter 2. In addition to being violent, clandestine, and values-based organizations, terrorist groups have other organizational features that amplify the importance of their leaders, such as the size and complexity of the organization, the leader's status as the group's founder, and whether the organization started from scratch or resorted to terrorism after an initial period of nonviolence. I generated hypotheses from these characteristics that could help evaluate how leadership decapitation affected the survival rate of terrorist groups.

Chapter 4 tested these hypotheses against an original data set, the largest open source data set of its kind, to see how leadership decapitation affected the survival rate of terrorist groups. To do so, I used a Cox proportional hazard model, the most widely used model for studying survival analysis and a model that can accommodate right-censored data. The findings from the statistical analysis confirmed many of the initial hypotheses and provide useful information for policymakers to consider when crafting counterterrorism policy and strategy.

First, killing or capturing the head leader significantly increases the mortality rate for terrorist groups. Decapitated groups are more than eight times as likely to end as groups that are never decapitated. This is a robust finding that holds in a variety of settings, no matter how one chooses to specify the duration of the decapitation effect on the terrorist group (i.e., the effect endures indefinitely after the decapitation, lasts for two years after decapitation, or is limited to only the year in which decapitation occurs).

Second, the timing of the leadership decapitation matters. Older groups mitigate the effect that decapitation has on their chances of survival. The earlier decapitation occurs in a group's life cycle, the more likely the group will end. When the effect of decapitation is allowed to linger indefinitely after a group loses its leader, the quantitative analysis showed that, on average, decapitated groups were greater than eight times more likely to end than nondecapitated groups. After approximately ten years, this effect was reduced by half, and after approximately twenty years, it is possible that leadership decapitation can have no effect on the group's mortality rate. Therefore, decapitating the group's leader as early as possible in the organization's life cycle provides the greatest chances of ending the group. Taking out the leader later in the group's life cycle may still help to facilitate organizational decline, but the magnitude of the effect will just be smaller.

Third, leadership change in terrorist groups also increases the mortality rate, regardless of what prompts the change. In other words, killing or capturing the group's leader increases the hazard rate, but so do leadership changes that occur due to natural causes, accidental death, mutual decisions between the group and the leader to voluntarily step down, or cases where the group forcibly removes the leader because of incompetence or a loss of confidence. Depending on how long the effect of decapitation is allowed to affect the organization, decapitating the founder has the potential to increase the hazard rate more than removing a successor will, but on average, there is no statistically significant difference between the two.

Fourth, ideology and size are less important in determining the longevity of terrorist groups than originally thought. Right-wing groups fare poorly in terms of duration, although they are severely underrepresented in the data set. Interestingly, it was often statistically impossible to say that religious groups were, on average, more or less resilient than ethno-nationalist groups. In the model that included an interaction term to see how decapitated groups differed according to ideology (chapter 4, Model 11), religious groups were over 74 percent more resilient than nationalist groups. However, this finding was balanced by one suggesting that religious groups that had experienced decapitation were almost five times more likely to end than decapitated nationalist groups. Although the variable capturing the size of the group was in the expected direction (i.e., an increase in group size would lead to a decrease in the mortality rate), it never achieved statistical significance by conventional standards (p-value < .05).

Finally, other variables that can regularly affect the duration of terrorist groups include the existence of rivals and allies, as well as the economic resources a state can bring to bear. Terrorist groups that have allies in the form of other terrorist groups are more resilient than groups that have to go it alone. Paradoxically, the existence of rival terrorist groups can also increase a group's chances for survival, a somewhat counterintuitive and interesting finding, but one that is in line with latest research in the field.[7] This fact suggests that groups facing rivals are forced to learn and adapt more quickly than groups without competitors. An alternative explanation might focus on the state's ability to counter multiple groups rather than organizational traits endogenous to the group. In other words, if the existence of allies forces the state to distribute its counterterrorism resources across multiple groups, then the existence of rivals forces the state to do the same. For example, Hamas and Fatah shared the same general goal of liberating Palestine from Israel, but they were bitter rivals competing for power, influence, and resources. In the end, Israel had to devote resources to combat both groups.

The variable measuring target state GDP per capita was a proxy for state counterterrorism capacity. Its effect remained statistically significant throughout all the models. On average, a one-unit change in the target states' GDP per capita increased the mortality rate of terrorist groups between 42 and 53 percent. Put another way, terrorist groups that targeted wealthier states with more resources available to devote to counterterrorism were more likely to die than groups that targeted poorer states.

Although democracies were disproportionately targeted by terrorist groups in this data set, the variable measuring the effect of Polity scores was never statistically significant. This fact weakens the argument that democracies are less suited to combat terrorist groups than their authoritarian counterparts. Additionally, the existence of a cofounder (43 of 207 groups) does not seem to matter in explaining group longevity after a decapitation.

The statistical analysis was able to show which variables were most important in affecting the duration of terrorist groups. It is difficult, however, to extract from the statistical model precisely how decapitations affect the group. In other words, what is it about leadership decapitation that contributes to organizational decline? Chapter 5 demonstrates the need for in-depth case studies to be used in conjunction with large-N statistical analyses in order to gain more traction in understanding decapitation effectiveness and how groups respond after the loss of their top leader.

Hamas served as an interesting test case for several reasons. First, it was a "least likely" case because the organization featured many characteristics identified in chapter 4 that should ostensibly reduce a group's mortality rate and make it more "decapitation proof." It also made for an important case because of the threat it poses to Israel and the fact that it has suffered several high-profile decapitations. Furthermore, the in-case variation that Hamas provides makes it a useful guinea pig of sorts for testing decapitation effectiveness. Since Israel changed its targeted killing policy to include targeting top political and ideological leaders in the middle of the second intifada, sixteen years after Hamas was founded, we can observe the before and after effects of that policy shift. Since Yasin was initially arrested, released eight years later, and then killed seven years after that, we are able to analyze two different methods of decapitation and long periods of time to evaluate other measures of organizational performance that relate to organizational decline.

The fact that Hamas was able to survive multiple decapitation events, including the loss of a very charismatic and competent founder in Yassin, should serve as a warning to policymakers that decapitation does not guarantee organizational collapse. What this case study does show, however, is that decapitation does not occur in a vacuum. Other events occurring around the same time a group is decapitated can determine whether a group is able to survive. For example, I am skeptical that Hamas would have enjoyed the operational and political success it enjoyed after 1997 if Yassin had remained in prison. Decapitating a group will increase its chances of collapse, but collapse also depends on additional factors. As mentioned previously, there are no "silver bullets" in counterterrorism, and decapitation strategies are no exception.

Policy Discussion

This study is agnostic when it comes to advocating leadership decapitation as a counterterrorism tactic for the United States and other nations. As Byman states, it is ultimately up to policymakers to determine if the benefits outweigh the costs in each particular case.[8] Additionally, definitions matter. It is not often clear what is meant when people talk about "effective" counterterrorism policies. It depends on what metrics of success are used to determine effectiveness. If effectiveness is measured in short-term reductions in the lethality, frequency, and number of terrorist attacks a group is able to conduct, then decapitation may not be the most preferable strategy.[9] A discussion of effectiveness, however, should avoid focusing solely on short-term metrics. As with any policy evaluation, metrics of success should be comprehensive and include long-term effects as well. We do this with policies in other fields such as health care, economics, and education, and we should do it in counterterrorism. The public needs to understand that some counterterrorism actions are going to have short-term negative consequences, but they may be sound strategies for success in the long run.

I advocate for alternative ways of conceptualizing the threat posed by terrorism and the methods by which we should combat that threat.[10] There are several traditional analytical frameworks that have influenced how policymakers view terrorism and counterterrorism. The war model, for example, sees terrorism as an act of war, and thus advocates for military solutions to the problem. Others use a criminal justice/legal model that views terrorism as a crime, which then leads policymakers to emphasize the police, judiciary, and law enforcement agencies in a particular counterterrorism strategy. Finally, some say that terrorism is not a criminal justice problem, but a political problem. Rather than emphasizing the police or the military in counterterrorism, the reconciliation model puts political reforms, negotiations, and diplomacy in the lead to address political grievances that give rise to terrorist groups and extremist behavior.

Inherent in all of these models, however, is the assumption that terrorism is like other national security threats that we have faced in the past, threats that the United States has solved, defeated, or vanquished. After all, the United States defeated fascism and totalitarianism in the world wars and communism in the Cold War, so why can't it defeat this threat in the same manner? I argue that terrorism is different. We should understand terrorism for what it is—an all but inevitable facet of modern life that can be managed but never fully eliminated—instead of what we want terrorism to be—another security threat that we can defeat and vanquish if we focus enough energy and attention on it.[11] Like other transregional threats we face today, such as climate change and pandemics, terrorism cannot be solved or defeated unilaterally by the United States or any other country.

Instead of comparing terrorism to previous national security threats and relying on traditional frameworks used in the past, I propose an alternative approach. Counterterrorism officials should take an epidemiological approach that views terrorism as a chronic disease like cancer rather than as a military, ideological, or sociopolitical problem. Counterterrorism policymakers and scholars can learn a great deal from how oncologists combat different varieties of cancer. There has been a tremendous learning curve in oncology over the past century, and counterterrorism officials can easily relate to the challenges and the mistakes that have been made in treating cancer.[12]

Can cancer treatments tell us anything about leadership decapitation and its effectiveness as a counterterrorism tool? Yes; in fact, the methodology used in chapter 4 to quantitatively analyze the effects of decapitation on terrorist group mortality is the same methodology used to evaluate cancer treatments. The difference, of course, is that in oncology, researchers are trying to find treatments that are going to help treat the disease and help extend the patient's life for as long as possible. Counterterrorism officials, however, have the opposite goal. Counterterrorism academics, policymakers, and practitioners are searching for the treatment or treatments that accelerate the death of the "patient."

Second, oncology can also help counterterrorism officials and researchers with historical perspective and hope for the future. In the early days of treating cancer, surgery was often the only tool in the toolbox, and doctors often operated under a "more is better" mentality when it came to removing cancerous tumors and tissue.[13] The same "more is better" mentality carried over when radiation and chemotherapy became new options for cancer treatment. Commenting on these early techniques, which left many cancer patients permanently deformed, disfigured, and often wishing they were dead, one oncologist said, "If we didn't kill the tumor we killed the patient."[14] While oncologists have dramatically improved cancer treatments today, many cancer patients can relate to American playwright Anna Deavere Smith, who once said, "Cancer therapy is like beating the dog with a stick to get rid of his fleas."[15]

While it is true that cancer treatments like chemotherapy and radiation have nasty side effects, including extreme nausea, hair loss, and weight loss, these are only short-term consequences. If we evaluated cancer treatments like chemotherapy and radiation therapy based solely on their negative short-term side effects, they would cease to exist as treatments. In the long term, however, doctors believe these methods give the patient the highest probability of survival and serve as the best ways to combat the disease.

Doctors are transparent and up-front with their patients about the short-term negative effects of these treatments, and patients know that these treatments are in their long-term interests.

If we believe that terrorism is a chronic ailment like cancer that is unlikely to be cured anytime soon, then it is imperative to conceptualize the terrorist threat and evaluate counterterrorism "treatments" in the same manner. Leadership decapitation involves a number of trade-offs, and the tactic has undeniable negative consequences in the short term. This study suggests that leadership decapitation is an effective tactic in causing organizational decline for terrorist groups in the long term. Evaluations of the tactic should therefore include a comprehensive cost-benefit analysis of the short- and long-term consequences. Moreover, just as oncologists were able to study and learn from countless clinical trials to tailor treatments for specific cancers, so too should scholars and policymakers with various counterterrorism tactics. Although counterterrorism officials do not have the luxury of conducting controlled clinical trials in the counterterrorism field, more can be done to rigorously evaluate different tactics to see what works, what does not, and in what optimal combination and sequence they should be employed. Oncologists are constantly tweaking treatments to dial in the optimum treatments and doses to combat cancer. Counterterrorism scholars should seek to do the same.

I am hesitant to make specific policy recommendations based on my analysis because there are important limitations to this study that deserve consideration. First, although I included controls that tried to show that it was leadership removal, and not some other variable, that increased the chances for organizational decline, this study could still suffer from an omitted variable problem. Because of the lack of information that is available when trying to open the black box of clandestine organizations like terrorist groups, the omitted variable problem is even more pronounced. Second, this study does not differentiate between cases where the state specifically targets the group's leader, such as a carefully planned assassination attempt, and cases where the leader is killed or captured by happenstance in some larger operation. In other words, it treats cases where the primary leader was killed by a sniper the same as cases where the state kills or captures entire portions of the group in a large-scale raid. In the latter case, we might expect groups to end much sooner than in the former case, but this study treats both cases the same. I leave it to future researchers to make this distinction and improve upon this work, although data availability may still be the crux of the problem.

Extensions to the Model and Conclusion

The findings in the statistical analysis were robust and, for the most part, consistent. Although the degree of statistical significance varied from one model to the next for some of the control variables, the variables for leadership decapitation were highly significant throughout, both statistically and substantively. Therefore, to refine our understanding of how terrorist groups end, researchers should focus on supplying the model with more detailed and accurate information. Unfortunately, most of this information is not publicly available, so it will most likely be up to policymakers to either provide scholars with better information or take the models in this dissertation and conduct their analyses in classified settings. Either way, the following are a few suggestions for improving the model.

First, governments should have more detailed information about group-specific characteristics than open source researchers. For example, in my model I used the maximum group size as a proxy for a terrorist group's operational capability and its ability to absorb losses. However, a group's size changes over time, and thus so should its capabilities, but this fact is not reflected in my model. Since Cox models can accommodate time-varying covariates (e.g., both of the variables for GDP per capita and Polity scores changed over time), adding this information to the model should provide a better fit of the data. The same could be said for a group's ideology and current allies and rivals. In my model, these variables remain fixed and are independent of time, when they should actually be dependent on time. Government intelligence agencies should also have a better understanding of how salient a particular ideology is for a certain group. More detailed and accurate data about these groups will only improve the model.

Second, even if states do not always have the most detailed and accurate information about every group that poses a threat to them, they should know precisely how they are allocating resources to combat each group. In my model, GDP per capita served as a proxy for a state's counterterrorism capacity. This was an admittedly rough measure, but it was used because states are understandably hesitant to disclose the size and scope of their counterterrorism bureaucracies. Detailed information about how many counterterrorism resources—namely, time and organizational bandwidth—are being devoted to particular groups can provide policymakers with a better understanding of the relationship between resource allocation and counterterrorism effectiveness, regardless of how the latter is defined. For example, assume the effect of leadership decapitation holds, even with the addition of more detailed and accurate information into the Cox model, and that removing a terrorist leader significantly increases the mortality rate in the first five years of an organization's life cycle but drops precipitously thereafter. In this situation, states can allocate their resources accordingly, spending substantially more to decapitate the leader early in the organization's life cycle and then shifting resources to other counterterrorism tactics that are more likely to bring about organizational decline as the group ages. Just as cancer treatments are constantly refined to maximize the life expectancy of the patient, counterterrorism strategies should be reevaluated to maximize the terrorist group's mortality rate.[16] Similarly, decisions concerning leadership decapitation, if a state chooses to employ the tactic, should be group specific. As this study has shown, counterterrorism strategies that are effective in dissolving one particular group may not work against another group.

Third, this study shows that leadership turnover by any means produces effects in the mortality rate of terrorist groups that are similar to those produced by decapitation. If this finding holds after better data are included in the model, then states can focus on other ways, including nonviolent methods, to produce leadership change within terrorist groups. There are a number of ways that states can target group cohesion and increase dissension in the ranks.[17] Israel attempted to do exactly this when it aired video footage of Barghouti, the leader of the al-Aqsa Martyrs Brigade, eating in his prison cell during a supposed hunger strike that he had personally organized days before.[18] States that do not want to employ decapitation strategies for moral or ethical reasons can then develop their own methods for triggering leadership succession.

Finally, policymakers must weigh the advantages and disadvantages of keeping detailed information about terrorist groups to themselves or releasing it for scholars to analyze. Retaining this information may keep terrorist groups in the dark about how much the state knows about their organizations, but on the other hand, it also prevents scholars from obtaining the information they need to do first-class studies on important topics in terrorism. Scholars from a variety of disciplines are bringing the latest methodologies to bear on the study of terrorism, including advanced statistical analysis, formal modeling, network analysis, and computer simulations. However, the findings derived from using these advanced methods are only as good as the information available to them. When terrorism scholars do not have access to reliable, accurate, and current data, both scholars and policymakers suffer in the end. Scholars can only make inferences based on the information they have available to them. If this information is not accurate, then their findings will not reflect reality. Policymakers using these scholarly findings to inform decision making may be making less-than-efficient policy decisions at best, and unnecessarily putting people's lives in danger at worst. At the end of the day, my hope is that the methods used in this study can be used and improved upon, together with the best information available, to inform the next generation of scholars and policymakers.

APPENDIX

Terrorist Groups by Category

TABLE A.1
Groups that have NOT ended* and have NOT experienced decapitation

Group	Start
al-Badr	2000
Alex Boncayao Brigade (ABB)	1984
All Tripura Tiger Force (ATTF)	1990
al-Qaeda	1988
Ansar al-Sunnah (Followers of the Tradition)	2003
Armed Revolutionary Forces of Colombia (FARC)	1966
Army of God	1982
Barisan Revolusi Nasional Melayu Pattani (BRN)	1963
Communist Party of India-Maoist (CPI-Maoist)	2004
Corsican National Liberation Front (FLNC)	1976
Democratic Front for the Liberation of Palestine (DFLP, formerly PDFLP)	1969
EZLN	1983
Fallujah Mujahideen	2003
Hizb ul-Mujahideen	1989
Islamic Army in Iraq (IAI)	2003

TABLE A.1 (*Continued*)

Group	Start
Islamic Jihad Uzbekistan (IJG) or Islamic Jihad Union (IJU)	2004
Jamaat al-Fuqra	1980
Janatantrik Terai Mukti Morcha (JTMM)	2004
Karbi Longri North Cachar People's Resistance (KNPR)	2004
Kayin National Union (KNU)	1959
Liberation Tigers of Tamil Eelam (LTTE)	1977
Lord's Resistance Army	1992
Mahdi Amy	2003
Movement for the Emancipation of the Niger Delta (MEND)	2006
Moro Islamic Liberation Front (MILF)	1984
Moro National Liberation Front (MNLF)	1972
National Liberation Front of Tripura (NLFT)	1989
People's Liberation Army II	1989
Popular Front for the Liberation of Palestine—General Command (PFLP-GC)	1968
Runda Kumpalan Kecil (RKK)	2005
Taliban	1994
Ulster Defence Association (UDA) / Ulster Freedom Fighters	1974
United Liberation Front of Assam (ULFA)	1990

*For all these groups, the observation period ended in 2008.

TABLE A.2
Groups that have NOT ended* AND have experienced decapitation

Group	Start
Abu Sayyaf Group	1991
al-Aqsa Martyrs Brigade	2000
al-Qaeda in Mesopotamia (in the Land of the Two Rivers)	2004
al-Qaeda Organization in the Islamic Maghreb (formerly (GSPC)	1996
Ansar al-Islam (AI)	2001
Asbat al-Ansar	1989

TABLE A.2 (*Continued*)

Group	Start
Babbar Khalsa International (BKI)	1978
Baloch Liberation Army (BLA)	2004
Basque Homeland and Freedom (ETA)	1958
Dagestani Shari'ah Jamaat	2002
Hamas	1987
Harakat ul-Jihad-i-Islami (HUJI)	1980
Harakat ul-Mujaheddin (HuM)	1985
Hezbollah	1983
Islamic Movement of Uzbekistan (IMU)	1998
Jaish-e-Mohammed (JEM)	2000
Jamatul Mujahedin Bangladesh (JMB)	2002
Jamiat ul-Mujahideen (JuM)	1990
Jemaah Islamiya Organization (JI)	1993
Kumpulan Mujahidin Malaysia (KMM)	1995
Kurdistan Worker's Party (PKK)	1974
Lashkar-e-Jhangvi (LeJ)	1996
Lashkar-e-Taiba (LeT)	1990
Morrocan Islamic Combat Group (GICM)	2003
National Liberation Army of Colombia (ELN)	1964
New People's Army (NPA)	1969
Palestinian Islamic Jihad (PIJ)	1981
Popular Front for the Liberation of Palestine (PFLP)	1967
Popular Resistance Committees (PRC)	2000
Purbo Banglar Communist Party (PBCP)	1995
Real IRA (RIRA)	1998
Riyad us-Saliheyn Martyrs Brigade	2002
Shining Path	1980
Sipah-e-Sahaba/Pakistan (SSP)	1985
Special Purpose Islamic Regiment (SPIR)	1996
Turkish Communist Party/Marxist-Leninist (TKP/ML)	1972

*For all these groups, the observation period ended in 2008.

TABLE A.3
Groups that have ended* and DID NOT experience decapitation

Group	Start	End*
al-Fatah	1959	1992
al-Ittihaad al-Islami (AIAI)	1991	2004
Argentine Anti-Communist Alliance (AAA)	1973	1976
Armed Forces of National Liberation (FALN)	1974	1985
Black Liberation Army (BLA)	1971	1985
Black Panthers (West Bank/Gaza)	1986	1995
Black September	1970	1974
Bodo Liberation Tigers (BLT)	1996	2003
Breton Liberation Front (FLB II—ARB)	1971	1978
Breton Liberation Front (FLB III—ARB)	1985	2000
Communist Party of Nepal-Maoist (CPN-M)	1996	2006
Continuity Irish Republican Army (CIRA)	1986	2005
Dima Halam Daoga (DHD)	1996	2002
Egyptian Islamic Jihad (EIJ)	1978	2001
Eritrean Liberation Front (ELF)	1961	1991
Farabundo Marti National Liberation Front (FMLN)	1980	1992
Free Aceh Movement (GAM)—Part I	1975	1991
Free Aceh Movement (GAM)—Part II	1999	2005
Guatemalan National Revolutionary Union (URNG)	1982	1996
Guerrilla Army of the Poor (EGP)	1975	1997
Harkat ul-Ansar (HUA)	1993	2002
Justice Commandos of the Armenian Revolutionary Army	1975	1983
Kosovo Liberation Army (KLA)	1992	1999
Lebanese National Resistance Front (LNRF)	1982	1991
Libyan Islamic Fighting Group (LIFG)	1995	2006
Maoist Communist Center	1975	2004
Muttahida Qami Movement (MQM)—initially Mohajir Qaumi Movement (MQM)	1990	2002
National Democratic Front of Bodoland (NDFB)	1988	2005
National Patriotic Front of Liberia	1984	1995

TABLE A.3 (*Continued*)

Group	Start	End*
National Socialist Council of Nagaland-Isak-Muivah (NSCN-IM)	1988	1997
Official IRA (OIRA)	1969	1975
Palestine Liberation Front (PLF)	1977	1996
Palestine Liberation Organization (PLO)	1964	1995
Pattani United Liberation Organization (PULO)	1968	1997
People's Liberation Forces (FPL)	1970	1979
People's Revolutionary Army (ERP)	1972	1992
Rebel Armed Forces (FAR)	1962	1996
Revolutionary Cells (RZ)	1973	1992
Revolutionary United Front (RUF)	1991	2002
Sudan People's Liberation Army (SPLA)	1983	2005
Tera Lliure (TL)	1979	1991
Ulster Volunteer Force (UVF)	1966	2007
United Self-Defense Forces of Colombia (AUC)	1997	2006
Weatherman	1969	1975

*End date is date of last attack; however, the observation period ended in 2008.

TABLE A.4
Groups that have ended* AND experienced decapitation

Group	Start	End*
2nd of June Movement	1971	1980
Action Directe (Direct Action)	1979	1987
African National Congress (ANC)	1961	1990
al Gama'a al-Islamiya (also Al-Jihad)	1991	1997
Al-Qaeda in the Arabian Peninsula (AQAP)	2003	2006
al-Umar Mujahideen (AUM)	1989	2002
al-Zulfikar	1977	1981
Amal Group—Islamic Amal	1975	1992
April 19 Movement (M-19)	1974	1989

(*continued*)

TABLE A.4 (*Continued*)

Group	Start	End*
Arab Communist Organization (ACO)	1974	1975
Armed Forces of National Resistance (FARN)	1975	1980
Armed Islamic Group (AIG)	1992	2001
Armed Proletarian Nuclei (NAP)	1974	1977
Armed Revolutionary Nuclei (and former Black Order)	1977	1981
Armenian Secret Army for the Liberation of Armenia (ASALA)	1975	1997
Aum Shinrikyo	1994	1995
Baader-Meinhof Group	1968	1977
Black Panthers	1966	1972
Cinchoneros Popular Liberation Movement (MLPC)	1980	1991
Committee of Solidarity with Arab and Middle East Political Prisoners (CSPPA)	1986	1987
Communist Combatant Cells (CCC)	1984	1985
Fatah Revolutionary Council/Black June (Abu Nidal group)	1974	2002
First of October Anti-Fascist Resistance Group (GRAPO)	1975	2000
Guatemalan Party of Labour (PGT)	1949	1996
Harakat al-Shuhada'a al-Islamiyah	1996	1997
Hector Riobe Brigade	1982	1984
Independent Armed Revolutionary Movement (MIRA)	1969	1970
International Revolution Action Group (GARI)	1974	1975
Iparretarrak	1973	1998
Irish National Liberation Army—General HQ Faction	1995	1996
Irish National Liberation Army (INLA)	1974	1998
Islamic Great Eastern Raiders Front (IBDA-C)	1970	2008
Islamic Salvation Front (FIS)	1989	1999
Jagrata Muslim Janata Bangladesh	1998	2007
Japanese Red Army	1971	2000
Jewish Defense League (JDL)	1968	2001
Jewish Underground	1980	1984
Kach and Kahana Chai	1973	1994
Khmer Rouge	1951	1998

TABLE A.4 (*Continued*)

Group	Start	End*
Lautaro Youth Movement (MJL)	1987	1994
Lebanese Armed Revolutionary Faction (FARL)	1979	1984
Lebanese Socialist Revolutionary Organization	1973	1974
Lorenzo Zelaya Popular Revolutionary Forces (FPRLZ)	1980	1988
Loyalist Volunteer Force (LVF)	1996	2005
Macheteros (Boricua Popular/Peoples Army)	1978	1989
Manuel Rodriquez Revolutionary or Patriotic Front (FPMR)	1983	1989
Marxist-Leninist Armed Propaganda Unit	1973	1980
May 19th Communist Order (May 19th)	1983	1985
Montoneros	1970	1979
Moujahidin-e-Khalq (MEK)	1971	2001
Movement for Self Determination & Independence for the Canary Islands Archipelago (MPAIAC)	1977	1979
Movement of the Revolutionary Left (MIR)	1965	1994
Movsar Baryayev Gang	1998	2002
New Red Brigades/Communist Combatant Party (BR-PCC)	1989	2003
November 17, also Revolutionary Organization 17 November (RO-N17)	1975	2002
October 8 Revolutionary Movement (MR-8)	1968	1972
Omega-7	1974	1983
Orange Volunteers (OV)	1998	2001
People Against Gangsterism and Drugs (PAGAD)	1996	2002
People's Liberation Army	1978	1982
People's Revolutionary Army (ERP) II	1969	1977
People's Revolutionary Organization (ORP)	1992	1997
People's Revolutionary Struggle (ELA)	1971	1990
People's War Group (PWG)	1980	2004
Peronist Armed Forces (FAP)	1967	1974
Polisario Front	1973	1991
Popular Forces of 25 April (FP-25)	1980	1986
Popular Front for the Liberation of Palestine—Special Ops Group (PFLP-SOG)	1972	1978

(*continued*)

TABLE A.4 (*Continued*)

Group	Start	End*
Popular Liberation Army (EPL)	1967	1991
Popular Revolutionary Army	1996	2008
Prima Linea	1976	1982
Provisional Irish Republican Army (PIRA)	1969	2005
Red Army Faction (RAF)	1977	1992
Red Brigades (BR)—Brigate Rosse	1969	1984
Red Flag (Bandera Roja)	1969	1996
Red Hand Defenders	1998	2008
Revolutionary People's Liberation Front (DHKP/C)	1978	1993
Revolutionary Popular Vanguard (VPR)	1968	1973
Salafia Jihadia	1996	2004
Self-Defense Groups of Cordoba and Uraba (ACCU)	1994	1997
September 23rd Communist League	1973	1982
Students Islamic Movement of India (SIMI)	2001	2008
Tawhid and Jihad	1999	2008
The National Union for the Total Independence of Angola (UNITA)	1966	2002
The Order	1982	1984
Tupac Amaru Revolutionary Movement (MRTA)	1984	1997
Tupac Katari Guerrilla Army (EGTK)	1991	1993
Tupamaros National Liberation Movement (MLN)	1968	1972
Turkish Hezbollah	1989	2000
Turkish People's Liberation Army (TPLA)	1969	1980
Turkish People's Liberation Front (TPLA-F)	1971	1973
Turkish Worker Peasant Liberation Army (TWPLA)	1971	1973
Zarate Willka Armed Forces of Liberation	1988	1989

*End date is date of last attack; however, the observation period ended in 2008.

Notes

1. Introduction

1. Barack Obama, "Remarks by the President on Osama bin Laden," May 1, 2011, https://www.whitehouse.archives.gov/the-press-office/2011/05/02/remarks-president-osama-bin-laden.
2. I define terrorist groups as organizations consisting of more than one person that have engaged in violence with a political purpose that is aimed at evoking a psychological reaction in an audience that extends beyond the targeted victims. My definition does not include "lone wolf" terrorists (e.g., Ted Kaczynski) because my focus is on the organizational dynamics of terrorist organizations.
3. Steven R. David, "Fatal Choices: Israel's Policy of Targeted Killings," *Mideast Security and Policy Studies*, no. 51 (September 2002): 1–26; Steven R. David, "Israel's Policy of Targeted Killings," *Ethics and International Affairs* 17, no. 1 (Spring 2003): 120; Mohammed M. Hafez and Joseph M. Hatfield, "Do Targeted Assassinations Work? A Multivariate Analysis of Israeli Counter-Terrorism Effectiveness During Al-Aqsa Uprising," *Studies in Conflict and Terrorism* 29, no. 4 (June 2006): 359–82; Boaz Ganor, *The Counter-Terrorism Puzzle: A Guide for Decision Makers* (New Brunswick, NJ: Transaction, 2005), 128; Daniel Byman, "Do Targeted Killings Work?" *Foreign Affairs* 85, no. 2 (March–April 2006): 95–111.
4. Byman, "Do Targeted Killings Work?"
5. Jenna Jordan, "When Heads Roll: Assessing the Effectiveness of Leadership Decapitation," *Security Studies* 18, no. 4 (October–December 2009): 721; Robert A. Pape, "The Strategic Logic of Suicide Terrorism," *American Political Science Review* 97, no. 3 (August 2003): 14.
6. David, "Israel's Policy of Targeted Killings"; Byman, "Do Targeted Killings Work?"

7. Greg Miller, "Under Obama, an Emerging Global Apparatus for Drone Killing," *Washington Post*, December 27, 2011.
8. Gordon Lubold and Shane Harris, "Trump Broadens CIA Powers, Allows Deadly Drone Strikes," *Wall Street Journal*, March 13, 2017; Charlie Savage and Eric Schmitt, "Trump Administration Is Said to Be Working to Loosen Counterterrorism Rules," *New York Times*, March 12, 2017.
9. Byman, "Do Targeted Killings Work?"
10. Jordan, "When Heads Roll," 723; Jenna Jordan, "Attacking the Leader, Missing the Mark," *International Security* 38 no. 4 (Spring 2014): 7–38; David, "Fatal Choices"; Pape, "The Strategic Logic of Suicide Terrorism."
11. Edward H. Kaplan, Alex Mintz, Shaul Mishal, and Claudio Samban, "What Happened to Suicide Bombings in Israel? Insights from a Terror Stock Model," *Studies in Conflict and Terrorism* 28, no. 3 (August 2005): 225–35.
12. Kaplan et al., "What Happened to Suicide Bombings in Israel?," 230; Audrey Kurth Cronin, "How al-Qaida Ends: The Decline and Demise of Terrorist Groups," *International Security* 31, no. 1 (Summer 2006): 22.
13. David, "Israel's Policy of Targeted Killings," 8.
14. Daniel L. Byman and Kenneth M. Pollack, "Let Us Now Praise Great Men: Bringing the Statesmen Back In," *International Security* 25, no. 4 (Spring 2001): 107–46.
15. Byman and Pollack, "Let Us Now Praise Great Men," 108; Kenneth N. Waltz, *Man, the State, and War* (New York: Columbia University Press, 1959).
16. Carol McCann and Ross Pigeau, *The Human in Command: Exploring the Modern Military Science* (New York: Kluwer Academic/Plenum, 2000), 4.
17. Byman and Pollack, "Let Us Now Praise Great Men," 108.
18. Jeffrey Pfeffer, "The Ambiguities of Leadership," *Academy of Management Review* 12, no. 1 (January 1977): 104–12.
19. Richard E. Neustadt, *Presidential Power* (New York: Macmillan, 1960); James David Barber, *The Presidential Character: Predicting Performance in the White House* (Upper Saddle River, NJ: Prentice-Hall, 1972); Alexander L. George, *Presidential Decision-making in Foreign Policy: The Effective Use of Information and Advice* (Boulder, CO: Westview, 1980).
20. Terry Moe, "Presidents, Institutions, and Theory," in *Researching the Presidency: Vital Questions, New Approaches*, ed. G. C. I. Edwards, J. H. Kessel, and B. A. Rockman (Pittsburgh, PA: University of Pittsburgh Press, 1993), 337–86.
21. Moe, "Presidents, Institutions, and Theory"; Moe, "The Politicized Presidency," in *The New Direction in American Politics*, ed. J. E. Chubb and P. E. Peterson (Washington, DC: Brookings Institution, 1985), 235–72.
22. Robert A. Dahl, *Who Governs? Democracy and Power in an American City* (New Haven, CT: Yale University Press, 1974), 95–96.
23. Kenneth A. Shepsle and Mark S. Bonchek, *Analyzing Politics: Rationality, Behavior, and Institutions* (New York: Norton, 1997), 380.
24. Margaret G. Hermann and Joe D. Hagan, "International Decision Making: Leadership Matters," *Foreign Policy* 110 (1998): 124–25.
25. Pfeffer, "The Ambiguities of Leadership"; James R. Meindl, Sanford B. Ehrlich, and Janet M. Dukerich, "The Romance of Leadership," *Administrative Science Quarterly*

30 (1985): 78–102; James R. Meindl and Sanford B. Ehrlich, "The Romance of Leadership and the Evaluation of Organizational Performance," *Academy of Management Journal* 30, no. 1 (1987): 91–109; David V. Day and Robert G. Lord, "Executive Leadership and Organizational Performance: Suggestions for a New Theory and Methodology," *Journal of Management* 14, no. 3 (1988): 453–64.
26. Nan Weiner and Timothy A. Mahoney, "A Model of Corporate Performance as a Function of Environmental, Organizational, and Leadership Influences," *Academy of Management Journal* 24, no. 3 (1981): 453–70.
27. Gerald R. Salancik and Jeffrey Pfeffer, "Constraints on Administrative Discretion: The Limited Influence of Mayors on City Budgets," *Urban Affairs Quarterly* 12 (1977): 475–98.
28. Oscar Grusky, "Administrative Succession in Formal Organizations," *Social Forces* 39, no. 2 (December 1960): 105–15; and Oscar Grusky, "Managerial Succession and Organizational Effectiveness," *American Journal of Sociology* 69, no. 1 (July 1963): 21–31.
29. Meindl et al., "The Romance of Leadership"; Meindl and Ehrlich, "The Romance of Leadership and the Evaluation of Organizational Performance."
30. Pfeffer, "The Ambiguities of Leadership"; Meindl et al., "The Romance of Leadership."
31. Day and Lord, "Executive Leadership and Organizational Performance."
32. Pfeffer, "The Ambiguities of Leadership."
33. Noam Wasserman, "Founder-CEO Succession and the Paradox of Entrepreneurial Success," *Organization Science* 14, no. 2 (2003): 149–72.
34. Richard J. Chasdi, *Serenade of Suffering: A Portrait of Middle East Terrorism, 1968–1993* (Lanham, MD: Lexington, 1999).
35. The God's Army, a terrorist group operating in Myanmar from 1997 to 2001, serves as an extreme example of this unique type of leadership. Its two leaders were supposedly twelve-year-old twins when the group was founded. They were chosen because of their alleged black tongues and animist powers, which followers believed made them bullet-proof and impervious to land mines. See Richard Ehrlich, "Burma's 'God's Army' No More," *Asian Pacific Post*, July 28, 2006.
36. Pfeffer, "The Ambiguities of Leadership," 107.
37. Meindl and Ehrlich, "The Romance of Leadership and the Evaluation of Organizational Performance," 91.
38. Paul J. DiMaggio and Walter W. Powell, "The Iron Cage Revisited: Institutional Isomorphism and Collective Rationality in Organizational Fields," *American Sociological Review* 48, no. 2 (April 1983): 147–60.
39. We should expect long-lasting groups such as the Irish Republican Army and Fatah to have internal traditions and norms that follow-on leaders continue and carry on.
40. Martha Crenshaw, "Why Violence Is Rejected or Renounced: A Case Study of Oppositional Terrorism," in *A Natural History of Peace*, ed. Thomas Gregor (Nashville, TN: Vanderbilt University Press, 1996), 249–72; J. K. Zawodny, "Infrastructures of Terrorist Organizations," *Conflict Quarterly* 1, no. 4 (Spring 1981): 24–31.
41. Pfeffer, "The Ambiguities of Leadership"; Meindl et al., "The Romance of Leadership"; Meindl and Ehrlich, "The Romance of Leadership and the Evaluation of Organizational Performance."

42. Meindl et al., "The Romance of Leadership," 100.
43. Pfeffer, "The Ambiguities of Leadership,"108.
44. William B. Quandt, *Revolution and Political Leadership: Algeria, 1954–1968* (Cambridge, MA: MIT Press, 1969); Mostafa Rejai and Kay Phillips, *Leaders of Revolution* (Beverly Hills, CA: Sage, 1979); Mostafa Rejai and Kay Phillips, *World Revolutionary Leaders* (New Brunswick, NJ: Rutgers University Press, 1983).
45. Donatella della Porta, *Social Movements, Political Violence, and the State: A Comparative Analysis of Italy and Germany* (Cambridge: Cambridge University Press, 1995); Ronald R. Aminzade, Jack A. Goldstone, and Elizabeth J. Perry, "Leadership Dynamics and Dynamics of Contention," in *Silence and Voice in the Study of Contentious Politics*, ed. Ronald R. Aminzade, Jack A. Goldstone, Doug McAdam, Elizabeth J. Perry, William H. Sewell, Sidney Tarrow, and Charles Tilly (New York: Cambridge University Press, 2001); Colin Barker, Alan Johnson, and Michael Lavalette, "Leadership Matters: An Introduction," in *Leadership in Social Movements*, ed. C. Barker, A. Johnson, and M. Lavalette (Manchester, UK: Manchester University Press, 2001), 126–54; Aldon Morris and Suzanne Staggenborg, "Leadership in Social Movements," in *The Blackwell Companion to Social Movements*, ed. D. A. Snow, S. A. Soule, and H. Kriesi (Malden, MA: Blackwell, 2004); Sharon Erickson Nepstad and Clifford Bob, "When Do Leaders Matter? Hypotheses on Leadership Dynamics in Social Movements," *Mobilization: An International Journal* 11, no. 1 (2006): 1–22.
46. Aminzade et al., "Leadership Dynamics and Dynamics of Contention," 143.
47. Nepstad and Bob, "When Do Leaders Matter?"
48. Some scholars suggest that groups like al-Qaeda and other groups with Salafist ideologies are part of a larger, broader social movement. See Marc Sageman, *Understanding Terror Networks* (Philadelphia: University of Pennsylvania Press, 2004). However, as will be discussed later, there are important differences between terrorist group leaders and those of social movements. Additionally, I, like several other scholars of terrorism, do not find the social movement analogy very compelling, mainly because al-Qaeda and others promoting the Salafist ideology do not enjoy the groundswell of mainstream support that the civil rights movement and other social movements throughout history have enjoyed.
49. Edna F. Reid and Hsinchun Chen, "Mapping the Contemporary Terrorism Research Domain," *International Journal of Human-Computer Studies* 65 (2007): 42–56.
50. Todd Sandler, "Collective Action and Transnational Terrorism," *The World Economy* 26, no. 6 (2003): 779–802; Alan B. Krueger and Jitka Maleckova, "Education, Poverty and Terrorism: Is There a Causal Connection?" *Journal of Economic Perspectives* 17, no. 4 (2003): 119–44; David C. Rapoport, "The Four Waves of Modern Terrorism," in *Attacking Terrorism: Elements of a Grand Strategy*, ed. A. K. Cronin and J. M. Ludes (Washington, DC: Georgetown University Press, 2004); James A. Piazza, "Rooted in Poverty? Terrorism, Poor Economic Development, and Social Cleavages," *Terrorism and Political Violence* 18, no. 1 (2006): 159–77; Alan B. Krueger, *What Makes a Terrorist* (Princeton, NJ: Princeton University Press, 2007).
51. Krueger, *What Makes a Terrorist*, 37.
52. Martha Crenshaw, "Innovation: Decision Points in the Trajectory of Terrorism," in *Terrorist Innovations in Weapons of Mass Effect: Preconditions, Causes and Predictive*

Indicators, ed. Maria Rasmussen and Mohammed Hafez (Washington, DC: The Defense Threat Reduction Agency, 2010), 35–50.
53. Martha Crenshaw, *Terrorism in Context* (University Park: Pennsylvania State University Press, 1995).
54. Krueger and Maleckova, "Education, Poverty and Terrorism"; Claude Berrebi, "Evidence About the Link Between Education, Poverty and Terrorism Among Palestinians," *Peace Economics, Peace Science and Public Policy* 13, no. 1 (2007): 1–36; Efraim Benmelech, Claude Berrebi, and Esteban F. Klor, "Economic Conditions and the Quality of Suicide Terrorism," *Journal of Politics* 74, no. 1 (2012): 1–16.
55. Martha Crenshaw, "The Psychology of Political Terrorism," in *Political Psychology*, ed. M. G. Hermann (San Francisco: Jossey-Bass, 1986), 379–413; Gordon H. McCormick, "Terrorist Decision Making," *Annual Review of Political Science* 6 (June 2003): 473–507; Jacob N. Shapiro, *The Terrorist's Dilemma* (Princeton, NJ: Princeton University Press, 2013).
56. Catherine L. Wang and Pervaiz K. Ahmed, "Organizational Learning: A Critical Review," *The Learning Organization* 10, no. 1 (2003): 8–17.
57. Graham T. Allison, "Conceptual Models and the Cuban Missile Crisis," *American Political Science Review* 63, no.3 (1969): 689–718.
58. Paul K. Davis and Brian Michael Jenkins, *Deterrence and Influence in Counterterrorism* (Washington, DC: RAND, 2002), 9. Italics original.
59. It should be noted that Crenshaw has been calling for more emphasis on the organizational approach to understanding terrorism since 1985. Martha Crenshaw, "An Organizational Approach to the Analysis of Political Terrorism," *Orbis* 29, no. 3 (1985): 465–89; Martha Crenshaw, "Theories of Terrorism: Instrumental and Organizational Approaches," *Journal of Strategic Studies* 10, no. 4 (1987): 13–31. See also Marissa Reddy Pynchon and Randy Borum, "Assessing Threats of Targeted Violence: Contributions from Social Psychology," *Behavioral Science and the Law* 17 (1999): 339–55.
60. According to Asal and Rethemeyer in their 2008 article, "the organizational level analysis has not been a major area of investigation." See Victor Asal and R. Karl Rethemeyer, "The Nature of the Beast: Organizational Structures and the Lethality of Terrorist Attacks," *Journal of Politics* 70, no. 2 (2008): 446–47.
61. Ami Pedahzur, *Suicide Terrorism* (Cambridge: Polity, 2005), 158.
62. Pedahzur, *Suicide Terrorism*, 193.
63. Diego Gambetta, "Can We Make Sense of Suicide Missions?" in *Making Sense of Suicide Missions*, ed. D. Gambetta (Oxford: Oxford University Press, 1995), 260. Italics original.
64. Pedahzur, *Suicide Terrorism*, 158.
65. Pedahzur, 159.
66. Pedahzur, 158, 176.
67. Pedahzur, 172–74.
68. Sageman, *Understanding Terror Networks*; Marc Sageman, *Leaderless Jihad: Terror Networks in the Twenty-First Century* (Philadelphia: University of Pennsylvania Press, 2008); Ethan Bueno de Mesquita, "The Quality of Terror," *American Journal of Political Science* 49, no. 3 (2005): 515–30; Max Abrahms, "What Terrorists Really Want: Terrorist

Motives and Counterterrorism Strategy," *International Security* 32, no. 4 (2008): 78–105; Eli Berman and David D. Laitin, "Religion, Terrorism and Public Goods: Testing the Club Model," in *Journal of Public Economics* 92, no. 10–11 (2008): 1942–67.

69. Marc Sageman states that there has been too much emphasis on terrorist group leaders. "Journalists and scholars tend to focus on leaders" because, unlike most foot soldiers, leaders are "people they can investigate" (Sageman, *Understanding Terror Networks*, 66). However, Sageman does not reference any academic works that *do* concentrate on terrorist group leaders. Conversely, I have found the opposite trend.

70. Abrahms, "What Terrorists Really Want."

71. Abrahms, "What Terrorists Really Want"; Jon Elster, "Motivations and Beliefs in Suicide Missions," in *Making Sense of Suicide Missions*, ed. D. Gambett (Oxford: Oxford University Press, 2005).

72. Max Abrahms, "Why Terrorism Does Not Work," *International Security* 31, no. 2 (2006): 42–78.

73. Abrahms, "Why Terrorism Does Not Work," 42–78.

74. Jerrold M. Post, "Terrorist Psycho-logic: Terrorist Behavior as a Product of Psychological Forces," in *Origins of Terrorism*, ed. W. Reich (Washington, DC: Woodrow Wilson Center, 1990), 25.

75. McCormick, "Terrorist Decision Making"; Jeff Victoroff, "Mind of the Terrorist: A Review and Critique of Psychological Approaches," *Journal of Conflict Resolution* 49, no. 3 (2005): 3–42.

76. For a review, see McCormick, "Terrorist Decision Making."

77. McCormick, "Terrorist Decision Making," 495.

78. McCormick, 495.

79. Berman and Laitin, "Religion, Terrorism and Public Goods."

80. Abrahms, "What Terrorists Really Want."

81. Pedahzur, *Suicide Terrorism*, 166–68.

82. Sageman, *Understanding Terror Networks*. Also, for an example of how influential high-level leaders are to radicalizing a group, see the May 2009 report by the International Crisis Group (ICG). The report details the emergence of the Palembang Group, a terrorist group based in Singapore, especially the role played by its two top leaders, Fajar Taslim and Sulthon Qolbi (alias Ustad Asadollah), who started the group from scratch. The report concludes that "the one lesson from the Palembang jama'ah is that groups with no prior history of involvement in violence or exposure to jihadist ideology can be radicalized through persuasive leaders." See International Crisis Group, "Indonesia: Radicalisation of the 'Palembang Group,' " in *Asia Briefing No. 92* (Jakarta, Indonesia: International Crisis Group, 2009), 14.

83. Asal and Rethemeyer, "The Nature of the Beast."

84. In a recent *New York Times* article detailing the choices young Algerians face in joining terrorist groups such as the Salafist Group for Preaching and Combat (GSPC), now officially affiliated with al-Qaeda, a high school senior with a long family history of military service tells how GSPC recruiters wooed him briefly into their organization for several days before his imam eventually found out and persuaded him not to join. This story is telling in two regards. First, the boy was not a religious ideologue and came from a strong family background, yet the recruiter

had convinced him "that soldiers, like his own father, are apostates and should be killed." Second, it shows the power and influence religious clerics have at these lower levels. They can foil the recruitment process or act as an accelerant. Of his recruiters, the boy said, "They really convince you." See Michael S. Slackman, "In Algeria, a Tug of War for Young Minds," *New York Times*, June 23, 2008.

85. Evidence from Iraq indicates that terrorist groups have recruited and coerced women to join their ranks as early as 2008, especially for suicide missions. One Iraqi girl who failed to detonate her suicide vest told American investigators that she was drugged with a sedative before being laden with the explosives and pushed toward a U.S. checkpoint (Thom Shanker, "New Lessons for the Army on Iraq Duty," *New York Times*, February 18, 2009). Leaders drugging their followers, especially prospective suicide attackers, may not be that uncommon. Pedahzur claims that this tactic was commonly used by terrorist groups in Chechnya as well. See Pedahzur, *Suicide Terrorism*, 175.

86. There is a lot of recent work on this subject. For a review paper, see Martha Crenshaw, "Evaluating the Effectiveness of Counterterrorism" (paper presented at the *International Studies Association Fiftieth Annual Convention*, New York City, NY, 2009). For a critique on the metrics used to evaluate counterterrorism's effectiveness, see Alexander Spencer, "The Problems of Evaluating Counter-Terrorism," UNISCI Discussion Paper No. 12 (October 2006).

87. Martha Crenshaw, "How Terrorism Declines," *Terrorism and Political Violence* 3, no. 1 (1991): 69–87.

88. Cronin, "How al-Qaida Ends."

89. Steve Hutchinson and Pat O'Malley, *How Terrorist Groups Decline* (Ottawa: Canadian Centre for Intelligence and Security Studies, Norman Paterson School of International Affairs, Carleton University, 2007), 3.

90. Secretary of Defense Donald Rumsfeld, as quoted by Mark Danner, "Taking Stock of the Forever War," *New York Times Magazine*, September 11, 2005.

91. David D. Laitin and Jacob N. Shapiro, "The Political, Economic, and Organizational Sources of Terrorism," in *Terrorism, Economic Development, and Political Openness*, ed. P. Keefer and N. Loayza (Cambridge: Cambridge University Press, 2008).

92. Crenshaw, "How Terrorism Declines"; Sandler, "Collective Action and Transnational Terrorism"; Spencer, "The Problems of Evaluating Counter-Terrorism"; Crenshaw, "Evaluating the Effectiveness of Counterterrorism."

93. Spencer, "The Problems of Evaluating Counter-Terrorism"; Raphael Perl, *Combating Terrorism: The Challenge of Measuring Effectiveness*, CRS Report for Congress, March 12, 2007.

94. Daniel Byman, "Scoring the War on Terrorism," *The National Interest*, Summer 2003, 67–75.

95. Crenshaw, "How Terrorism Declines."

96. Audrey Kurth Cronin, *Ending Terrorism: Lessons for Defeating al-Qaeda* (Abingdon, Oxford: International Institute for Strategic Studies, 2008).

97. Perl, *Combating Terrorism*.

98. Cronin gives seven broad explanations in the "How al-Qaida Ends" article, but she has narrowed them down to six in more recent publications, such as *Ending Terrorism: Lessons for Defeating al-Qaeda*.

99. Cronin, *Ending Terrorism*, 29.
100. Cronin, "How al-Qaida Ends," 18.
101. Cronin, "How al-Qaida Ends," 18. See also Colonel John M. Collins, *Assassination and Abduction as Tools of National Policy* (Norfolk, VA: Armed Forces War College, 1965); Stephen Hosmer, *Operations Against Enemy Leaders* (Santa Monica, CA: RAND, 2001); Grahm H. Turbiville Jr., "Hunting Leadership Targets in Counterinsurgency and Counterterrorist Operations," *Joint Special Operations University* 7, no. 6 (2007): 1–102.
102. Robert Pape, *Bombing to Win* (Ithaca, NY: Cornell University Press, 1996).
103. Pape, *Bombing to Win*, 80.
104. Paul Bracken, *The Command and Control of Nuclear Forces* (New Haven, CT: Yale University Press, 1983); Howard Tamashiro, "The Danger of Nuclear Diplomatic Decapitation," *Air University Review* 35 (September–October, 1984): 74–79.
105. Bracken, *The Command and Control of Nuclear Forces*, 234.
106. Hosmer, *Operations Against Enemy Leaders*.
107. Moyar Moyar, *Phoenix and the Birds of Prey: Counterinsurgency and Counterterrorism in Vietnam* (Lincoln: University of Nebraska Press, 1997).
108. Robert E. Venkus, *Raid on Qaddafi* (New York: St. Martin's Press, 1992).
109. Raymond Bonner and Steve Levine, "After the Attack, the Guerillas: 'We Are Freedom Fighters,' Says a Leader of Militants," *New York Times*, August 27, 1998; Davis and Jenkins, *Deterrence and Influence in Counterterrorism*, 26.
110. Executive Office of the President, *The National Security Strategy of the United States of America*, Washington, DC, 2002, 5.
111. Executive Office of the President, *National Strategy for Combating Terrorism*, Washington, DC, February 2003, 6. Italics added.
112. Executive Office of the President, *National Strategy for Combating Terrorism*, February 2003, 6.
113. Executive Office of the President, *National Strategy for Combating Terrorism*, Washington, DC, September 2006, 11–12. Italics added.
114. This concept is compatible with some work done in organizational theory, particularly on leadership. In their article "The Romance of Leadership," Meindl et al. argue that leaders matter not so much because they can personally affect organizational performance, but because their followers believe their leaders matter. In other words, "the romanticized conception of leadership results from a biased preference to understand important but causally indeterminate and ambiguous organizational events and occurrences in terms of leadership." See Meindl et al., "The Romance of Leadership," 80.
115. U.S. Department of Defense, *National Military Strategy for the War on Terrorism*, 2006, 15.
116. Mark Mazzetti and Scott Shane, "CIA Had Plan to Assassinate Qaeda Leaders," *New York Times*, July 14, 1009.
117. There are numerous examples of policymakers using this language. For one example, then national security advisor Condoleezza Rice gave sworn testimony to the September 11th Commission in April 2004 that "the president had been told by the director of the Central Intelligence Agency that it was not going to be a silver

bullet to kill bin Laden, that you had to do much more." See "Transcript of Rice's 9/11 Commission Statement," CNN.com, May 19, 2004, accessed May 10, 2018, http://www.cnn.com/2004/ALLPOLITICS/04/08/rice.transcript/.
118. Cronin, *Ending Terrorism*, 27.
119. Cronin, "How al-Qaida Ends"; Cronin, *Ending Terrorism*; Turbiville, "Hunting Leadership Targets in Counterinsurgency and Counterterrorist Operations."
120. Dipal K. Gupta and Kusum Mundra, "Suicide Bombing as a Strategic Weapon: An Empirical Investigation of Hamas and Islamic Jihad," *Terrorism and Political Violence* 17 (2005): 573–98; Kaplan et al., "What Happened to Suicide Bombings in Israel?"; Byman, "The Decision to Begin Talks with Terrorists: Lessons for Policymakers," *Studies in Conflict and Terrorism* 29, no. 5 (2005): 403–414.
121. Alex S. Wilner, "Targeted Killings in Afghanistan: Measuring Coercion and Deterrence in Counterterrorism and Counterinsurgency," *Studies in Conflict and Terrorism* 33, no. 4 (2009): 307–29.
122. For an in-depth review of the literature, see Stephanie Carvin, "The Trouble with Targeted Killing," *Security Studies* 21, no. 3 (2012): 529–55.
123. Gupta and Mundra, "Suicide Bombing as a Strategic Weapon."
124. Kaplan et al., "What Happened to Suicide Bombings in Israel?"
125. Lisa Langdon, Alexander J. Sarapu, and Matthew Wells, "Targeting the Leadership of Terrorist and Insurgent Movements: Historical Lessons for Contemporary Policy Makers," *Journal of Public and International Affairs* 15 (Spring 2004): 59–78.
126. Langdon et al., "Targeting the Leadership of Terrorist and Insurgent Movements," 75.
127. Rapoport claims that most groups have fewer than fifty members but does not define what "most" means, nor does he provide empirical evidence to support this claim. That being said, in my original data set of terrorist groups, 49 had memberships under one hundred members, accounting for one-quarter of all groups. See David C. Rapoport, "Terrorism," in *Encyclopedia of Government and Politics*, ed. M. Hawkesworth and M. Kogan (London: Routledge, 1992), 1067.
128. Aaron Mannes, "Testing the Snake Head Strategy: Does Killing or Capturing Its Leaders Reduce a Terrorist Group's Activity?" *Journal of International Policy Solutions* 9 (Spring 2008):40–49.
129. "Right-censored data" refers to the groups in Mannes's data set that have experienced a decapitation event but have to be excluded from his analysis because five years had not elapsed by the time his study ended. Thus, Mannes has to exclude eight cases from his analysis. Since he only has sixty total observations, this is a sizable number of groups to omit. There are models other than linear regression that can accommodate right-censored data. These models will be further explained in chapter 4. In terms of the size of his data set, Mannes has 71 groups, while Jordan includes 169 groups in her data set and I include 207 groups in mine.
130. Gupta and Mundra, "Suicide Bombing as a Strategic Weapon."
131. Kaplan et al., "What Happened to Suicide Bombings in Israel?"
132. Laitin and Shapiro, "The Political, Economic, and Organizational Sources of Terrorism."
133. Lawrence Wright, *The Looming Tower* (New York: Knopf, 2006).
134. Ganor, *The Counter-Terrorism Puzzle*.

135. Jordan, "When Heads Roll"; Jordan, "Attacking the Leader, Missing the Mark."
136. In his book on suicide terrorism, Pedahzur came up with a similar conclusion. See Pedahzur, *Suicide Terrorism*.
137. Jordan, "When Heads Roll," 15. To her credit, Jordan explicitly recognizes this fact, but she feels it does not detract from her analysis in a significant way.
138. Jordan says her "cases were drawn from an encyclopedia on the history of terrorist organizations (Sloan and Anderson's *Historical Dictionary of Terrorism*), Lexis-Nexis searches of newspapers, the MIPT database, and the U.S. State Department's *Patterns of Global Terrorism*" (Jordan, "When Heads Roll," 15). However, if she took groups from all of these sources to populate her data set, she would have many more than 169 organizations. To use one example, the TOPS database, which was managed by MIPT up until March 2008, contains 856 terrorist groups. Go to TOPs database at http://www.start.umd.edu/gtd/features/TOPs.aspx. The Patterns of Global Terrorism series started in 1976, but its last publication was in 2003. Furthermore, Sloan and Anderson do not explain their coding criteria or how they selected individual groups to be in their book—entries in this dictionary include terms, events, individuals, and various groups from AD 66 to 1994. The authors do not even provide a total number of the groups in their book.
139. According to Box-Steffensmeir and Jones, "Censoring occurs whenever an observation's full event history is unobserved. Thus, we may fail to observe the termination or the onset of a spell. In this sense, censored observations are akin to missing data, insofar as the portion of the history that is censored is, in fact, missing. Right-censoring is commonly observed in event history data sets. Typically, we encounter right-censoring because the time-frame of a study or observation plan concludes prior to the completion or termination of survival times. The ubiquity of right-censoring in social science data sets provides a strong motivation for event history models. . . . The basic problem is that if censored and uncensored cases are treated equivalently, then parameter estimates from a model treating the duration time as a function of covariates may be misleading (that is, the relationship between the covariates and the duration times may be under- or over-stated). In general, the standard regression framework does not distinguish between uncensored and right-censored observations." See Janet M. Box-Steffensmeier and Bradford S. Jones, *Event History Modeling: A Guide for Social Sciences* (Cambridge: Cambridge University Press, 2004), 16.

    Jordan uses logistic regression, which the authors claim "is troublesome, because it belies the logic of duration modeling; usually, we are concerned both with the occurrence or nonoccurrence of some events as well as the length of time the unit survived until the event occurred. This strategy precludes this kind of information" (Box-Steffensmeier and Jones, *Event History Modeling*, 19).
140. For my study that ends in 2008, this number of terrorist groups is not inconsequential. I have eighty-five groups that were active as of 2006.
141. Box-Steffensmeier and Jones, *Event History Modeling*.
142. Louise Richardson, *What Terrorists Want* (New York: Random House, 2006), 45.
143. Rapoport, "Terrorism."

144. Seth G. Jones and Martin C. Libicki, *How Terrorist Groups End: Lessons for Countering al Qa'ida* (Santa Monica, CA: RAND, 2008); Brian J. Phillips, "Terrorist Group Cooperation and Longevity," *International Studies Quarterly* 58, no. 2 (2014): 336–47.
145. Crenshaw, "Why Violence Is Rejected or Renounced," 259.
146. Byman, "Do Targeted Killings Work?"
147. Executive Office of the President, *National Strategy for Combating Terrorism*, 2006, 8.
148. Crenshaw, "Why Violence Is Rejected or Renounced," 259.
149. Michael Kenney, *From Pablo to Osama* (University Park: Pennsylvania State University Press, 2007); Simon Romero, "Cocaine Trade Helps Rebels Reignite War in Peru," *New York Times*, March 18, 2009.
150. Romero, "Cocaine Trade Helps Rebels Reignite War in Peru."
151. Even in cases where the state has successfully destroyed most of the group, capturing or killing the leader is still considered to be important, even if only for symbolic reasons, to both the state and the group. For example, even though the Sri Lankan government had destroyed large portions of the LTTE and taken back more than 90 percent of the territory once controlled by the organization, it was not until the government killed longtime LTTE leader Velupillai Prabhakaran in May 2009 that it openly declared victory over the LTTE. Once Prabhakaran was declared dead, Sri Lanka's president boasted that he had finally liberated his country from terror.

2. Organizations and Leaders

1. Tom Huddleston Jr., "Theo Epstein's Perfect Response to the World's Greatest Leaders List," *Fortune*, March 23, 2017, http://fortune.com/2017/03/23/theo-epstein-worlds-greatest-leaders-response/.
2. Huddleston, "Theo Epstein's Perfect Response."
3. Gary Yukl, *Leadership in Organizations* (Upper Saddle River, NJ: Prentice Hall, 2002), 365. Note: Yukl calls this "a major controversy in the leadership literature."
4. For a review of the literature, see Yukl, *Leadership in Organizations*.
5. Yukl, *Leadership in Organizations*, 74.
6. Yukl, 74.
7. Yukl, 11–17.
8. James MacGregor Burns, *Leadership* (New York: Harper & Row, 1978).
9. Robert J. House and Jitendra V. Singh, "Organizational Behavior: Some New Directions for I/O Psychology," *Annual Review of Psychology* 38 (1987): 696.
10. Yukl, *Leadership in Organizations*, 241.
11. House and Singh, "Organizational Behavior," 696.
12. Michael D. Mumford, Jazmine Espejo, Samuel T. Hunter, Katrina E. Bedell-Avers, Dawn L. Eubanks, and Shane Connelly, "The Sources of Leader Violence: A Comparison of Ideological and non-Ideological Leaders," *Leadership Quarterly* 18, no. 3 (2007): 217–35.
13. Yukl, *Leadership in Organizations*, 74.

14. Glenn R. Carroll, "Dynamics of Publisher Succession in Newspaper Organizations," *Administrative Science Quarterly* 29, no. 1 (1984): 93–113.
15. Carroll, "Dynamics of Publisher Succession in Newspaper Organizations," 96. For previous work on organizational performance and leadership turnover in baseball teams, see Oscar Grusky, "Managerial Succession and Organizational Effectiveness," *American Journal of Sociology* 69 (1963): 21–31; Oscar Grusky, "Reply to Scapegoating in Baseball," *American Journal of Sociology* 70 (1964): 72–76.
16. Arlyn J. Melcher, "Leadership Models and Research Approaches," in *Leadership: The Cutting Edge*, ed. J. G. Hunt and L. L. Larson (Carbondale: Southern Illinois University Press, 1977), 98–99.
17. Melcher, "Leadership Models and Research Approaches," 108.
18. Richard E. Neustadt, *Presidential Power* (New York: Macmillan, 1960).
19. Alexander L. George and Juliette George, *Presidential Personality and Performance* (Boulder, CO: Westview, 1998).
20. Terry Moe, "The Politicized Presidency," in *The New Direction in American Politics*, ed. J. E. Chubb and P. E. Peterson (Washington, DC: Brookings Institution, 1985), 235–72. Terry Moe, "Presidents, Institutions, and Theory," in *Researching the Presidency: Vital Questions, New Approaches*, ed. G. C. I. Edwards, J. H. Kessel, and B. A. Rockman (Pittsburgh, PA: University of Pittsburgh Press, 1993), 337–86.
21. Terry Moe, "The Politics of Bureaucratic Structure," in *Can the Government Govern?*, ed. J. E. Chubb and P. E. Peterson (Washington, DC: Brookings Institution, 1989), 267.
22. Margaret Hermann, a political psychologist who has written extensively on leadership in political organizations, noted in 1986 that "the systematic study of political leadership remains in its infancy." See Margaret G. Hermann, "Ingredients of Leadership," in *Political Psychology*, ed. Margaret G. Hermann (San Francisco: Jossey-Bass, 1986), 167. A lot has been written on the subject of political leadership, and leadership in government in particular, in the twenty-three years since then, and one could argue that the systematic study of leadership in other types of organizations, such as social movements and terrorist organizations, is in its infancy today. Interestingly, in her discussion of the ingredients of political leadership, Hermann's first ingredient is the "context factors" that "set the limits within which leaders and those they are leading can operate" (170).
23. Colonel John M. Collins, *Assassination and Abduction as Tools of National Policy* (Norfolk, VA: Armed Forces War College, 1965); Stephen Hosmer, *Operations Against Enemy Leaders* (Santa Monica, CA: RAND, 2001).
24. Michael Kenney, *From Pablo to Osama* (University Park: Pennsylvania State University Press, 2007). It should be noted that Kenney's work on the adaptive learning by both terrorist groups and drug cartels is much more nuanced than these other works, and he correctly identifies several important distinctions between these types of organizations.
25. Lisa Langdon, Alexander J. Sarapu, and Matthew Wells, "Targeting the Leadership of Terrorist and Insurgent Movements: Historical Lessons for Contemporary Policy Makers," *Journal of Public and International Affairs* 15 (Spring 2004): 59–78.
26. One could argue that organizations like national militaries and local police forces practice the lawful use of force rather than violence per se. The former is seen as

being legitimate while the latter may be seen as illegitimate. Putting semantics aside, organizations that are deemed violent in this study are all regularly exposed to the danger of being hurt by others and have the capacity to inflict hurt on others, whether it is legitimate or not.

27. Michael A. Hogg and Dominic Abrams, *Social Identifications: A Social Psychology of Intergroup Relations and Group Processes* (London: Routledge, 1988).
28. Mancur Olson Jr., *The Logic of Collective Action* (Cambridge, MA: Harvard University Press, 1965).
29. I thank Martha Crenshaw for pointing out this important distinction.
30. Dara Cohen, *Rape During Civil War* (Ithaca, NY: Cornell University Press, 2016); Elisabeth Jean Wood, "Armed Groups and Sexual Violence: When Is Wartime Rape Rare?" *Politics and Society* 37, no. 1 (2009): 131–62. Of particular interest to this study is Wood's conclusion that effective leadership is better than other factors in explaining which armed groups are more likely to engage in sexual violence against civilians.
31. Jerrold M. Post, "Terrorist Psycho-logic: Terrorist Behavior as a Product of Psychological Forces," in *Origins of Terrorism*, ed. W. Reich (Washington, DC: Woodrow Wilson Center, 1990), 134.
32. To explain, one could argue that people working in certain professions, such as firefighters and coal miners, are more cohesive than members in other organizations because they face dangerous conditions and can be easily killed in the line of duty. In this case, these organizations face violent death, but they do not engage in violence against others. Compared to other types of organizations, such as militaries, gangs, and terrorist groups, nonviolent organizations exhibiting similar types of cohesion and bonding are certainly the exception, not the rule.
33. U.S. Army, *FM-1 The Army* (Washington, DC: U.S. Government Printing Office, 2005), 1–11. (The FM-1 was superseded by the ADP-1 in 2014, and the quoted material is no longer current, although it does discuss unlimited liability on page 2-6).
34. Pedahzur discusses how violent organizations such as terrorist groups and militaries share this unique cohesion built around dangerous missions in his book, *Suicide Terrorism*. See Ami Pedahzur, *Suicide Terrorism* (Cambridge: Polity, 2005), 41–42.
35. Walter F. Ulmer Jr., "Introduction," in *Leadership: The Warrior's Art*, ed. C. Kolenda (Carlisle, PA: Army War College Foundation, 2001), xxxii.
36. Scott H. Decker and Barrick Van Winkle, *Life in the Gang: Family, Friends, and Violence* (Cambridge: Cambridge University Press, 1996).
37. Richard M. Nixon, *Leadership* (New York: Warner, 1982), 36.
38. John C. "Doc" Bahnsen, "Charisma," in *Leadership: The Warrior's Art*, ed. C. Kolenda (Carlisle, PA: Army War College Foundation, 2001), 274.
39. Oscar Grusky, "Administrative Succession in Formal Organizations," *Social Forces* 39 (1960): 105–15.
40. Clandestineness in this sense refers to a group's desire to keep information about how it operates hidden from outsiders. It is not meant to imply that the group desires to be completely invisible to others. For example, terrorist groups often operate clandestinely, but they want their target audiences to know they exist and want credit for successful attacks. They want and need publicity, but they want and need to keep how they operate a secret to maintain operational security.

41. Donatella della Porta, *Social Movements, Political Violence, and the State: A Comparative Analysis of Italy and Germany* (Cambridge: Cambridge University Press, 1995).
42. Eli Berman, *Sect, Subsidy and Sacrifice: An Economist's View of Ultra-Orthodox Jews* (Jerusalem: The Hay Elyachar House, 1998).
43. Marc Galanter, *Cults: Faith, Healing, and Coercion* (New York: Oxford University Press, 1999).
44. Stuart Koschade, "A Social Network Analysis of Aum Shinrikyo: Understanding Terrorism in Australia," in *Social Change in the 21st Century* (Brisbane, Australia: QUT, 2005), 1–18.
45. Martha Crenshaw, "The Subjective Reality of the Terrorist: Ideological and Psychological Factors in Terrorism," in *Current Perspectives on International Terrorism*, ed. R. O. Slater and M. Stohl (Hong Kong: MacMillan, 1988), 38.
46. Della Porta, *Social Movements, Political Violence, and the State*, 119.
47. Della Porta, *Social Movements, Political Violence, and the State*, 33.
48. Mumford et al., "The Sources of Leader Violence," 234.
49. Della Porta, *Social Movements, Political Violence, and the State*, 177.
50. J. K. Zawodny, "Infrastructures of Terrorist Organizations," *Conflict Quarterly* 1, no. 4 (1981): 26.
51. Irving L. Janis, *Victims of Groupthink* (Boston: Houghton-Mifflin, 1972).
52. Zawodny, "Infrastructures of Terrorist Organizations," 30.
53. Decker and Van Winkle, *Life in the Gang*, 271.
54. Crenshaw, "The Subjective Reality of the Terrorist," 38.
55. Ronald R. Aminzade, Jack A. Goldstone, and Elizabeth J. Perry, "Leadership Dynamics and Dynamics of Contention," in *Silence and Voice in the Study of Contentious Politics*, ed. Ronald R. Aminzade, Jack A. Goldstone, Doug McAdam, Elizabeth J. Perry, William H. Sewell, Sidney Tarrow, and Charles Tilly (New York: Cambridge University Press, 2001), 132.
56. Kenney, *From Pablo to Osama*.
57. Crenshaw, "The Subjective Reality of the Terrorist," 37.
58. Brian A. Jackson, "Organizational Learning and Terrorist Groups," Working paper, RAND, 2004, 3.
59. Kenney, *From Pablo to Osama*, 13.
60. Jackson, "Organizational Learning and Terrorist Groups," 23.
61. I am assuming an open systems approach here, where the "environment" refers to the external environment. This is in contrast to the close system approach that some scholars use to study organizational learning, where concern is only for processes internal to the group.
62. Catherine L. Wang and Pervaiz K. Ahmed, "Organizational Learning: A Critical Review," *The Learning Organization* 10, no. 1 (2003): 8–17.
63. Jackson, "Organizational Learning and Terrorist Groups," 45.
64. Jackson, "Organizational Learning and Terrorist Groups," 46.
65. Bruce Hoffman, "The Myth of Grass-Roots Terrorism," *Foreign Affairs* 87, no. 3 (2008): 133–38.
66. Decker and Van Winkle, *Life in the Gang*, 100
67. Jackson, "Organizational Learning and Terrorist Groups," 21.

68. Kenney, *From Pablo to Osama*, 16.
69. Kenney, *From Pablo to Osama*, 37.
70. Jackson, "Organizational Learning and Terrorist Groups," 22.
71. Mark Stout, Jessica M. Huckabey, John R. Schindler, and Jim Lacey, *The Terrorist Perspectives Project: Strategic and Operational Views of Al Qaida and Associated Movements* (Annapolis, MD: Naval Institute Press, 2008); see also https://ctc.usma.edu/harmony-program/.
72. Ed Blanche, "An Al Qaeda Rolodex: A Vast Treasure Trove of Captured Documents and Records Provides a Unique Insight into the Foreign Jihadis Fighting in Iraq, Prompting the US Military to Reassess How It Views Al Qaeda," *The Middle East*, March 2008, 7–10.
73. This trade-off is part of the principal-agent problem that all terrorist group leaders face. For an excellent discussion of this topic, see Jacob N. Shapiro, "The Terrorist's Challenge: Security, Efficiency, and Control" (PhD diss., Stanford University, 2007); and Jacob N. Shapiro, *The Terrorist's Dilemma: Managing Violent Covert Organizations* (Princeton, NJ: Princeton University Press, 2013).
74. Others refer to this type of organizational learning as "learning by doing." For more on organizational learning in general, see Barbara Levitt and James G. March, "Organizational Learning," *Annual Review of Sociology* 14 (1988): 319–40. For organizational learning in terrorist groups, see Brian A. Jackson, John C. Baker, Kim Cragin, John Parachini, Horacio R. Trujillo, and Peter Chalk, *Aptitude for Destruction: Organizational Learning in Terrorist Groups and Its Implications for Combating Terrorism* (Santa Monica, CA: RAND, 2005).
75. Kenney, *From Pablo to Osama*, 166.
76. Kenney, *From Pablo to Osama*, 154.
77. Kenney, *From Pablo to Osama*, 188.
78. Crenshaw, "The Subjective Reality of the Terrorist," 19.
79. Steven R. David, "Fatal Choices: Israel's Policy of Targeted Killings," *Mideast Security and Policy Studies*, no. 51 (September 2002): 13.
80. Jonathan B. Tucker, "Historical Trends Related to Bioterrorism: An Empirical Analysis," *Emerging Infectious Diseases* 5, no. 4 (1999): 4.
81. Aminzade et al., "Leadership Dynamics and Dynamics of Contention."
82. Zawodny, "Infrastructures of Terrorist Organizations," 28. Italics original.
83. Robert J. House, "A 1976 Theory of Charismatic Leadership," in *Leadership: The Cutting Edge*, ed. J. G. Hunt and L. L. Larson (Carbondale: Southern Illinois University Press, 1977), 189–207; House and Singh, "Organizational Behavior"; Mumford et al., "The Sources of Leader Violence." Mumford et al. and others outline the differences between charismatic leaders and ideological leaders; however, in this study, the two types are synonymous. The emphasis in this study is between charismatic/ideological leaders and noncharismatic/nonideological leaders. Another way of thinking about it is in terms of value- versus performance-based leadership.
84. Aminzade et al., "Leadership Dynamics and Dynamics of Contention," 152.
85. House and Singh, "Organizational Behavior," 686.
86. House, "A 1976 Theory of Charismatic Leadership."

87. Eugene P. H. Furtado and Vijay Karan, "Causes, Consequences, and Shareholder Wealth Effects of Management Turnover: A Review of the Empirical Evidence," *Financial Management* 19, no. 2 (1990): 60–75.
88. House and Singh, "Organizational Behavior," 691.
89. House, "A 1976 Theory of Charismatic Leadership," 204.
90. Bernard M. Bass, *Leadership Beyond Expectations* (New York: Free Press, 1985).
91. Shapiro, "The Terrorist's Challenge."
92. Crenshaw, "The Subjective Reality of the Terrorist," 19.
93. Crenshaw, "The Subjective Reality of the Terrorist," 19.
94. Crenshaw, "The Subjective Reality of the Terrorist," 19; see also Martha Crenshaw, "Why Violence Is Rejected or Renounced: A Case Study of Oppositional Terrorism," in *A Natural History of Peace*, ed. T. Gregor (Nashville, TN: Vanderbilt University Press, 1996), 263.
95. Max Weber, *The Theory of Social and Economic Organizations* (New York: Free Press, 1947), 363–73.
96. Lorne L. Dawson, "Crises of Charismatic Legitimacy and Violent Behavior in New Religious Movements," in *Cults, Religion, and Violence*, ed. D. G. Bromley and J. G. Melton (Cambridge: Cambridge University Press, 2002), 83.
97. Dawson, "Crises of Charismatic Legitimacy and Violent Behavior," 83.
98. The Terrorist Organization Profiles (TOPs) data collection provided background information on more than 850 organizations that have been known to engage in terrorist activity around the world during the last four decades. Included for each organization was information on bases of operations, organizational strength, ideology, and goals. These data were collected for the Terrorism Knowledge Base (TKB), managed by the Memorial Institute for the Prevention of Terrorism (MIPT) until March 2008. The database is currently housed at the National Consortium for the Study of Terrorism and Responses to Terrorism (START), which is based at the University of Maryland. START has neither reviewed nor verified these data, but it used to make that data set publicly available as a service to the homeland security community. For more, go to their TOPs database at http://www.start.umd.edu/gtd/features/TOPs.aspx.
99. Marshall W. Meyer and Lynne G. Zucker, *Permanently Failing Organizations* (Newbury Park, CA: Sage, 1989).
100. Bass, *Leadership Beyond Expectations*.
101. Kenney, *From Pablo to Osama*, 9–10.
102. Kenney, *From Pablo to Osama*, 10–11.
103. Meyer and Zucker, *Permanently Failing Organizations*.
104. Kenney, *From Pablo to Osama*, 44.
105. Decker and Van Winkle, *Life in the Gang*.
106. However, it would be possible for groups to use violence for a certain period of time and then stop, resorting to only peaceful acts thereafter. For example, some groups have started out as political parties and then devolved into terrorist groups and vice versa. See Aila Matanock, *Electing Peace: From Civil Conflict to Political Participation* (Cambridge, MA: Cambridge University Press, 2017).
107. Audrey Kurth Cronin, *Ending Terrorism: Lessons for Defeating al-Qaeda* (Abingdon, Oxford: International Institute for Strategic Studies, 2008); Simon Romero,

"Cocaine Trade Helps Rebels Reignite War in Peru," *New York Times*, March 18, 2009.
108. Elizabeth Barham, "Towards a Theory of Values-Based Labeling," *Agriculture and Human Values* 19 (2002): 349–60.
109. In his study of leadership succession of newspaper editors, Carroll coded the publisher control structures of each newspaper to determine whether they were run by a dominant individual, family, group, or corporation. He found that "transfers within positions in which authority is concentrated (i.e. dominant individual to dominant individual) should be the most precarious. These transfers also contain the potential for vast organizational change following succession." The only statistically significant variable in this case was the dominant individual, and in his conclusion, Carroll noted that "the empirical findings also suggested that succession is most precarious when the transfer of control occurs from and between organizations controlled by individuals." See Carroll, "Dynamics of Publisher Succession in Newspaper Organizations," 112. Since most violent organizations are hierarchically structured, and many have dominant individuals at the top, this conclusion, even though it was derived from the "left side" of the cube, supports my hypothesis that leadership succession in violent organizations is more precarious than in nonviolent organizations.
110. For example, on Blackwater's now-defunct website, prerequisites for employment as a Tier 1 contractor included a "minimum eight-years experience in either SOCCOM/JSOC/Intelligence field(s)." Prospective employees needed to be "retired or released from active duty within the last twenty-four months, or [had] maintained their skills sets through other independent contracting opportunities."
111. U.S. Army, *FM-1 The Army*, 1-11.
112. These were originally taken from Blackwater's website (http://blackwatersecurity.com/ employment.html) in 2009 and 2010.
113. Peter W. Singer, *Can't Win with 'Em, Can't Go to War Without 'Em: Private Military Contractors and Counterinsurgency* (Washington, DC: Brookings Institution, 2007).
114. John A. Nagl, David H. Petraeus, and James F. Amos, *The U.S. Army/Marine Corps Counterinsurgency Field Manual: U.S. Army Field Manual No. 3–24*, Marine Corps Warfighting Publication No. 3–33.5 (Chicago: University of Chicago Press, 2007).
115. Singer, *Can't Win with 'Em, Can't Go to War Without 'Em*.
116. Singer, *Can't Win with 'Em, Can't Go to War Without 'Em*, 8.
117. Singer.
118. Singer, 10.
119. Singer, 10.
120. Kenney, *From Pablo to Osama*, 10.
121. Quoted in Joseph N. Felter, "Preface," in *Cracks in the Foundation: Leadership Schisms in al-Qa'ida 1989–2006*, ed. J. N. Felter (West Point, NY: Combating Terrorism Center at West Point, 2007), i.
122. Noam Wasserman, "Founder-CEO Succession and the Paradox of Entrepreneurial Success," *Organization Science* 14, no. 2 (2003): 149.
123. Carroll, "Dynamics of Publisher Succession in Newspaper Organizations."
124. Carroll, "Dynamics of Publisher Succession in Newspaper Organizations," 94.

125. See, for example, Donald B. Trow, "Executive Succession in Small Companies," *Administrative Science Quarterly* 6 (1961): 228–39.
126. Bruce W. Johnson, Robert P. Magee, Nandu J. Nagarajan, and Harry A. Newman, "An Analysis of the Stock Price Reaction to Sudden Executive Deaths," *Journal of Accounting and Economics* 7 (1985): 151–74; Dan L. Worrell, Wallace N. Davidson III, P. R. Chandy, and Sharon L. Garrison, "Management Turnover Through Deaths of Key Executives: Effects on Investor Wealth," *Academy of Management Journal* 29, no. 4 (1986): 674–94.
127. Donald L. Helmich, "Organizational Growth and Succession Patterns," *Academy of Management Journal* 17, no. 4 (1974): 771–75.
128. Grusky, "Managerial Succession and Organizational Effectiveness."
129. Jenna Jordan, "When Heads Roll: Assessing the Effectiveness of Leadership Decapitation," *Security Studies* 18, no. 4 (October–December 2009): 719–55.
130. Edward H. Kaplan, Alex Mintz, Shaul Mishal, and Claudio Samban, "What Happened to Suicide Bombings in Israel? Insights from a Terror Stock Model," *Studies in Conflict and Terrorism* 28, no. 3 (August 2005): 225–35; Dipal K. Gupta and Kusum Mundra, "Suicide Bombing as a Strategic Weapon: An Empirical Investigation of Hamas and Islamic Jihad," *Terrorism and Political Violence* 17 (2005): 573–98; Aaron Mannes, "Testing the Snake Head Strategy: Does Killing or Capturing Its Leaders Reduce a Terrorist Group's Activity?" *Journal of International Policy Solutions* 9 (Spring 2008): 40–49.
131. Worrell et al., "Management Turnover Through Deaths of Key Executives."
132. Johnson et al., "An Analysis of the Stock Price Reaction to Sudden Executive Deaths," 152.
133. Johnson et al., "An Analysis of the Stock Price Reaction to Sudden Executive Deaths."
134. Worrell et al., "Management Turnover Through Deaths of Key Executives."
135. Johnson et al., "An Analysis of the Stock Price Reaction to Sudden Executive Deaths."
136. Worrell et al., "Management Turnover Through Deaths of Key Executives."
137. Worrell et al., "Management Turnover Through Deaths of Key Executives," 688.
138. John A. Cope, *Colombia's War: Toward a New Strategy*, Strategic Forum No. 194 (Washington, DC: Institute for National Strategic Studies, National Defense University, 2002, 1–8.
139. Cope, *Colombia's War*, 4.
140. Cope, *Colombia's War*, 8.
141. Victor Hyder, *Decapitation Operations: Criteria for Targeting Enemy Leadership* (Fort Leavenworth, KS: School of Advanced Military Studies, United States Army Command and General Staff College, 2004), 45.
142. Russell Crandall, *Driven by Drugs: U.S. Policy Towards Colombia* (Boulder, CO: Lynne Rienner, 2002), 117.
143. Decker and Van Winkle, *Life in the Gang*, 97.
144. Decker and Van Winkle, *Life in the Gang*, 98.
145. Decker and Van Winkle, 97.
146. Decker and Van Winkle, 98.
147. TOPs database at http://www.start.umd.edu/gtd/features/TOPs.aspx.

3. Leadership in Terrorist Organizations

1. This is not his real name, but his pen name. For more on this operation, see Dalton Fury, *Kill Bin Laden* (New York: St. Martin's, 2008).
2. "Elite Officer Recalls Bin Laden Hunt," *60 Minutes*, video, 13:22, October 5, 2008, https://www.cbsnews.com/news/elite-officer-recalls-bin-laden-hunt/.
3. Fury, *Kill Bin Laden*.
4. Roman D. Ortiz, "The Human Factor in Insurgency: Recruitment and Training in the Revolutionary Armed Forces of Colombia (FARC)," in *The Making of a Terrorist: Recruitment, Training, and Root Causes*, ed. J. J. F. Forest (Westport, CT: Praeger Security International, 2006), 275.
5. Deborah Amos, "Islamic State Defector: If You Turn Against ISIS, They Will Kill You," National Public Radio, September 25, 2014.
6. Jerrold M. Post, Ehud Sprinzak, and Laurita M. Denny, "The Terrorists in Their Own Words: Interviews with 35 Incarcerated Middle Eastern Terrorists," *Terrorism and Political Violence* 15, no. 1 (2003): 178.
7. Ami Pedahzur, *Suicide Terrorism* (Cambridge: Polity, 2005), 174.
8. John C. "Doc" Bahnsen, "Charisma," in *Leadership: The Warrior's Art*, ed. C. Kolenda (Carlisle, PA: Army War College Foundation, 2001), 274.
9. Richard J. Chasdi, *Serenade of Suffering: A Portrait of Middle East Terrorism, 1968–1993* (Lanham, MD: Lexington Books, 1999).
10. Gary Yukl, *Leadership in Organizations* (Upper Saddle River, NJ: Prentice Hall, 2002), 241.
11. James M. Burns, *Leadership* (New York: Harper & Row, 1978).
12. Arthur J. Deikman, "The Psychological Power of Charismatic Leaders in Cults and Terrorist Organizations," in *The Making of a Terrorist: Recruitment, Training, and Root Causes*, ed. J. J. F. Forest (Westport, CT: Praeger Security International, 2006), 76.
13. Yukl, *Leadership in Organizations*, 242.
14. Yukl, *Leadership in Organizations*, 243.
15. Brian Crozier, *The Rebels* (Boston: Beacon Press, 1960); Walter Laqueur, "The Terrorism to Come," *Policy Review* 126 (August–September 2004).
16. Yukl, *Leadership in Organizations*, 242.
17. Gordon H. McCormick, "Terrorist Decision Making," *Annual Review of Political Science* 6 (2003): 473–507; Mette Eilstrup-Sangiovanni and Calvert Jones, "Assessing the Dangers of Illicit Networks: Why al-Qaida May Be Less Threatening than Many Think," *International Security* 33, no. 2 (2008): 7–44.
18. As one former navy intelligence analyst noted, "Terrorist organizations do not have organizational charts. They have relationships, and if you can understand those relationships you have gained valuable intelligence." See Bryan Bender, "Antiterrorism Agency Taps Boston-Area Brains," *Boston Globe*, March 28, 2007.
19. Marc Galanter and James J. F. Forest, "Cults, Charismatic Groups, and Social Systems: Understanding the Transformation of Terrorist Recruits," in *The Making of a Terrorist: Recruitment, Training, and Root Causes*, ed. J. J. F. Forest (Westport, CT: Praeger Security International, 2006), 34–50.

20. Michael Kenney, *From Pablo to Osama* (University Park: Pennsylvania State University Press, 2007), 145.
21. Patrick Seale, *Abu Nidal: A Gun for Hire* (London: Hutchinson, 1992).
22. Duane R. Clarridge, *A Spy for All Seasons* (New York: Scribner, 1997), 336.
23. Clarridge, *A Spy for All Seasons*, 336; Christopher C. Harmon, "The Myth of the Invincible Terrorist," *Policy Review* 142 (April–May 2007): 57.
24. Seale, *Abu Nidal*, 290.
25. Harmon, "The Myth of the Invincible Terrorist," 1.
26. Rukmini Callimachi, "ISIS and the Lonely Young American," *New York Times*, July 28, 2015.
27. Irving L. Janis, *Victims of Groupthink* (Boston: Houghton-Mifflin, 1972).
28. McCormick, "Terrorist Decision Making."
29. Bruce Hoffman, "The Leadership Secrets of Osama bin Laden," *Atlantic Monthly*, April 2003, https://www.theatlantic.com/magazine/archive/2003/04/the-leadership-secrets-of-osama-bin-laden/302702/.
30. Hoffman, "The Leadership Secrets of Osama bin Laden."
31. Robert J. House and Jitendra V. Singh, "Organizational Behavior: Some New Directions for I/O Psychology," *Annual Review of Psychology* 38 (1987): 686.
32. Burns, *Leadership*.
33. Max Weber, *The Theory of Social and Economic Organizations* (New York: Free Press, 1947).
34. Walter Pincus, "Zarqawi Is Said to Swear Allegiance to Bin Laden," *Washington Post*, October 19, 2004, A16.
35. Louis Meixler, "Iraq Inspiring Copycat Beheadings," Associated Press, November 6, 2004.
36. Meixler, "Iraq Inspiring Copycat Beheadings."
37. Meixler.
38. You can find this letter on the Combating Terrorism Center's website. The letter is from Zawahiri to Zarqawi, dated July 9, 2005, and released by the Office of the Director of National Intelligence on October 11, 2005. Go to https://ctc.usma.edu/app/uploads/2013/10/Zawahiris-Letter-to-Zarqawi-Translation.pdf.
39. Meixler, "Iraq Inspiring Copycat Beheadings."
40. Steven Stalinsky, " 'Jihadi Porn' Puts Beheadings Online," *New York Sun*, June 28, 2006.
41. An alternative explanation for why beheadings suddenly stopped focuses on the criticism of the tactic by Zarqawi's lifelong mentor, Abu Muhammad al-Maqdisi. Not only did Zarqawi and Maqdisi have a long history together, dating back to the early 1990s when they first met in Peshawar, Pakistan, but Maqdisi was also considered to be "the most influential jihadi thinker alive" according to Will McCants of the Combating Terrorism Center at West Point. See Lawrence Wright, "The Master Plan," *New Yorker*, September 11, 2006, https://www.newyorker.com/magazine/2006/09/11/the-master-plan. Maqdisi served as the spiritual guide for Zarqawi's Al-Tawhid, the name of the group before Zarqawi pledged allegiance to bin Laden and joined al-Qaeda (they would later become what is known as al-Qaeda in Iraq). Maqdisi published several statements admonishing his former protégé for conducting suicide attacks, targeting fellow Muslims (namely, Shiites), and conducting beheadings (see Wright, "The Master Plan"; also Gabriel Weimann, "Virtual Disputes: The Use of

the Internet for Terrorist Debates," *Studies in Conflict and Terrorism* 29 [2006]: 623–39). However, Maqdisi had been criticizing Zarqawi since July 2004, and Zarqawi "angrily refuted Maqdisi's remarks" each time, including in several online website postings and audio statements (Wright, "The Master Plan," 5). In July 2005, Zarqawi attacked Maqdisi personally, "arguing that although Al-Maqdisi had been his mentor, he, Al-Zarqawi, did not follow Al-Maqdisi's teachings but rather followed the advice of other ulama whom he trusted more. Moreover, Al-Maqdisi, argued Al-Zarqawi, had no right to criticize the fighters in Iraq because he had not taken part in the Jihad in Iraq" (Weimann, "Virtual Disputes," 628). Thus, it is unlikely that Zarqawi stopped the beheadings because of Maqdisi's criticism. This was not the first time the protégé disobeyed Maqdisi. Maqdisi had been a staunch opponent of suicide bombings for decades, but "suicide bombings became a trademark of Zarqawi's operation, despite Maqdisi's condemnation of the practice (Wright, "The Master Plan," 5). It also should be noted that Zawahiri levied the same criticism concerning killing Shiites and the gruesome beheadings, and did so from a safe haven in Pakistan, yet Zarqawi did not publicly refute this criticism as he had done with Maqdisi.
42. This is especially interesting considering the measured tone Zawahiri uses in his letter so as not to anger and insult Zarqawi. Zawahiri recognizes the fact that Zarqawi is on the front lines of the fight while he and other al-Qaeda leaders such as bin Laden are in hiding. Zawahiri writes, "I repeat that I see the picture from afar, and I repeat that you see what we do not see. No doubt you have the right to defend yourself, the mujahedeen, and Muslims in general and in particular against any aggression or threat of aggression. . . . One who monitors from afar lacks many of the important details that affect decision-making in the field." https://ctc.usma.edu/app/uploads/2013/10/Zawahiris-Letter-to-Zarqawi-Translation.pdf.
43. Louise Richardson, *What Terrorists Want* (New York: Random House, 2006), 45.
44. Pedahzur, *Suicide Terrorism*, 179.
45. Pedahzur, *Suicide Terrorism*.
46. Pedahzur, 180.
47. Pedahzur, 174.
48. Bryan C. Price, "Terrorism as Cancer: How to Combat an Incurable Disease," *Terrorism and Political Violence*, June 9, 2017, 1–25.
49. Post et al., "The Terrorists in Their Own Words," 183.
50. Post et al., "The Terrorists in Their Own Words," 181, italics added.
51. Post et al., 176.
52. Albert Bandura, "Training for Terrorism Through Selective Moral Disengagement," in *The Making of a Terrorist: Recruitment, Training, and Root Causes*, ed. J. J. F. Forest (Westport, CT: Praeger Security International, 2006), 34–50.
53. Jerrold M. Post, "Killing in the Name of God: Osama bin Laden and Al Qaeda," in *Know Thy Enemy: Profiles of Adversary Leaders and Their Strategic Cultures*, ed. B. R. Schneider and J. M. Post (Maxwell Air Force Base, AL: U.S. Government Printing Office, 2003), 17–40.
54. Mohammed M. Hafez, "Martyrdom Mythology in Iraq: How Jihadists Frame Suicide Terrorism in Videos and Biographies," *Terrorism and Political Violence* 19 (2007): 102.
55. Pedahzur, *Suicide Terrorism*, 160.

56. Pedahzur, *Suicide Terrorism*, 159–60.
57. Quintan Wiktorowicz and John Kaltner, "Killing in the Name of Islam: Al-Qaeda's Justification for September 11," *Middle East Policy* 10, no. 2 (2003): 76–92; Bandura, "Training for Terrorism Through Selective Moral Disengagement."
58. The document, "A Statement from Qaidat al-Jihad Regarding the Mandates of the Heroes and the Legality of the Operations in New York and Washington," has been made available in both Arabic and English at www.mepc.org.
59. Wiktorowicz and Kaltner, "Killing in the Name of Islam," 90.
60. Erica Goode, "A Day of Terror; Attackers Believed to Be Sane," *New York Times*, September 12, 2001.
61. Max Abrahms, "Why Terrorism Does Not Work," *International Security* 31, no. 2 (2006): 42–78.
62. Martha Crenshaw, "Why Violence Is Rejected or Renounced: A Case Study of Oppositional Terrorism," in *A Natural History of Peace*, ed. T. Gregor (Nashville, TN: Vanderbilt University Press, 1996), 268; Franco Ferracuti, "Ideology and Repentance: Terrorism in Italy," in *Origins of Terrorism: Psychologies, Ideologies, Theologies, States of Mind*, ed. W. Reich (Washington, DC: Woodrow Wilson Center, 1990), 59–64.
63. Ferracuti, "Ideology and Repentance," 63.
64. Marshall W. Meyer and Lynne G. Zucker, *Permanently Failing Organizations* (Newbury Park, CA: Sage, 1989).
65. Meyer and Zucker, *Permanently Failing Organizations*, 93.
66. *The Mind of the Terrorist: Individual and Group Psychology of Terrorist Behavior, Hearing Before the Subcommittee on Emerging Threats and Capabilities, Senate Armed Services Committee*, 107th Cong. 1 (2001) (statement of Jerrold M. Post, Professor, George Washington University).
67. Some do not consider the armed wing of the African National Congress (ANC), which Mandela led in the early 1960s, to be a terrorist group. As with many nationalist/separatist terrorist groups, perception is in the eye of the beholder when it comes to labeling the group as a terrorist organization. As the phrase goes, one man's terrorist is another man's freedom fighter. With that said, the Terrorism Knowledge Base and the Global Terrorism Database list the ANC as a terrorist organization that conducted 254 attacks after 1970.
68. *The Mind of the Terrorist*. Although leaders of nationalist/separatist terrorist groups often find it easier to attain positions of authority following their tenure in terrorist organizations, it is telling, that many strongly deny their affiliation with their former groups. This is especially true for many Irish politicians such as Gerry Adams and Martin McGuiness, who deny their leadership roles in the IRA. Additionally, no leaders of anarchist or right-wing groups went into politics, and nationalist and religious terrorist group leaders outnumber left-wing groups by a 3:1 margin.
69. Glenn R. Carroll, "Dynamics of Publisher Succession in Newspaper Organizations," *Administrative Science Quarterly* 29, no. 1 (1984): 93–113; Jacob N. Shapiro, *The Terrorist's Dilemma* (Princeton, NJ: Princeton University Press, 2013).
70. Bryan C. Price, "Removing the Devil You Know: Unraveling the Puzzle Behind Leadership Decapitation and Terrorist Group Duration" (PhD diss., Stanford University, 2009).

71. Amnesty International, *Bolivia: Awaiting Justice: Torture, Extrajudicial Executions and Legal Proceedings* (London: Amnesty International, September 1996), 1, https://www.amnesty.org/download/Documents/164000/amr180091996en.pdf.
72. Martha Crenshaw, "An Organizational Approach to the Analysis of Political Terrorism," *Orbis* 29, no. 3 (1985): 489.
73. Bruce Hoffman, "The Leadership Secrets of Osama bin Laden," *Atlantic Monthly*, April 2003. Italics added.
74. Crenshaw, "Why Violence Is Rejected or Renounced: A Case Study of Oppositional Terrorism," in *A Natural History of Peace*, ed. T. Gregor (Nashville, TN: Vanderbilt University Press, 1996), 259.
75. Culture in this sense entails both the formal and the informal cultures that exist in organizations. For more on how group norms constrain the leader, see Sidney Verba, *Small Groups and Political Behavior* (Princeton, NJ: Princeton University Press, 1961), chap. 8, 185–205. For a comprehensive look at culture and organizations, see Richard J. Harrison and Glenn R. Carroll, *Culture and Demography in Organizations* (Princeton, NJ: Princeton University Press, 2006).
76. Peter J. Boettke, Christopher Coyne, and Peter T. Leeson, "Institutional Stickiness and the New Development Economics," *American Journal of Economics and Sociology* 67, no. 2 (2008): 331–58.
77. Ortiz, "The Human Factor in Insurgency," 275.
78. For one interesting example, Aum Shinrikyo's leader allegedly modeled his organizational structure after the Japanese government, complete with the requisite number of ministries, so there could be a "smooth transition" when the group took over. See Stuart Koschade, "A Social Network Analysis of Aum Shinrikyo: Understanding Terrorism in Australia," in *Social Change in the 21st Century* (Brisbane, Australia: QUT, 2005), 6.
79. Paul Joosse, "Leaderless Resistance and Ideological Inclusion: The Case of the Earth Liberation Front," *Terrorism and Political Violence* 19 (2007): 351–68.
80. Shapiro, *The Terrorist's Dilemma*.
81. Arthur S. Stinchcombe, "Organizations and Social Structure," in *Handbook of Organizations*, ed. J. G. March (Chicago: Rand-McNally, 1965), 142–93.
82. Edgar H. Schein, "The Role of the Founder in the Creation of Organizational Culture," *Organizational Dynamics* 12, no. 1 (1983): 13–28.
83. Schein, "The Role of the Founder," 18.
84. Carroll, "Dynamics of Publisher Succession in Newspaper Organizations."
85. Schein, "The Role of the Founder."
86. Shapiro, *The Terrorist's Dilemma*.
87. Luther Gulick, "Notes on the Theory of Organization," in *Papers on the Science of Administration*, ed. Luther Gulick and Lydal Urwick (New York: Institute of Public Administration, Columbia University, 1937), 191–95.
88. *Global Proliferation of Weapons of Mass Destruction: Hearings Before the Permanent Subcommittee on Investigations of the Committee on Governmental Affairs*, United States Senate, 104th Cong. 1 (1995).
89. Ortiz, "The Human Factor in Insurgency."

90. As Shapiro noted, the downside is that leaders often have to sacrifice operational security if they insist on operating only in a face-to-face manner (see Shapiro, *The Terrorist's Dilemma*).
91. Audrey Kurth Cronin, "How al-Qaida Ends: The Decline and Demise of Terrorist Groups," *International Security* 31, no. 1 (Summer 2006): 7–48; Cronin, *Ending Terrorism: Lessons for Defeating al-Qaeda* (Abingdon, Oxford: International Institute for Strategic Studies, 2008); Aaron Mannes, "Testing the Snake Head Strategy: Does Killing or Capturing Its Leaders Reduce a Terrorist Group's Activity?" *Journal of International Policy Solutions* 9 (Spring 2008): 40–49; Jenna Jordan, "When Heads Roll: Assessing the Effectiveness of Leadership Decapitation," *Security Studies* 18, no. 4 (October–December 2009): 719–55; Patrick Johnston, "Does Decapitation Work? Assessing the Effectiveness of Leadership Targeting in Counterinsurgency Campaigns," *International Security* 36, no. 4 (Spring 2012): 47–79; Jenna Jordan, "Attacking the Leader, Missing the Mark," *International Security* 38, no. 4 (Spring 2014): 7–38.
92. Walter Laqueur, *The Terrorism Reader: A Historical Anthology* (New York: New American Library, 1978).
93. Cronin, "How al-Qaida Ends," 48.
94. Walter Enders and Todd Sandler, *The Political Economy of Terrorism* (New York: Cambridge University Press, 2006), 245.
95. Price, "Terrorism as Cancer."
96. Martha Crenshaw, "Evaluating the Effectiveness of Counterterrorism" (paper presented at the International Studies Association Fiftieth Annual Convention, New York, February 15–18, 2009), 24.
97. Marc Sageman, *Leaderless Jihad: Terror Networks in the Twenty-First Century* (Philadelphia: University of Pennsylvania Press, 2008).
98. Sageman and other supporters of the "bunch of guys" theory often contend that the Internet has become a "virtual training camp" for the next generation of jihadist militants. However, after studying many of the terrorist networks operating in Europe during the mid-2000s, including the so-called home-grown terrorist cells that performed attacks in London and Madrid, Nesser thinks the threat from individuals who radicalize via the Internet is overblown and mischaracterized. In a 2008 article, Nesser stated, "Looking more closely at the cases, one will find that, in terms of operational training and preparation, the activists interacted face-to-face with organized mujahidin, and traveled in order to obtain real-life training and develop necessary skills." See Petter Nesser, "How Did Europe's Global Jihadis Obtain Training for Their Militant Causes?," *Terrorism and Political Violence* 20 (2008): 248.
99. Daveed Gartenstein-Ross and Kyle Dabruzzi, "Is Al-Qaeda's Central Leadership Still Relevant?," *Middle East Quarterly* (Spring 2008): 27.
100. For a spirited critique of the "bunch of guys" theory, see Bruce Hoffman, "The Myth of Grass-Roots Terrorism: Why Osama bin Laden Still Matters," *Foreign Affairs* 87, no. 3 (2008): 133–38.
101. Executive Office of the President, *National Strategy for Combating Terrorism*, February 2003; Executive Office of the President, *National Strategy for Combating Terrorism*,

September 2006; Executive Office of the President, *National Strategy for Counterterrorism*, June 2011.
102. Seth G. Jones and Martin C. Libicki, *How Terrorist Groups End: Lessons for Countering al Qa'ida* (Santa Monica, CA: RAND, 2008).
103. Cronin, *Ending Terrorism*.
104. Mannes, "Testing the Snake Head Strategy."
105. Lawrence Wright, *The Looming Tower* (New York: Knopf, 2006).
106. Vahid Brown, *Cracks in the Foundation: Leadership Schisms in al-Qa'ida from 1989–2006* (West Point, NY: Combating Terrorism Center, 2007), 22.
107. Kenney, *From Pablo to Osama*; Barbara Levitt and James G. March, "Organizational Learning," *Annual Review of Sociology* 14 (1988): 319–40.
108. Daniel Byman, "Do Targeted Killings Work?" *Foreign Affairs* 85, no. 2 (March 2006): 103–4.
109. For a review of this literature, see J. Bendor, A. Glazer, and T. Hammond, "Theories of Delegation," *Annual Review of Political Science* 4 (2001): 235–69.
110. Shapiro, *The Terrorist's Dilemma*.
111. Pedahzur, *Suicide Terrorism*, 176.
112. Stephanie Hanson, *MEND: The Niger Delta's Umbrella Militant Group* (Washington, DC: Council on Foreign Relations, 2007).
113. Byman, "Do Targeted Killings Work?"
114. Byman, "Do Targeted Killings Work?," 104.
115. Shapiro, *The Terrorist's Dilemma*.
116. Sageman, *Leaderless Jihad*; John Arquilla and David Ronfeldt, *Networks and Netwars: The Future of Terror, Crime, and Militancy* (Santa Monica, CA: RAND, 2001).
117. Eilstrup-Sangiovanni and Jones, "Assessing the Dangers of Illicit Networks."
118. Eilstrup-Sangiovanni and Jones, "Assessing the Dangers of Illicit Networks," 21.
119. Byman, "Do Targeted Killings Work?"
120. Byman, "Do Targeted Killings Work?"
121. Grahm H. Turbiville Jr., "Hunting Leadership Targets in Counterinsurgency and Counterterrorist Operations," *Joint Special Operations University* 7, no. 6 (2007): 1–102.
122. Maria Elena García, *Making Indigenous Citizens: Identities, Education, and Multicultural Development in Peru* (Stanford, CA: Stanford University Press, 2005), 48.
123. Laurie Copans, "Film Shows Barghouti Eating During Hunger Strike," *Jerusalem Post*, August 19, 2004, 3.
124. Byman, "Do Targeted Killings Work?"
125. Jordan, "When Heads Roll"; Jordan, "Attacking the Leader, Missing the Mark."
126. Catherine Lotrionte, "When to Target Leaders," *Washington Quarterly* 26, no. 3 (2003): 73–86; Edward H. Kaplan, Alex Mintz, Shaul Mishal, and Claudio Samban, "What Happened to Suicide Bombings in Israel? Insights from a Terror Stock Model," *Studies in Conflict and Terrorism* 28 (2005): 225–35; Byman, "Do Targeted Killings Work?"; Jordan, "When Heads Roll."
127. Steven R. David, *Fatal Choices: Israel's Policy of Targeted Killings*, Mideast Security and Policy Studies No. 51 (Ramat Gan, Israel: Begin-Sadat Center for Strategic Studies, 2002), 1–26; Boaz Ganor, *The Counter-Terrorism Puzzle* (New Brunswick, NJ: Transaction, 2005); Byman, "Do Targeted Killings Work?"

128. Stephen Hosmer, *Operations Against Enemy Leaders* (Santa Monica, CA: RAND, 2001); David Kilcullen and Andrew Exum, "Death from Above, Outrage Down Below," *New York Times*, May 16, 2009.
129. Byman, "Do Targeted Killings Work?"
130. Byman, "Do Targeted Killings Work?"
131. Paul Staniland, "Defeating Transnational Insurgencies: The Best Offense Is a Good Fence," *Washington Quarterly* 29, no. 1 (2005–2006): 21–40.
132. For an interesting and well-told example of the political fallout stemming from a failed decapitation mission, see Ganor's discussion in chapter 5 of the failed attempt by Israel to kill Hamas leader Khaled Mashaal. See Ganor, *The Counter-Terrorism Puzzle*, 122–25.
133. Schein, "The Role of the Founder," 22.
134. Carroll, "Dynamics of Publisher Succession in Newspaper Organizations."
135. Carroll, "Dynamics of Publisher Succession in Newspaper Organizations."
136. Mannes, "Testing the Snake Head Strategy."
137. Langdon et al., "Targeting the Leadership of Terrorist and Insurgent Movements."
138. Mannes, "Testing the Snake Head Strategy," 45.
139. Jordan, "When Heads Roll"; Jordan, "Attacking the Leader, Missing the Mark."

4. Quantitative Analysis of Leadership Decapitation in Terrorist Groups

1. Lisa Langdon, Alexander J. Sarapu, and Matthew Wells, "Targeting the Leadership of Terrorist and Insurgent Movements: Historical Lessons for Contemporary Policy Makers," *Journal of Public and International Affairs* 15 (Spring 2004): 59–78; Aaron Mannes, "Testing the Snake Head Strategy: Does Killing or Capturing Its Leaders Reduce a Terrorist Group's Activity?" *Journal of International Policy Solutions* 9 (Spring 2008): 40–49.
2. Gary LaFree and Laura Dugan, "Introducing the Global Terrorism Database," *Terrorism and Political Violence* 19 (2007): 181–204; Victor Asal and R. Karl Rethemeyer, "The Nature of the Beast: Organizational Structures and the Lethality of Terrorist Attacks," *Journal of Politics* 70, no. 2 (2008): 437–49.
3. See Michael Kenney, *From Pablo to Osama* (University Park: Pennsylvania State University Press, 2007).
4. Ariel Merari, "Academic Research and Government Policy on Terrorism," *Terrorism and Political Violence* 3 (1991): 88–102.
5. LaFree and Dugan, "Introducing the Global Terrorism Database," 183; Kenney, *From Pablo to Osama*; Lionel Beehner, "America's Useless Terrorism List," *Los Angeles Times*, October 20, 2008.
6. An interesting and telling example of this point comes from West Point's Combating Terrorism Center (CTC), which has become a leading force since its inception in 2003 in translating captured documents from terrorist groups into English and getting them declassified and into the hands of scholars. However, making this information

public means it can get into the hands of terrorists too, as demonstrated by an al-Qaeda propaganda video that specifically referenced a report published by the CTC in 2006. Zawahiri, the speaker in the video, reads and criticizes two paragraphs from the report while a graphic of the CTC emblem is displayed in the background. Also, Kenney provides compelling evidence that other clandestine organizations such as drug trafficking cartels use the mass media and government reports to better understand counterdrug operations (Kenney, *From Pablo to Osama*, 59).

7. Kenney, *From Pablo to Osama*, 160.
8. Mannes, "Testing the Snake Head Strategy"; Jenna Jordan, "When Heads Roll: Assessing the Effectiveness of Leadership Decapitation," *Security Studies* 18, no. 4 (October–December 2009): 719–55; Human Security Report Project, *Human Security Brief 2007* (Vancouver, BC: Simon Fraser University, 2008).
9. Asal and Rethemeyer, "The Nature of the Beast."
10. Alexander Spencer, "The Problems of Evaluating Counter-Terrorism," UNISCI Discussion Paper No. 12 (October 2006); David D. Laitin and Jacob N. Shapiro, "The Political, Economic and Organizational Sources of Terrorism," in *Terrorism, Economic Development, and Political Openness*, ed. P. Keefer and N. Loayza (Cambridge: Cambridge University Press, 2008), 209–32; Mannes, "Testing the Snake Head Strategy"; Bryan C. Price, "Targeting Top Terrorists," *International Security* 36, no. 4 (Spring 2012): 9–36.
11. National Consortium for the Study of Terrorism and Responses to Terrorism (START), Global Terrorism Database [Data file], 2017, https://www.start.umd.edu/gtd.
12. LaFree and Dugan say they received funding from the Department of Homeland Security in April 2006 to recover the missing data, but as of February 24, 2009, no incidents from 1993 showed up in the GTD. See LaFree and Dugan, "Introducing the Global Terrorism Database," 186.
13. Asal and Rethemeyer, "The Nature of the Beast," 447.
14. Glenn R. Carroll, "Dynamics of Publisher Succession in Newspaper Organizations," *Administrative Science Quarterly* 29, no. 1 (1984): 6.
15. The Terrorist Organization Profiles (TOPs) data collection provided background information on more than 850 organizations that have been known to engage in terrorist activity around the world during the last four decades. Included for each organization was information on bases of operations, organizational strength, ideology, and goals. These data were collected for the Terrorism Knowledge Base (TKB), which was managed by the Memorial Institute for the Prevention of Terrorism (MIPT) until March 2008. The database is currently housed at the National Consortium for the Study of Terrorism and Responses to Terrorism (START), which is based at the University of Maryland. START has neither reviewed nor verified these data, but it used to make that data set publicly available as a service to the homeland security community. For more, go to the TOPs database at http://www.start.umd.edu/gtd/features/TOPs.aspx.
16. LaFree and Dugan, "Introducing the Global Terrorism Database," 187.
17. For an exampleof criticism directed toward then Governor Romney, see http://www.dialoginternational.com/dialog_international/2007/06/index.html, last accessed May 9, 2018.

18. START, GTD; Price, "Targeting Top Terrorists," 24; TOPs database at http://www.start.umd.edu/gtd/features/TOPs.aspx.
19. START, GTD; Price, "Targeting Top Terrorists," 24; TOPs database at http://www.start.umd.edu/gtd/features/TOPs.aspx.
20. START, GTD; TOPs database at http://www.start.umd.edu/gtd/features/TOPs.aspx.
21. See, for example, Asal and Rethemeyer, "The Nature of the Beast."
22. Some of these groups were founded prior to 1970, but all were active for at least part of the period between 1970 and 2008.
23. Langdon et al., "Targeting the Leadership of Terrorist and Insurgent Movements."
24. For comparison purposes, I have 48 groups with under 100 members in my data set.
25. Mannes, "Testing the Snake Head Strategy."
26. Jordan, "When Heads Roll."
27. Several data sets in political science employ similar filters. For example, many scholars studying civil wars use a coding criterion that includes conflicts with at least 1,000 total deaths and 100 deaths per year. I felt that limiting my data set to groups that have killed at least one person and conducted four attacks would be a fair demonstration of organizational capability.
28. Kenney, *From Pablo to Osama*, viii.
29. After my initial quantitative analysis, I ran my models again with these groups running continuously instead of having breaks in their organizational history. It resulted in no significant change.
30. Seth G. Jones and Martin C. Libicki, *How Terrorist Groups End: Lessons for Countering al Qa'ida* (Santa Monica, CA: RAND, 2008).
31. Clint Davis, "What Happened to the 52 'Most Wanted' Iraqis from the U.S. Military Card Deck?" *KSHB News*, April 22, 2015.
32. It is important to note that starting in the year the group executes its first attack, I assume the group becomes "at risk" by the state even though it may not have met all of the criteria for inclusion into the data set in this first year (i.e., conducted at least four attacks and killed at least one person). Some, of course, do. I thank Ken Schultz for bringing this to my attention.
33. START, GTD; TOPs database at http://www.start.umd.edu/gtd/features/TOPs.aspx.
34. Brian J. Phillips, "Terrorist Group Cooperation and Longevity," *International Studies Quarterly* 58, no. 2 (2014): 336–47.
35. Rober J. Chasdi, *Serenade of Suffering: A Portrait of Middle East Terrorism, 1968–1993* (Lanham, MD: Lexington Books, 1999), 106.
36. W. P. Barnett and D. G. McKendrick, "Why Are Some Organizations More Competitive than Others? Evidence from a Changing Global Market," *Administrative Science Quarterly* 49 (2004): 535–71.
37. Joseph K. Young and Laura Dugan, "Survival of the Fittest: Why Terrorist Groups Endure," Perspectives on Terrorism 8, no. 2 (2014): 1–23.
38. Brian J. Phillips, "Enemies with Benefits? Violent Rivalry and Terrorist Group Longevity," *Journal of Peace Research* 52, no. 1 (2015): 62–75.
39. Audrey Kurth Cronin, "No Silver Bullets: Explaining Research on How Terrorist Groups End," *CTC Sentinel* 3, no. 4 (2010): 16–18.

40. Brian Jackson's work on how difficult it is to label a particular terrorist organization as being purely hierarchical or purely decentralized speaks to this point. Ultimately, it comes down to a question of degree; rarely can one label a group as being purely hierarchical or decentralized. Instead, Jackson recommends looking at the quality and quantity of a group's command and control linkages to better understand the structure. This, however, is often difficult to accurately determine as well. For more, see Brian A. Jackson, "Groups, Networks, or Movements: A Command-and-Control-Driven Approach to Classifying Terrorist Organizations and Its Application to Al Qaeda," *Studies in Conflict and Terrorism* 29 (2006): 241–62.
41. Bruce Hoffman, "Rethinking Terrorism and Counterterrorism Since 9/11," *Studies in Conflict and Terrorism* 25 (2002): 303–16; Audrey Kurth Cronin, "Behind the Curve," *International Security* 27, no. 3 (2002–2003): 30–58; Mannes, "Testing the Snake Head Strategy"; Jordan, "When Heads Roll"; Jenna Jordan, "Attacking the Leader, Missing the Mark," *International Security* 38, no. 4 (Spring 2014): 7–38; Young and Dugan, "Survival of the Fittest."
42. Cronin, "Behind the Curve," 41–42.
43. Bruce Hoffman, *Inside Terrorism* (New York: Columbia University Press, 2006), 242–43.
44. Louise Richardson, *What Terrorists Want* (New York: Random House, 2006), 48.
45. Hutchinson and O'Malley, "How Terrorist Groups Decline," 2.
46. Jerrold M. Post, "Terrorist Psycho-logic: Terrorist Behavior as a Product of Psychological Forces," in *Origins of Terrorism*, ed. W. Reich (Washington, DC: Woodrow Wilson Center, 1990), 35.
47. Martha Crenshaw, "The Subjective Reality of the Terrorist: Ideological and Psychological Factors in Terrorism," in *Current Perspectives on International Terrorism*, ed. R. O. Slater and M. Stohl (Hong Kong: MacMillan, 1988), 27.
48. Jones and Libicki, *How Terrorist Groups End*.
49. As a robustness check, I also ran a Cox model with the ideologies as they were coded in the TOPs data set. Ideology in this data set was coded as nine types: anarchist, anti-globalist, socialist/communist, environmental, leftist, nationalist/separatist, racist, religious, right-wing conservative, right-wing reactionary, and other. Since there was no major change in the results and since the RAND typologies are easier to comprehend, I used the RAND ideologies.
50. Asal and Rethemeyer, "The Nature of the Beast"; Jordan, "When Heads Roll"; Max Abrahms and Philip B. K. Potter, "Explaining Terrorism: Leadership Deficits and Militant Group Tactics," *International Organization* 69 (Spring 2015): 311–42.
51. Jones and Libicki, *How Terrorist Groups End*.
52. Mannes, "Testing the Snake Head Strategy"; Jones and Libicki, *How Terrorist Groups End*.
53. James Fearon and David D. Laitin, "Ethnicity, Insurgency, and Civil War," *American Political Science Review* 97 (2003): 75–90.
54. Todd Sandler, "Collective Action and Transnational Terrorism," *The World Economy* 26, no. 6 (2003): 787.
55. For al-Qaeda, I used the GDP per capita of the United States, the United Kingdom, and Pakistan.

56. The UN has developed evaluation criteria for state counterterrorism capacity as per UN Resolution 1373, which made member states obligated to revise laws and enhance their law enforcement capability. Additionally, states were encouraged to become signatories of twelve counterterrorism conventions. However, a critical analysis of the UN's counterterrorism program identified several weaknesses. Not only are these criteria very vague (i.e., does a member state have "the administrative capacity to enforce various counter-terrorism mandates"?), but there are difficulties in evaluating compliance. According to the report, "Evaluating whether states are actually implementing these conventions and complying with the requirements of Resolution 1373 is a difficult challenge. There are no agreed criteria for evaluating implementation capabilities, or determining what additional steps a state should take to achieve compliance." See David Cortright, Alistair Millar, Linda Gerber, and George A. Lopez, "An Action Agenda for Enhancing the United Nations Program on Counter-Terrorism," Kroc Institute for International Peace Studies (September 2004), 5. Therefore, I did not find compliance with these conventions to be a better measure than GDP per capita.
57. Robert J. Art and Louise Richardson, *Democracy and Counterterrorism: Lessons from the Past* (Washington, DC: United States Institute of Peace, 2007); Ian O. Lesser, Bruce Hoffman, John Arquilla, David Ronfeldt, and Michele Zanini, *Countering the New Terrorism* (Santa Monica, CA: RAND, 1999); Paul Wilkinson, *Terrorism Versus Democracy* (London: Frank Cass, 2000); Doron Zimmerman and Andreas Wenger, *How States Fight Terrorism: Policy Dynamics in the West* (London: Lynne Rienner, 2007); Walter Enders and Todd Sandler, *The Political Economy of Terrorism* (New York: Cambridge University Press, 2006).
58. I thank Martha Crenshaw for pointing this out to me.
59. The correlations for the variables in this model can be found on my website.
60. Mannes, "Testing the Snake Head Strategy," 42.
61. Janet M. Box-Steffensmeier and Bradford S. Jones, *Event History Modeling: A Guide for Social Sciences* (Cambridge: Cambridge University Press, 2004).
62. Examples of works in political science that have used survival analysis are Bueno de Mesquita and Siverson, who looked at the survival rates of political leaders, and Bennett and Stam, who looked at the duration of military conflicts (Box-Steffensmeier and Jones, *Event History Modeling*, 21). Page Fortna used survival analysis to examine the effectiveness of peacekeeping operations. See Virginia Page Fortna, "Does Peacekeeping Keep Peace? International Intervention and the Duration of Peace After Civil War," *International Studies Quarterly* 48 (2004): 269–92.
63. Box-Steffensmeier and Jones, *Event History Modeling*, 21.
64. Box-Steffensmeier and Jones, *Event History Modeling*, 21.
65. Box-Steffensmeier and Jones, 13–14.
66. Box-Steffensmeier and Jones, 48.
67. Additionally, to avoid confusion, it should be noted that the standard errors reported below the hazard ratios are for the actual coefficients from which the hazard ratios were derived, not the hazard ratios themselves.
68. David C. Rapoport, "Terrorism," in *Encyclopedia of Government and Politics*, ed. M. Hawkesworth and M. Kogan (London: Routledge, 1992), 1067.

69. Bruce Hoffman, *Inside Terrorism*; Audrey Kurth Cronin, "How al-Qaida Ends: The Decline and Demise of Terrorist Groups," *International Security* 31, no. 1 (Summer 2006): 7–48; Hutchinson and O'Malley, "How Terrorist Groups Decline."
70. Rapoport, "Terrorism."
71. Rapoport, "Terrorism," 1067. Italics added.
72. Bryan C. Price, "Removing the Devil You Know: Unraveling the Puzzle Behind Leadership Decapitation and Terrorist Group Duration" (PhD diss., Stanford University, 2009); Price, "Targeting Top Terrorists."
73. Brian J. Phillips, "Do 90 Percent of Terrorist Groups Last Less Than a Year? Updating the Conventional Wisdom," *Terrorism and Political Violence* (September 2017), https://doi.org/10.1080/09546553.2017.1361411.
74. Asal and Rethemeyer, "The Nature of the Beast," 442.
75. Price, "Targeting Top Terrorists."
76. Jordan, "When Heads Roll."
77. This is because Cox models do not have an intercept term. All results are interpreted relative to the baseline hazard rate. For more, see Terry M. Therneau and Patricia M. Grambsch, *Modeling Survival Data: Extending the Cox Model* (New York: Springer, 2000).
78. TOPs database at http://www.start.umd.edu/gtd/features/TOPs.aspx.
79. Jones and Libicki, *How Terrorist Groups End*.
80. Jones and Libicki, *How Terrorist Groups End*, xiv.
81. Phillips, "Enemies with Benefits?"
82. See, for example, William Eubank and Leonard Weinberg, "Does Democracy Encourage Terrorism?" *Terrorism and Political Violence* 6, no. 4 (1994): 417–35; and Audrey Kurth Cronin, "Sources of Contemporary Terrorism," in *Attacking Terrorism: Elements of a Grand Strategy*, ed. A. K. Cronin and J. M. Ludes (Washington, DC: Georgetown University Press, 2004), 19–45.
83. Ortiz believes this is an important reason for the FARC's success in certain areas of Colombia. See Roman D. Ortiz, "The Human Factor in Insurgency: Recruitment and Training in the Revolutionary Armed Forces of Colombia (FARC)," in *The Making of a Terrorist: Recruitment, Training, and Root Causes*, ed. J. J. F. Forest (Westport, CT: Praeger Security International, 2006), 263–76.
84. The inclusion of the interaction term was also needed to satisfy the Cox proportional hazards assumption to determine whether time dependence was an issue in the models. After conducting a Schoenfeld's residual test, I found that the main explanatory variable, *Exp Decap*, violated the nonproportionality assumption. In order to "save" this variable, I had to include an interaction term of *Exp Decap* and time. For a more detailed discussion, see Price, "Removing the Devil You Know."
85. Thus, in subsequent years, the net effect of decapitation = $e^{(2.17 - (t_i \times 0.073))}$ where t represents time and i represents the years after decapitation.
86. If one or more of the cofounders were decapitated but the other(s) remained, I coded the group as still having their founder.
87. Cronin, "How al-Qaida Ends"; Hutchinson and O'Malley, "How Terrorist Groups Decline"; Audrey Kurth Cronin, *Ending Terrorism: Lessons for Defeating al-Qaeda*,

Adelphi Paper No. 394, International Institute for Strategic Studies (London: Routledge, 2008), 1–85.
88. Catherine Lotrionte, "When to Target Leaders," *Washington Quarterly* 26, no. 3 (2003): 73–86; Boaz Ganor, *The Counter-Terrorism Puzzle* (New Brunswick, NJ: Transaction, 2005); Scott Shane, "Government Hit Squads, Minus the Hits," *New York Times*, July 19, 2009; Mark Mazzetti and Scott Shane, "CIA Had Plan to Assassinate Qaeda Leaders," *New York Times*, July 14, 2009.
89. Cronin, "Ending Terrorism," 30.
90. Hutchinson and O'Malley, "How Terrorist Groups Decline," 6.
91. Ganor, *The Counter-Terrorism Puzzle*.
92. Ganor, *The Counter-Terrorism Puzzle*, 128.
93. Ganor, *The Counter-Terrorism Puzzle*.
94. This was done via chi-square testing.
95. Because no terrorist groups ended (in the same year) in the 11 cases where a leader died of natural causes, this variable does not show up in the results in table 4.9 This is because the model is incapable of estimating how leadership turnover in this way affects the hazard rate in that year.
96. Michael Eisenstadt, *"Preemptive Targeted Killings" as a Counterterror Tool: An Assessment of Israel's Approach* (Washington, DC: Washington Institute for Near East Policy, 2002); Steven R. David, *Fatal Choices: Israel's Policy of Targeted Killings*, Mideast Security and Policy Studies No. 51 (Ramat Gan, Israel: Begin-Sadat Center for Strategic Studies, 2002), 1–26; David Margolick, "Israel's Payback Principle," *Vanity Fair*, January 2003, 40; Michael Gross, "Fighting by Other Means in the Mideast: A Critical Analysis of Israel's Assassination Policy," *Political Studies* 51 (2003): 350–68; Daniel Byman, "Do Targeted Killings Work?" *Foreign Affairs* 85, no. 2 (March–April 2006): 95–111; Avi Kober, "Targeted Killing During the Second Intifada: The Quest for Effectiveness," *Journal of Conflict Studies* 27, no. 1 (2007): 76–93.
97. Jordan, "When Heads Roll," 754.
98. Jordan, "When Heads Roll."
99. See, for example, Art and Richardson, *Democracy and Counterterrorism*; Cronin, "No Silver Bullets."
100. Brian A. Jackson, John C. Baker, Kim Cragin, John Parachini, Horacio R. Trujillo, and Peter Chalk, *Aptitude for Destruction: Organizational Learning in Terrorist Groups and Its Implications for Combating Terrorism* (Santa Monica, CA: RAND, 2005); Kenney, *From Pablo to Osama*.
101. Martha Crenshaw, "How Terrorism Declines," *Terrorism and Political Violence* 3, no. 1 (1991): 79.
102. Jordan, "Attacking the Leader, Missing the Mark."
103. Ganor, *The Counter-Terrorism Puzzle*.
104. Jarret M. Brachman and William F. McCants, *Stealing Al-Qa'ida's Playbook* (West Point, NY: Combating Terrorism Center, 2006); Jacob N. Shapiro, "The Terrorist's Challenge: Security, Efficiency, and Control" (PhD diss., Stanford University, 2007); Joseph N. Felter, *Cracks in the Foundation: Leadership Schisms in al-Qa'ida 1989–2006* (West Point, NY: Combating Terrorism Center, 2007).
105. Jordan, "When Heads Roll," 24.

5. The Effects of Leadership Decapitation on Hamas

1. Brian Jackson, "Groups, Networks, or Movements: A Command-and-Control-Driven Approach to Classifying Terrorist Organizations and Its Application to Al Qaeda," *Studies in Conflict and Terrorism* 29 (2006): 241–62.
2. For example, the Revolutionary Popular Vanguard (VPR), a Brazilian left-wing terrorist group that operated in the late 1960s and early 1970s, quickly collapsed after suffering the loss of its charismatic leader, Carlos Lemarca. See Jamie Wright and Joan Dassin, *Torture in Brazil: A Shocking Report on the Pervasive Use of Torture by Brazilian Military Governments, 1964–1979* (Austin: University of Texas Press, 1998), 95. Lemarca had been a captain in the Brazilian military and convinced other members of the military to join his outfit. He stole arms and equipment from his previous military unit in order to start his terrorist campaign against the regime. Because of his charisma and experience as a military tactician, the group successfully carried out several high-profile attacks against the Brazilian military and kidnapped three high-level diplomats from Japan, Germany, and Switzerland; one of these kidnappings resulted in the release of several VPR members from prison. See Paulo Freire and Donaldo Pereira Macedo, *Letters to Cristina: Reflections on My Life and Work* (New York: Routledge, 1996), 203. The group was able to endure a massive military onslaught from the Brazilian government in 1970, including a battle near the VPR's training facility outside São Paulo that included thousands of Brazilian regulars supported by air power (TOPs profile on VPR). However, after Lemarca was killed by government forces on September 17, 1971, the group rapidly disintegrated (Wright and Dassin, *Torture in Brazil*, 95). Group infighting increased and security became lax after Lemarca was killed, which allowed a government double agent, Cabo Anselmo, to infiltrate the group. Anselmo hand-fed the Brazilian authorities information that allegedly led to two hundred arrests, and the group's coup de grâce occurred in Recife, where he led the remaining members of the organization into a government ambush (Freier and Macedo, *Letters to Cristina*, 203). The group never recovered.
3. Alexander L. George and Andrew Bennett, *Case Studies and Theory Development in the Social Sciences* (Cambridge, MA: MIT Press, 2005), 80.
4. Although George and Bennett generally recommend against single case studies and prefer the focused comparison case study method, which compares and contrasts multiple "like" observations that differ only on one variable (and preferably on the main independent variable in question), I had difficulty finding case studies in my data set that met these criteria (for more on case study selection, see George and Bennett, *Case Studies and Theory Development in the Social Sciences*). Ideally, I would have preferred to do a focused comparison of terrorist groups that differed only by their exposure to leadership decapitation and were similar in all other regards (i.e., operated within the same state during the same time period, espoused a similar ideology, featured the same leadership structure, had a comparable number of allies and rivals, and were of a similar size). However, it was difficult to find similar groups that only differed on their experience with leadership decapitation. Additionally, a

lack of public information on many of these groups prevented an in-depth comparison of the micro-level processes that I am interested in finding via the case study method. See Jacob N. Shapiro, "The Terrorist's Challenge: Security, Efficiency, and Control" (PhD diss., Stanford University, 2007), 15.

5. Azzam Tamimi, *Hamas: A History from Within* (Northampton, MA: Olive Branch Press, 2007).
6. Bruce Hoffman, "Rethinking Terrorism and Counterterrorism Since 9/11," *Studies in Conflict and Terrorism* 25 (2002): 303–16; Audrey Kurth Cronin, "How al-Qaida Ends: The Decline and Demise of Terrorist Groups," *International Security* 31, no. 1 (Summer 2006): 7–48.
7. Shapiro, "The Terrorist's Challenge."
8. Matthew Levitt, "Hamas Social Welfare: In the Service of Terror," in *The Making of a Terrorist: Recruitment, Training, and Root Causes*, ed. J. J. F. Forest (Westport, CT: Praeger Security International, 2006), 120–35.
9. George and Bennett, *Case Studies and Theory Development in the Social Sciences.*
10. According to David, Israel has used targeted killings to advance its political interests since its inception in 1948. See Steven R. David, "Fatal Choices: Israel's Policy of Targeted Killings," *Mideast Security and Policy Studies*, no. 51 (September 2002): 3. Many people are familiar with Israel's campaign to kill the perpetrators of the 1972 Munich Olympics massacre, which was depicted on film in the movie *Munich*. However, despite its long history with decapitation strategies, Israel has pursued an open policy of targeted killing only since the second intifada began in 2000 (David, "Fatal Choices," 1). Its methods of decapitating terrorist leaders vary, ranging from arrest and incarceration to laser-guided missiles fired from F-16s and Apache helicopters. It has even used surreptitious methods one would expect to see in a Bond film. Yahya Ayyash, the premier bomb maker in Hamas and nicknamed "the Engineer," was famously killed when Israeli agents blew up a booby-trapped cell phone. The current leader of Hamas, Khaled Mashal, narrowly escaped death by lethal injection when a Mossad assassination attempt was botched in 1997. See Boaz Ganor, *The Counter-Terrorism Puzzle: A Guide for Decision Makers* (New Brunswick, NJ: Transaction, 2005), 122–25; Paul McGeough, *Kill Khalid: The Failed Mossad Assassination of Khalid Mishal and the Rise of Hamas* (New York: New Press, 2009).
11. Michael Eisenstadt, " 'Preemptive Targeted Killings' as a Counterterror Tool: An Assessment of Israel's Approach" (Washington, DC: Washington Institute for Near East Policy, 2002), https://www.washingtoninstitute.org/policy-analysis/view/preemptive-targeted-killings-as-a-counterterror-tool-an-assessment-of-israe; David, "Fatal Choices"; Ganor, *The Counter-Terrorism Puzzle*; Daniel Byman, "Do Targeted Killings Work?" *Foreign Affairs* 85, no. 2 (March–April 2006): 102–4; Avi Kober, "Targeted Killing During the Second Intifada: The Quest for Effectiveness," *Journal of Conflict Studies* 27, no. 1 (2007): 76–93.
12. Michael Gross, "Fighting by Other Means in the Mideast: A Critical Analysis of Israel's Assassination Policy," *Political Studies* 51 (2003): 350–68.
13. Edward H. Kaplan, Alex Mintz, Shaul Mishal, and Claudio Samban, "What Happened to Suicide Bombings in Israel? Insights from a Terror Stock Model," *Studies in Conflict and Terrorism* 28, no. 3 (August 2005): 225–35; David Margolick, "Israel's

Payback Principle," *Vanity Fair*, January 2003, 40; Byman, "Do Targeted Killings Work?"; Kober, "Targeted Killing During the Second Intifada."
14. Jenna Jordan, "When Heads Roll: Assessing the Effectiveness of Leadership Decapitation," *Security Studies* 18, no. 4 (October–December 2009): 719–55.
15. Other potential case study candidates that also target Israel include Fatah (including the al-Aqsa Martyrs Brigade, which was created by Fatah as a counterweight to Hamas) and the Palestinian Islamic Jihad (PIJ). Fatah has a long and impressive history, but it did not make for an interesting case study because it never experienced a decapitation event involving its primary leader. The PIJ began in the late 1970s and lost its primary leader, Fathi Shaqaqi, to assassination by Israeli authorities in October 1995. "The organization limped along for several years, unable to mount any serious attacks against Israeli interests" (David, "Fatal Choices," 4). However, the group was largely inactive during the five-year period following Shaqaqi's death, and as a result, not much is known about the organization. It did not conduct any major attacks during this time. When the second intifada began in 2000, the group returned to action and is believed to be led by Ramadan Shallah and longtime spiritual leader Abd al-Aziz Awda from its headquarters in Damascus, Syria. See Holly Fletcher, *Backgrounder: Palestinian Islamic Jihad* (Washington, DC: Council on Foreign Relations, 2008).
16. Tamimi, *Hamas*.
17. Zaki Chehab, *Inside Hamas: The Untold Story of the Militant Islamic Movement* (New York: Nation Books, 2007), 16.
18. Tamimi, *Hamas*.
19. Tamimi, *Hamas*, 16.
20. Chehab, *Inside Hamas*, 17–18.
21. Shaul Mishal and Avraham Sela, *The Palestinian Hamas: Vision, Violence, and Coexistence* (New York: Columbia University Press, 2000), 19.
22. Tamimi, *Hamas*, 17.
23. Levitt, "Hamas Social Welfare," 124–29.
24. Tamimi, *Hamas*, 37.
25. Tamimi, *Hamas*, 122. Levitt also references Palestinian author Khaled Hroub, who believes Yasin was instrumental in creating the following groups: Yahya al-Ghuoul's Mujahideen of Mifraqa Group, Salah Shehadah's Group Number 44, and Muhammad Sharathah's Group Number 101.
26. Chehab, *Inside Hamas*.
27. Tamimi, *Hamas*, 46–47.
28. As a side note, Yasin also learned about whom he could trust in his organization. Yasin was not present when the arms deal was compromised. Israeli intelligence agents allegedly used torture to extract information from those initially arrested. The foot soldiers who were initially arrested eventually gave up the names of their superiors until Israeli intelligence worked their way up to Yasin's two lieutenants, who were the only two group members who knew Yasin was involved with the arms deal. One of the lieutenants, Dr. Ibrahim al-Maqadmah, caved under torture and gave up Yasin. The other, Salah Shihadah, never gave up Yasin. Not surprisingly, Shihadah went on to become the commander of Yasin's military wing, the Izz

ad-Din al-Qassam Brigades (Tamimi, *Hamas*, 46–47). The same type of repayment of loyalty was awarded to Muhammad al-Sharatiha, who also refused to give up Yasin "under severe interrogation" (Tamimi, *Hamas*, 57). Sharatiha was later given command of an even smaller, more elite military wing of Hamas called Cell 101. Although these acts of loyalty may seem inconsequential, these types of trials by fire allowed Yasin to learn a great deal about whom he could trust within his organization, not just in terms of loyalty but also in terms of competence. Events like this enabled Yasin to put the absolutely best people in the most important positions within his organization well before the group started its violent resistance.

29. Chehab, *Inside Hamas*, 23. The name Hamas is actually an acronym for Harakat Al Mokawama Al Islamiya (in English, Islamic Resistance Movement). In Arabic, though, *hamas* is another word for "zeal," a word the founders thought embodied their movement.
30. Tamimi, *Hamas*, 53.
31. Chehab, *Inside Hamas*, 30.
32. Yehudit Barsky, "Focus on Hamas: Terror by Remote Control," *Middle East Quarterly* 3, no. 2 (June 1996): 3.
33. Jonathan Schanzer, *Hamas vs. Fatah: The Struggle for Palestine* (New York: Palgrave MacMillan, 2008), 26.
34. Tamimi, *Hamas*, 61.
35. Tamimi, *Hamas*, 58.
36. Tamimi, *Hamas*, 58.
37. Barsky, "Focus on Hamas," 3.
38. Tamimi, *Hamas*, 60.
39. Mishal and Sela, *The Palestinian Hamas*, 58.
40. Tracing the organizational roots of a group like Hamas is not difficult. However, for many of the groups in my data set, determining an accurate start date would be problematic. As evidence of how difficult this is, many entries in the TOPs database have start dates such as "1970s," early "1980s," and so on.
41. Schanzer, *Hamas vs. Fatah*.
42. Mishal and Sela, *The Palestinian Hamas*, 22.
43. Sharon Erickson Nepstad and Clifford Bob, "When Do Leaders Matter? Hypotheses on Leadership Dynamics in Social Movements," *Mobilization: An International Journal* 11, no. 1 (2006): 1–22.
44. Barsky, "Focus on Hamas."
45. Barsky, "Focus on Hamas."
46. Barsky, "Focus on Hamas."
47. Barsky, "Focus on Hamas."
48. Eli Berman and David D. Laitin, "Religion, Terrorism and Public Goods: Testing the Club Model," *Journal of Public Economics* 92, nos. 10–11 (2008): 1942–67.
49. Tamimi, *Hamas*.
50. Tamimi, *Hamas*, 66.
51. Gross, "Fighting by Other Means in the Mideast."
52. Tamimi, *Hamas*, 67–68.
53. Mishal and Sela, *The Palestinian Hamas*, 66.

54. Tamimi, *Hamas*, 69.
55. The large increase in the average number of fatalities and injuries per attack in 1997 requires explanation. Of the three attacks attributed to Hamas that year, its simultaneous July 30 suicide bombings on a Jerusalem market killed 15 and wounded 170 victims, by far its deadliest attack during this time period.
56. Khlaed Hroub, *Hamas* (London: Pluto Press, 2006); Shapiro, "The Terrorist's Challenge."
57. This assumption does not always hold either. For example, groups hoping to assassinate a leader may be trying to kill one person only. The same could be said for groups that kidnap a lone individual for ransom or execute an individual for propaganda purposes. However, scholars are generally interested in how many attacks a group commits and how lethal these attacks are (see Victor Asal and R. Karl Rethemeyer, "The Nature of the Beast: Organizational Structures and the Lethality of Terrorist Attacks," *Journal of Politics* 70, no. 2 [2008]: 437–49).
58. Byman, "Do Targeted Killings Work?"; Kober, "Targeted Killing During the Second Intifada."
59. Because the GTD does not have data for any group in 1993 due to a filing error, I used data from the Committee for Accuracy in Middle East Reporting in America for 1993.
60. Margolick, "Israel's Payback Principle"; Kober, "Targeted Killing During the Second Intifada."
61. Writing in January 2003 and prior to Israel's policy shift, Margolick noted, "The Israelis have never targeted top political leaders, such as Arafat or Sheikh Ahmed Yassin of Hamas—in part because, as one prominent Israeli politician says, dying at its hands is 'the wet dream of a terror leader.' Instead, Israelis say they've focused on operational types: the suicide bombers themselves and, more often, the people making bombs for them or sending them on their way" (Margolick, "Israel's Payback Principle," 2).
62. For a detailed account of this affair, see McGeough, *Kill Khalid*.
63. Tamimi, *Hamas*; Chehab, *Inside Hamas*.
64. Wendy Kristiansen, "Challenge and Counterchallenges: Hamas' Response to Oslo," *Journal of Palestine Studies* 28, no. 3 (1999): 19–36.
65. Mishal and Sela, *The Palestinian Hamas*.
66. Kristiansen, "Challenge and Counterchallenges," 28.
67. Kristiansen, "Challenge and Counterchallenges," 28.
68. Kristiansen, "Challenge and Counterchallenges," 29.
69. Reven Paz, *Hamas Analyzes Its Terrorist Activity* (Herzliya, Israel: International Institute for Counter-Terrorism, 1999), accessed May 10, 2018, https://www.ict.org.il/Article.aspx?ID=774#gsc.tab=0.
70. Kristiansen, "Challenge and Counterchallenges"; Hroub, *Hamas*.
71. Tamimi, *Hamas*, 115.
72. Levitt, "Hamas Social Welfare."
73. Shapiro, "The Terrorist's Challenge."
74. Tamimi, *Hamas*.
75. Tamimi, *Hamas*, 117.

76. Barsky, "Focus on Hamas," 4.
77. Nepstad and Bob, "When Do Leaders Matter?"
78. Dipak K. Gupta and Kusum Mundra, "Suicide Bombing as a Strategic Weapon: An Empirical Investigation of Hamas and Islamic Jihad," *Terrorism and Political Violence* 17 (2005): 573–98. Note: Kaplan et al. argue the exact opposite and suggest that targeted killings increase the recruitment ("terror stock") of Palestinian terrorist groups. This, they argue, ultimately leads to an increase in suicide bombings. See Kaplan et al., "What Happened to Suicide Bombings in Israel?"
79. Gupta and Mundra, "Suicide Bombing as a Strategic Weapon," 585.
80. Gupta and Mundra define political provocations as "nonviolent yet highly significant symbolic gestures, which are either deliberately designed or have the effect of igniting passion within the Palestinian community against Israeli authorities" (Gupta and Mundra, "Suicide Bombing as a Strategic Weapon," 579).
81. Byman, "Do Targeted Killings Work?"
82. Cronin, "How al-Qaida Ends."
83. David, "Fatal Choices"; Byman, "Do Targeted Killings Work?"
84. Ganor, *The Counter-Terrorism Puzzle*; Byman, "Do Targeted Killings Work?"
85. This evidence was found in an Australian government report that provided evidence in order to put PIJ on its terrorist list. For the report, go to http://archive.is/dUv2a.
86. Mishal and Sela, *The Palestinian Hamas*, 66. Mishal and Sela claim that "it was no coincidence that Hamas's first suicide operation was carried out shortly after the deportees had returned to the occupied territories" and that Hamas and PIJ adopted almost identical procedures for preparing candidates for suicide missions.
87. Chehab, *Inside Hamas*, 106–7.
88. According to Chehab, there was a lot of discontent between the Qassam Brigades and the political leaders of Hamas. The leaders of the Qassam Brigades complained that they were not getting financial support and that communications were sparse and contradictory (Chehab, *Inside Hamas*, 109–10).
89. Tamimi, *Hamas*.
90. Kober, "Targeted Killing During the Second Intifada," 76.
91. Kober, "Targeted Killing During the Second Intifada."
92. Byman, "Do Targeted Killings Work?"
93. Eisenstadt, *"Preemptive Targeted Killings" as a Counterterror Tool*.
94. Ami Pedahzur, *Suicide Terrorism* (Cambridge: Polity, 2005), 170.
95. Pedahzur, *Suicide Terrorism*.
96. START, GTD, http://www.start.umd.edu/gtd/features/TOPs.aspx.
97. David, "Fatal Choices," 7.
98. William Safire, "Sharon Enters Armistice Talks," *New York Times*, February 4, 2002, A23.
99. Ganor, *The Counter-Terrorism Puzzle*, 71–72.
100. Kober, "Targeted Killing During the Second Intifada."
101. Byman, "Do Targeted Killings Work?"
102. Byman, "Do Targeted Killings Work?"
103. Tamimi, *Hamas*, 167.
104. Chehab, *Inside Hamas*, 120.

105. Chehab, *Inside Hamas*, 120.
106. Chehab, *Inside Hamas*.
107. Chehab, *Inside Hamas*; Hroub, *Hamas*.
108. Kristiansen, "Challenge and Counterchallenges," 28.
109. Chehab, *Inside Hamas*; Tamimi, *Hamas*, 111–117.
110. Chehab, *Inside Hamas*, 36.
111. Kristiansen, "Challenge and Counterchallenges," 31.
112. Hroub, *Hamas*.
113. Erik Schechter, "Where Have All the Bombers Gone?" *Jerusalem Post*, August 9, 2004, 11.
114. Greg Myre, "In Loss of Leaders, Hamas Discovers a Renewed Strength," *New York Times*, April 25, 2004.
115. Byman, "Do Targeted Killings Work?" 17.
116. James Bennet, "Israelis Say Hamas Is Not Able to Mount Major Retaliation," *New York Times*, March 27, 2004.
117. Bennet, "Israelis Say Hamas Is Not Able to Mount Major Retaliation," A3.
118. START, GTD.
119. Matthew Levitt, "Hamas from Cradle to Grave," *Middle East Quarterly* 11, no. 1 (2004): 3.
120. Kenneth W. Stein, "Yassin's Assassination," *La Vanguardia*, April 1, 2004.
121. Byman, "Do Targeted Killings Work?"; Kober, "Targeted Killing During the Second Intifada."
122. B'Tselem lists only the information about those killed and does not attribute these deaths to attacks by specific groups.
123. https://www.btselem.org/statistics/fatalities/before-cast-lead/by-date-of-event.
124. Byman, "Do Targeted Killings Work?"
125. Byman, "Do Targeted Killings Work?," 5; see also Kober, "Targeted Killing During the Second Intifada."
126. Kober, "Targeted Killing During the Second Intifada."
127. IICC, Intelligence and Terrorism Information Center, *Hamas's Military Buildup in the Gaza Strip* (Ramat Hasharon: Israel Intelligence Heritage and Commemoration Center, 2007).
128. Kober, "Targeted Killing During the Second Intifada."
129. Byman, "Do Targeted Killings Work?," 5.
130. Byman, "Do Targeted Killings Work?"
131. Byman, "Do Targeted Killings Work?"
132. IICC, *Hamas's Military Buildup in the Gaza Strip*.
133. Paz, *Hamas Analyzes Its Terrorist Activity*; Shapiro, "The Terrorist's Challenge."
134. Hroub, *Hamas*; Chehab, *Inside Hamas*.
135. Joshua L. Gleis and Benedetta Berti, *Hezbollah and Hamas* (Baltimore, MD: Johns Hopkins University Press, 2002), 147.
136. Hroub, *Hamas*.
137. Khaled Abu Toameh, "Analysis: Hamas Desperate for Lull," *Jerusalem Post*, January 6, 2009.
138. Abu Toameh, "Analysis: Hamas Desperate for Lull."

139. This point supports Jordan's theory that domestic support is one of the key factors in explaining a group's resilience against catastrophic collapse following a decapitation event. See Jordan, "When Heads Roll."
140. Jordan, "When Heads Roll." For an exception, see Gupta and Mundra, "Suicide Bombing as a Strategic Weapon."
141. START, GTD.
142. START, GTD.
143. Schechter, "Where Have All the Bombers Gone?"
144. Byman, "Do Targeted Killings Work?"
145. Asaf Zussman and Noam Zussman, "Assassinations: Evaluating the Effectiveness of an Israeli Counterterrorism Policy Using Stock Market Data," *Journal of Economic Perspectives* 20, no. 2 (2006): 193–206; Kober, "Targeted Killing During the Second Intifada."
146. David, "Fatal Choices"; Zussman and Zussman, "Assassinations."
147. The Tamil Tigers will be an interesting test case for future scholars. The group's leader, Velupillai Prabhakaran, was killed May 18, 2009. Like Yasin, he was a very charismatic and influential leader of the Sri Lankan separatist group. As an indication of how important he was to the LTTE, a group that Jones and Libicki estimate to be over ten thousand strong, the top Sri Lankan military official announced after Prabhakaran's death, "We can announce very responsibly that we have liberated the whole country from terrorism." See Ravi Nessman, "Sri Lanka Says War Over, Rebel Leader Killed," Associated Press, May 18, 2009.

6. Conclusion: Policy Implications and Future Research

1. Audrey Kurth Cronin, "How al-Qaida Ends: The Decline and Demise of Terrorist Groups," *International Security* 31, no. 1 (Summer 2006): 7–48; Jenna Jordan, "When Heads Roll: Assessing the Effectiveness of Leadership Decapitation," *Security Studies* 18, no. 4 (October–December 2009): 719–55; Patrick Johnston, "Does Decapitation Work? Assessing the Effectiveness of Leadership Targeting in Counterinsurgency Campaigns," *International Security* 36, no. 4 (Spring 2012): 47–79; Jenna Jordan, "Attacking the Leader, Missing the Mark," *International Security* 38, no. 4 (Spring 2014): 7–38; Bryan C. Price, "Targeting Top Terrorists," *International Security* 36, no. 4 (Spring 2012): 9–36; Max Abrahms and Philip B. K. Potter, "Explaining Terrorism: Leadership Deficits and Militant Group Tactics," *International Organization* 69 (Spring 2015): 311–42.
2. Stephen Hosmer, *Operations Against Enemy Leaders* (Santa Monica, CA: RAND, 2001); Michael Kenney, *From Pablo to Osama* (University Park: Pennsylvania State University Press, 2007).
3. Executive Office of the President, *National Strategy for Combating Terrorism*, Washington, DC, February 2003, 11.
4. Jordan, "When Heads Roll."
5. Edward H. Kaplan, Alex Mintz, Shaul Mishal, and Claudio Samban, "What Happened to Suicide Bombings in Israel? Insights from a Terror Stock Model," *Studies in Conflict and Terrorism* 28, no. 3 (August 2005): 225–35.
6. Hosmer, *Operations Against Enemy Leaders*; Lisa Langdon, Alexander J. Sarapu, and Matthew Wells, "Targeting the Leadership of Terrorist and Insurgent Movements:

Historical Lessons for Contemporary Policy Makers," *Journal of Public and International Affairs* 15 (Spring 2004): 59–78.
7. Brian J. Phillips, "Enemies with Benefits? Violent Rivalry and Terrorist Group Longevity," *Journal of Peace Research* 52, no. 1 (2015): 62–75.
8. Daniel Byman, "Do Targeted Killings Work?" *Foreign Affairs* 85, no. 2 (March–April 2006): 95–111.
9. Aaron Mannes, "Testing the Snake Head Strategy: Does Killing or Capturing Its Leaders Reduce a Terrorist Group's Activity?" *Journal of International Policy Solutions* 9 (Spring 2008): 40–49.
10. Bryan C. Price, "Terrorism as Cancer: How to Combat an Incurable Disease," *Terrorism and Political Violence*, June 9, 2017, 1–25.
11. Price, "Terrorism as Cancer."
12. Price, "Terrorism as Cancer."
13. Siddhartha Mukherjee, *The Emperor of All Maladies: A Biography of Cancer* (New York: Scribner, 2010).
14. Mukherjee, *The Emperor of All Maladies*, 143.
15. Quoted in Mukherjee, *The Emperor of All Maladies*, 305.
16. For instance, see Price, "Terrorism as Cancer."
17. Jacob N. Shapiro, *The Terrorist's Dilemma* (Princeton, NJ: Princeton University Press, 2013).
18. Laurie Copans, "Film Shows Barghouti Eating During Hunger Strike," *Jerusalem Post*, August 19, 2004, 3.

Bibliography

Abrahms, Max. "What Terrorists Really Want: Terrorist Motives and Counterterrorism Strategy." *International Security* 32, no. 4 (2008): 78–105.

Abrahms, Max. "Why Terrorism Does Not Work." *International Security* 31, no. 2 (2006): 42–78.

Abrahms, Max, and Philip B. K. Potter. "Explaining Terrorism: Leadership Deficits and Militant Group Tactics." *International Organization* 69 (Spring 2015): 311–42.

Allison, Graham T. "Conceptual Models and the Cuban Missile Crisis." *American Political Science Review* 63, no. 3 (1969): 689–718.

Aminzade, Ronald R., Jack A. Goldstone, and Elizabeth J. Perry. "Leadership Dynamics and Dynamics of Contention." In *Silence and Voice in the Study of Contentious Politics*, edited by R. R. Aminzade, J. A. Goldstone, D. McAdam, E. J. Perry, W. H. Sewell, S. Tarrow, and C. Tilly, 126–54. New York: Cambridge University Press, 2001.

Amnesty International. "Bolivia Awaiting Justice: Torture, Extrajudicial Executions and Legal Proceedings." London: Amnesty International, August 31, 1996.

Amos, Deborah. "Islamic State Defector: If You Turn Against ISIS, They Will Kill You." National Public Radio. September 25, 2014. https://www.npr.org/sections/parallels/2014/09/25/351436894/islamic-state-defector-if-you-turn-against-isis-they-will-kill-you.

Anderson, Sean, and Stephen Sloan. *Historical Dictionary of Terrorism*. Metuchen, NJ: Scarecrow Press, 1995.

Arquilla, John, and David Ronfeldt. *Networks and Netwars: The Future of Terror, Crime, and Militancy*. Santa Monica, CA: RAND, 2001.

Art, Robert J., and Louise Richardson. *Democracy and Counterterrorism: Lessons from the Past.* Washington, DC: United States Institute of Peace Press, 2001.

Asal, Victor, and R. Karl Rethemeyer. "The Nature of the Beast: Organizational Structures and the Lethality of Terrorist Attacks." *Journal of Politics* 70, no. 2 (2008): 446–47.

Ashworth, Scott, Joshua D. Clinton, Adam Meirowitz, and Kristopher W. Ramsay. "Design, Inference, and the Strategic Logic of Suicide Terrorism." *American Political Science Review* 102, no. 2 (2008): 269–77.

Bahnsen, John C. "Charisma." In *Leadership: The Warrior's Art*, edited by C. Kolenda, 259–76. Carlisle, PA: Army War College Foundation Press, 2001.

Bandura, Albert. "Training for Terrorism Through Selective Moral Disengagement." In *The Making of a Terrorist: Recruitment, Training, and Root Causes*, edited by J. J. F. Forest, 34–50. Westport, CT: Praeger Security International, 2006.

Barber, James David. *The Presidential Character: Predicting Performance in the White House.* Upper Saddle River, NJ: Prentice-Hall, 1972.

Barham, Elizabeth. "Towards a Theory of Values-Based Labeling." *Agriculture and Human Values* 19 (2002): 349–60.

Barker, Colin, Alan Johnson, and Michael Lavalette. "Leadership Matters: An Introduction." In *Leadership in Social Movements*, edited by C. Barker, A. Johnson, and M. Lavalette, 126–54. Manchester, UK: Manchester University Press, 2001.

Barnett, W. P., and D. G. McKendrick. "Why Are Some Organizations More Competitive than Others? Evidence from a Changing Global Market." *Administrative Science Quarterly* 49 (2004): 535–71.

Barsky, Yehudit. "Focus on Hamas: Terror by Remote Control." *Middle East Quarterly* (June 1996). https://www.meforum.org/articles/other/focus-on-hamas-terror-by-remote-control.

Bass, Bernard M. *Leadership Beyond Expectations.* New York: Free Press, 1985.

Beehner, Lionel. "America's Useless Terrorism List." *Los Angeles Times*, October 20, 2008.

Bender, Bryan. "Antiterrorism Agency Taps Boston-Area Brains." *Boston Globe*, March 28, 2007.

Bendor, J., A. Glazer, and T. Hammond. "Theories of Delegation." *Annual Review of Political Science* 4 (2001): 235–69.

Benmelech, Efraim, Claude Berrebi, and Esteban F. Klor. "Economic Conditions and the Quality of Suicide Terrorism." *Journal of Politics* 74, no. 1 (2012): 1–16.

Bennet, James. "Israelis Say Hamas Is Not Able to Mount Major Retaliation." *New York Times*, March 27, 2004.

Bergen, Peter, and Alex Reynolds. "Blowback Revisited." *Foreign Affairs* 84, no. 6 (November– December 2005): 2–6.

Berman, Eli. *Sect, Subsidy and Sacrifice: An Economist's View of Ultra-Orthodox Jews.* Jerusalem: The Hay Elyachar House, 1998.

Berman, Eli, and David D. Laitin. "Religion, Terrorism and Public Goods: Testing the Club Model." *Journal of Public Economics*, 92, nos. 10–11 (2008): 1942–67.

Berman, Eli, Jacob N. Shapiro, and Joseph N. Felter. "Can Hearts and Minds Be Bought? The Economics of Counterinsurgency in Iraq." *Journal of Public Economy* 119, no. 4 (August 2011): 766–819.

Blanche, Ed. "An Al Qaeda Rolodex: A Vast Treasure Trove of Captured Documents and Records Provides a Unique Insight into the Foreign Jihadis Fighting in Iraq, Prompting the US Military to Reassess How It Views Al Qaeda." *The Middle East*, March 2008.

Bloom, Mia M. *Dying to Kill: The Allure of Suicide Terror*. New York: Columbia University Press, 2005.

Bloom, Mia M. "Palestinian Suicide Bombing: Public Support, Market Share, and Outbidding." *Political Science Quarterly* 119, no. 1 (2004): 61–89.

Boettke, Peter J., Christopher Coyne, and Peter T. Leeson. "Institutional Stickiness and the New Development Economics." *American Journal of Economics and Sociology* 67, no. 2 (2008): 331–358.

Bonner, Raymond, and Steve Levine. "After the Attack, the Guerillas: 'We Are Freedom Fighters,' Says a Leader of Militants." *New York Times*, August 27, 1998.

Borum, Randy, and Michael Gelles. "Al-Qaeda's Operational Evolution: Behavioral and Organizational Perspectives." *Behavioral Sciences and the Law* 23 (2005): 467–83.

Box-Steffensmeier, Janet M., and Bradford S. Jones. *Event History Modeling: A Guide for Social Sciences*. Cambridge: Cambridge University Press, 2004.

Brachman, Jarret M., and William F. McCants. *Stealing Al-Qa'ida's Playbook*. West Point, NY: Combating Terrorism Center, 2006.

Bracken, Paul. *The Command and Control of Nuclear Forces*. New Haven, CT: Yale University Press, 1983.

Brimley, Shawn. "Tentacles of Jihad: Targeting Transnational Support Networks." *Parameters* 36 (Summer 2006): 30–46.

Bromley, David G., and J. Gordon Melton. *Cults, Religion and Violence*. Cambridge: Cambridge University Press, 2002.

Bryman, Alan. *Charisma and Leadership in Organizations*. London: Sage, 1992.

Bueno de Mesquita, Ethan. "The Quality of Terror." *American Journal of Political Science* 49, no. 3 (2005): 515–30.

Burns, James M. *Leadership*. New York: Harper & Row, 1978.

Burns, James M. *Transforming Leadership*. New York: Atlantic Monthly Press, 2003.

Byman, Daniel. "The Decision to Begin Talks with Terrorists: Lessons for Policymakers." *Studies in Conflict and Terrorism* 29 (2006): 403–14.

Byman, Daniel. "Do Targeted Killings Work?" *Foreign Affairs* 85, no. 2 (March–April 2006): 95–111.

Byman, Daniel. "Scoring the War on Terrorism." *The National Interest* 73 (Summer 2003): 75–84.

Byman, Daniel L., and Kenneth M. Pollack. "Let Us Now Praise Great Men: Bringing the Statesman Back In." *International Security* 25, no. 4 (2001): 107–46.

Callimachi, Rukmini. "ISIS and the Lonely Young American." *New York Times*, July 28, 2015.

Carley, Kathleen M., Ju-Sung Lee, and David Krackhardt. "Destabilizing Networks." *Connections* 23, no. 2 (2002): 79–92.

Carroll, Glenn R. "Dynamics of Publisher Succession in Newspaper Organizations." *Administrative Science Quarterly* 29, no.1 (1984): 93–113.

Carvin, Stephanie. "The Trouble with Targeted Killing." *Security Studies* 21, no. 3 (August 2012): 529–55.

Chasdi, Richard J. *Serenade of Suffering: A Portrait of Middle East Terrorism, 1968–1993*. Lanham: Lexington Books, 1999.

Chehab, Zaki. *Inside Hamas: The Untold Story of the Militant Islamic Movement*. New York: Nation Books, 2007.

Clarridge, Duane R. *A Spy for All Seasons*. New York: Scribner, 1997.

Cohen, Dara. "Explaining Sexual Violence During Civil War: Evidence from Sierra Leone (1991–2002)." Paper presented at the annual meeting of the American Political Science Association, Chicago, IL, August 30, 2007.

Cohen, Roger. "After the War on Terror." *New York Times*, January 29, 2009.

Collins, John M. *Assassination and Abduction as Tools of National Policy*. Norfolk, VA: Armed Forces War College, 1965.

Copans, Laurie. "Film Shows Barghouti Eating During Hunger Strike." *Jerusalem Post*, August 19, 2004.

Cope, John A. *Colombia's War: Toward a New Strategy*. Strategic Forum No. 194 (October 2002). https://www.hsdl.org/?abstract&did=458781.

Cortright, David. "A Critical Evaluation of the UN Counter-Terrorism Program: Accomplishments and Challenges." Paper presented at Global Enforcement Regimes: Transnational Organized Crime, International Terrorism and Money Laundering, Amsterdam, April 28–29, 2005.

Crandall, Russell. *Driven by Drugs: U.S. Policy Towards Colombia*. Boulder, CO: Lynne Rienner, 2002.

Crenshaw, Martha. "The Causes of Terrorism." *Comparative Politics* 13, no. 4 (1981): 379–99.

Crenshaw, Martha. "Counterterrorism Policy and the Political Process." *Studies in Conflict and Terrorism* 24 (2001): 329–37.

Crenshaw, Martha. "Evaluating the Effectiveness of Counterterrorism." Paper presented at the International Studies Association Fiftieth Annual Convention, New York, February 15–18, 2009.

Crenshaw, Martha. "Explaining Suicide Terrorism: A Review Essay." *Security Studies* 16, no. 1 (2007): 133–62.

Crenshaw, Martha. "How Terrorism Declines." *Terrorism and Political Violence* 3, no. 3 (1991): 69–87.

Crenshaw, Martha. "Innovation: Decision Points in the Trajectory of Terrorism." In *Terrorist Innovations in Weapons of Mass Effect: Preconditions, Causes and Predictive Indicators*, edited by Maria Rasmussen and Mohammed Hafez, 35–50. Washington, DC: The Defense Threat Reduction Agency, 2010.

Crenshaw, Martha. "An Organizational Approach to the Analysis of Political Terrorism." *Orbis* 29, no. 3 (1985): 465–89.

Crenshaw, Martha. "The Psychology of Political Terrorism." In *Political Psychology*, edited by M. G. Hermann, 379–413. San Francisco: Jossey-Bass, 1986.

Crenshaw, Martha. "The Subjective Reality of the Terrorist: Ideological and Psychological Factors in Terrorism." In *Current Perspectives on International Terrorism*, edited by R. O. Slater and M. Stohl, 12–46. Hong Kong: MacMillan, 1988.

Crenshaw, Martha. "Why America? The Globalization of Civil War." *Current History* 100 (December 2001): 425–32.

Crenshaw, Martha. "Why Violence Is Rejected or Renounced: A Case Study of Oppositional Terrorism." In *A Natural History of Peace*, edited by T. Gregor, 249–72. Nashville, TN: Vanderbilt University Press, 1996.

Crenshaw, Martha. "Theories of Terrorism: Instrumental and Organizational Approaches." *Journal of Strategic Studies* 10, no. 4 (1987): 13–31.

Cronin, Audrey Kurth. "Behind the Curve." *International Security* 27, no. 3 (2002–2003): 30–58.

Cronin, Audrey Kurth. *Ending Terrorism: Lessons for Defeating al-Qaeda*. Abingdon, Oxford: International Institute for Strategic Studies, 2008.

Cronin, Audrey Kurth. "How al-Qaida Ends: The Decline and Demise of Terrorist Groups." *International Security* 31, no. 1 (2006): 7–48.

Cronin, Audrey Kurth. "No Silver Bullets: Explaining Research on How Terrorist Groups End." *CTC Sentinel* 3, no. 4 (2010): 16–18.

Cronin, Audrey Kurth. "Sources of Contemporary Terrorism." In *Attacking Terrorism: Elements of a Grand Strategy*, edited by A. K. Cronin and J. M. Ludes, 19–45. Washington, DC: Georgetown University Press, 2004.

Crozier, Brian. *The Rebels*. Boston: Beacon Press, 1960.

Dahl, Robert A. *Who Governs? Democracy and Power in an American City*. New Haven, CT: Yale University Press, 1974.

Danner, Mark. "Taking Stock of the Forever War." *New York Times Magazine*, September 11, 2005.

Davis, Clint. "What Happened to the 52 'Most Wanted' Iraqis from the U.S. Military Card Deck?" *KSHB News*, April 22, 2015.

Davis, Paul K., and Brian Michael Jenkins. *Deterrence and Influence in Counterterrorism.* Washington, DC: RAND, 2002.

Dawson, Lorne L. "Crises of Charismatic Legitimacy and Violent Behavior in New Religious Movements." In *Cults, Religion, and Violence*, edited by D. G. Bromley and J. G. Melton, 80–101. Cambridge: Cambridge University Press, 2002.

Day, David V., and Robert G. Lord. "Executive Leadership and Organizational Performance: Suggestions for a New Theory and Methodology." *Journal of Management* 14, no 3. (1988): 453–64.

Decker, Scott H., and Barrick Van Winkle. *Life in the Gang: Family, Friends, and Violence.* Cambridge: Cambridge University Press, 1996.

Deikman, Arthur J. "The Psychological Power of Charismatic Leaders in Cults and Terrorist Organizations." In *The Making of a Terrorist: Recruitment, Training, and Root Causes*, edited by J. J. F. Forest, 51–70. Westport, CT: Praeger Security International, 2006.

Della Porta, Donatella. *Social Movements, Political Violence, and the State: A Comparative Analysis of Italy and Germany.* Cambridge: Cambridge University Press, 1995.

DiMaggio, Paul J., and Walter W. Powell. "The Iron Cage Revisited: Institutional Isomorphism and Collective Rationality in Organizational Fields." *American Sociological Review* 48, no. 2 (April 1983): 147–60.

Dirks, Kurt T. "Trust in Leadership and Team Performance: Evidence from NCAA Basketball." *Journal of Applied Psychology* 85, no. 6 (2000): 1004–12.

Ehrlich, Richard. "Burma's 'God's Army' No More." *Asian Pacific Post*, July 28, 2006.

Eilstrup-Sangiovanni, Mette, and Calvert Jones. "Assessing the Dangers of Illicit Networks: Why al-Qaida May Be Less Threatening Than Many Think." *International Security* 33, no. 2 (2008): 7–44.

Eisenstadt, Michael. *"Preemptive Targeted Killings" as a Counterterror Tool: An Assessment of Israel's Approach.* Washington, DC: Washington Institute for Near East Policy, 2002.

"Elite Officer Recalls Bin Laden Hunt," *60 Minutes*, October 5, 2008. Video, 13:22. https://www.cbsnews.com/news/elite-officer-recalls-bin-laden-hunt/.

Elster, Jon. "Motivations and Beliefs in Suicide Missions." In *Making Sense of Suicide Missions*, edited by D. Gambetta, 233–58. Oxford: Oxford University Press, 2005.

Enders, Walter, and Todd Sandler. *The Political Economy of Terrorism.* New York: Cambridge University Press, 2006.

Eubank, William, and Leonard Weinberg. "Does Democracy Encourage Terrorism?" *Terrorism and Political Violence* 6, no. 4 (1994): 417–35.

Fearon, James, and David D. Laitin. "Ethnicity, Insurgency, and Civil War." *American Political Science Review* 97, no. 1 (2003): 75–90.

Felter, Joseph N. *Cracks in the Foundation: Leadership Schisms in al-Qa'ida 1989–2006.* West Point, NY: Combating Terrorism Center, 2007.

Ferracuti, Franco. "Ideology and Repentance: Terrorism in Italy." In *Origins of Terrorism: Psychologies, Ideologies, Theologies, States of Mind*, edited by W. Reich, 59–64. Washington, DC: Woodrow Wilson Center Press, 1990.

Fletcher, Holly. *Backgrounder: Palestinian Islamic Jihad*. Washington, DC: Council on Foreign Relations, 2008. https://www.cfr.org/backgrounder/palestinian-islamic-jihad.

Flynn, Stephen E. "America the Resilient." *Foreign Affairs* 87, no. 8 (March–April 2008): 2–8.

Fortna, Virginia Page. "Does Peacekeeping Keep Peace? International Intervention and the Duration of Peace After Civil War." *International Studies Quarterly* 48 (2004): 269–92.

Fox, John. "Cox Proportional-Hazards Regression for Survival Data." In *An R and S-Plus Companion to Applied Regression*, edited by J. Fox, 1–20. Thousand Oaks, CA: Sage, 2002.

Freire, Paulo, and Donaldo Pereira Macedo. *Letters to Cristina: Reflections on My Life and Work*. New York: Routledge, 1996.

Frenkel, Sheera. "Olmert, Netanyahu Clash over Hamas and Golan Heights." *Jerusalem Post*, February 13, 2007.

Furtado, Eugene P. H., and Vijay Karan. "Causes, Consequences, and Shareholder Wealth Effects of Management Turnover: A Review of the Empirical Evidence." *Financial Management* 19, no. 2 (1990): 60–75.

Fury, Dalton. *Kill Bin Laden*. New York: St. Martin's Press, 2008.

Galanter, Marc. *Cults: Faith, Healing, and Coercion*. New York: Oxford University Press, 1999.

Galanter, Marc, and James J. F. Forest. "Cults, Charismatic Groups, and Social Systems: Understanding the Transformation of Terrorist Recruits." In *The Making of a Terrorist: Recruitment, Training, and Root Causes*, edited by J. J. F. Forest, 34–50. Westport, CT: Praeger Security International, 2006.

Gall, Carlotta. "Taliban Commander Is Face of Rising Threat." *New York Times*, June 17, 2008.

Gambetta, Diego. "Can We Make Sense of Suicide Missions?" In *Making Sense of Suicide Missions*, edited by D. Gambetta, 259–99. Oxford: Oxford University Press, 2005.

Ganor, Boaz. *The Counter-Terrorism Puzzle*. New Brunswick, NJ: Transaction, 2005.

García, María Elena. *Making Indigenous Citizens: Identities, Education, and Multicultural Development in Peru*. Stanford, CA: Stanford University Press, 2005.

Garfield, Andrew. "PIRA Lessons Learned: A Model of Terrorist Leadership Succession." *Low Intensity Conflict and Law Enforcement* 11, nos. 2–3 (2004): 271–84.

Gartenstein-Ross, Daveed, and Kyle Dabruzzi. "Is Al-Qaeda's Central Leadership Still Relevant?" *Middle East Quarterly* 15, no. 2 (Spring 2008): 27–36.

Gause, F. Gregory III. "Can Democracy Stop Terrorism?" *Foreign Affairs* 84, no. 5 (September–October 2005): 62–76.

George, Alexander L. "Case Studies and Theory Development: The Method of Structured, Focused Comparison." In *Diplomacy*, edited by P. G. Lauren, 95–124. New York: Free Press, 1979.

George, Alexander L. *Presidential Decisionmaking in Foreign Policy: The Effective Use of Information and Advice*. Boulder, CO: Westview Press, 1980.

George, Alexander L., and Andrew Bennett. *Case Studies and Theory Development in the Social Sciences*. Cambridge, MA: MIT Press, 2005.

George, Alexander L., and Juliette George. *Presidential Personality and Performance*. Boulder, CO: Westview Press, 1998.

Gleis, Joshua L., and Benedetta Berti. *Hezbollah and Hamas*. Baltimore, MD: Johns Hopkins University Press, 2012.

Goode, Erica. "A Day of Terror; Attackers Believed to Be Sane." *New York Times*, September 12, 2001.

Goodwin, Jeff. "A Theory of Categorical Terrorism." *Social Forces* 84, no. 4 (2006): 2027–46.

Gordon, Philip H. "Can the War on Terror Be Won?" *Foreign Affairs* 86, no. 6 (November–December 2007): 53–66.

Gouldner, Alvin W. *Patterns of Industrial Bureaucracy*. New York: Free Press, 1954.

Grazda, Edward. "Searching for Mullah Omar." *Vanity Fair* no. 510 (February 2003): 139. https://www.vanityfair.com/news/2003/02/mullah200302.

Gross, Michael. "Fighting by Other Means in the Mideast: A Critical Analysis of Israel's Assassination Policy." *Political Studies* 51, no. 2 (2003): 350–68.

Grusky, Oscar. "Administrative Succession in Formal Organizations." *Social Forces* 39 (1960): 105–15.

Grusky, Oscar. "Managerial Succession and Organizational Effectiveness." *American Journal of Sociology* 69 (1963): 21–31.

Grusky, Oscar. "Reply to Scapegoating in Baseball." *American Journal of Sociology* 70, no. 1 (1964): 72–76.

Gulick, Luther. "Notes on the Theory of Organization." In *Papers on the Science of Administration*, edited by Luther Gulick and Lydal Urwick, 191–95. New York: Institute of Public Administration, Columbia University, 1937.

Gupta, Dipak K., and Kusum Mundra. "Suicide Bombing as a Strategic Weapon: An Empirical Investigation of Hamas and Islamic Jihad." *Terrorism and Political Violence* 17, no. 4 (2005): 573–98.

Gupta, Vipin, Ian C. MacMillan, and Gita Surie. "Entrepreneurial Leadership: Developing and Measuring a Cross-Cultural Construct." *Journal of Business Venturing* 19, no. 2 (2004): 241–60.

Hafez, Mohammed M. "Martyrdom Mythology in Iraq: How Jihadists Frame Suicide Terrorism in Videos and Biographies." *Terrorism and Political Violence* 19, no. 1 (2007): 95–115.

Hafez, Mohammed M., and Joseph M. Hatfield. "Do Targeted Assassinations Work? A Multivariate Analysis of Israeli Counter-terrorism Effectiveness During Al-Aqsa Uprising." *Studies in Conflict and Terrorism* 29, no. 4 (June 2006): 359–82.

Hanson, Stephanie. *MEND: The Niger Delta's Umbrella Militant Group*. Washington, DC: Council on Foreign Relations, March 21, 2007. https://www.cfr.org/backgrounder/mend-niger-deltas-umbrella-militant-group.

Harmon, Christopher C. "The Myth of the Invincible Terrorist." *Policy Review* 142 (April–May 2007): 57–74.

Harris, Lee. "Al Qaeda's Fantasy Ideology." *Policy Review* 114, no. 4 (August–September 2002): 19–25.

Harrison, J. Richard, and Glenn R. Carroll. *Culture and Demography in Organizations*. Princeton, NJ: Princeton University Press, 2006.

Hawkesworth, Mary, and Maurice Kogan. *Encyclopedia of Government and Politics*. Vol. 2. London: Routledge, 1992.

Hegghammer, Thomas. "Islamist Violence and Regime Stability in Saudi Arabia." *International Affairs* 84, no. 4 (2008): 701–15.

Hegghammer, Thomas. "The Origins of Global Jihad: Explaining the Arab Mobilization to 1980s Afghanistan." Policy Brief. January 22, 2009. https://www.belfercenter.org/publication/origins-global-jihad-explaining-arab-mobilization-1980s-afghanistan.

Helmich, Donald L. "Organizational Growth and Succession Patterns." *Academy of Management Journal* 17, no. 4 (1974): 771–75.

Hendawi, Hamza. "Iraq Insurgents Post New Beheading Video." *AP Online*, June 11, 2006.

Hermann, Margaret G. "Ingredients of Leadership." In *Political Psychology*, edited by M. G. Hermann, 167–92. San Francisco: Jossey-Bass, 1986.

Hermann, Margaret G., and Joe D. Hagan. "International Decision Making: Leadership Matters." *Foreign Policy* 110 (Spring 1998): 124–37.

Hoffman, Bruce. *Inside Terrorism*. New York: Columbia University Press, 2006.

Hoffman, Bruce. "The Leadership Secrets of Osama bin Laden." *Atlantic Monthly* 291, no. 3 (April 2003): 26–27.

Hoffman, Bruce. "The Myth of Grass-Roots Terrorism." *Foreign Affairs* 87, no 3. (2008): 133–38.

Hoffman, Bruce. "Rethinking Terrorism and Counterterrorism Since 9/11." *Studies in Conflict and Terrorism* 25, no. 5 (2002): 303–16.

Hogg, Michael A., and Dominic Abrams. *Social Identifications: A Social Psychology of Intergroup Relations and Group Processes*. London: Routledge, 1988.

Hollander, Edwin P., and James W. Julian. "Contemporary Trends in the Analysis of Leadership Processes." *Psychological Bulletin* 71, no. 5 (1969): 387–97.

Hosmer, Stephen T. *Operations Against Enemy Leaders*. Santa Monica, CA: RAND, 2001.

House, Robert J. "A 1976 Theory of Charismatic Leadership." In *Leadership: The Cutting Edge*, edited by J. G. Hunt and L. L. Larson, 189–207. Carbondale: Southern Illinois University Press, 1977.

House, Robert J., and Jitendra V. Singh. "Organizational Behavior: Some New Directions for I/O Psychology." *Annual Review of Psychology* 38 (1987): 669–718.

Executive Office of the President. *The National Security Strategy of the United States of America*. Washington, DC, 2002. https://www.state.gov/documents/organization/63562.pdf.

Executive Office of the President. *National Strategy for Combating Terrorism*. February 2003. https://fas.org/irp/threat/ctstrategy.pdf.

Executive Office of the President. *National Strategy for Combating Terrorism*. September 2006. https://www.cbsnews.com/htdocs/pdf/NSCT0906.pdf.

Executive Office of the President. *National Strategy for Counterterrorism*. June 2011. https://obamawhitehouse.archives.gov/sites/default/files/counterterrorism_strategy.pdf.

Hroub, Khaled. *Hamas*. London: Pluto Press, 2006.

Huddleston, Tom, Jr. "Theo Epstein's Perfect Response to the World's Greatest Leaders List." *Fortune*, March 23, 2017. http://fortune.com/2017/03/23/theo-epstein-worlds-greatest-leaders-response/.

Human Security Research Group. *Human Security Brief 2007*. Vancouver, BC: Simon Fraser University, 2008. https://www.files.ethz.ch/isn/55856/HSRP_Brief_2007.pdf.

Hutchinson, Steve, and Pat O'Malley. *How Terrorist Groups Decline* (Ottawa: Canadian Centre for Intelligence and Security Studies, Norman Paterson School of International Affairs, Carleton University, 2007).

Hyder, Victor. "Decapitation Operations: Criteria for Targeting Enemy Leadership." Master's thesis, School of Advanced Military Studies, United States Army Command and General Staff College, Fort Leavenworth, KS, 2004.

International Crisis Group. "Indonesia: Radicalisation of the 'Palembang Group.'" *Asia Briefing*, no. 92 (May 2009). https://www.crisisgroup.org/asia/south-east-asia/indonesia/indonesia-radicalisation-palembang-group.

United Press International. "Terrorist Takes the Blame for '89 Killings." *Deseret News*, July 21, 1992. https://www.deseretnews.com/article/238232/TERRORIST-TAKES-THE-BLAME-FOR-89-KILLINGS.html.

Israel Intelligence Heritage and Commemoration Center. *Hamas's Military Buildup in the Gaza Strip*. April 2008. https://www.terrorism-info.org.il/Data/pdf/PDF1/hamas_080408_501786899.pdf.

Jackson, Brian A. "Groups, Networks, or Movements: A Command-and-Control-Driven Approach to Classifying Terrorist Organizations and Its Application to Al Qaeda." *Studies in Conflict and Terrorism* 29, no. 3 (2006): 241–62.

Jackson, Brian A. "Organizational Learning and Terrorist Groups." Working paper, RAND, February 2004. https://www.rand.org/content/dam/rand/pubs/working_papers/2004/RAND_WR133.pdf.

Jackson, Brian A., John C. Baker, Kim Cragin, John Parachini, Horacio R. Trujillo, and Peter Chalk. *Aptitude for Destruction: Organizational Learning in Terrorist Groups and Its Implications for Combating Terrorism.* Santa Monica, CA: RAND, 2005.

Janis, Irving L. *Victims of Groupthink.* Boston: Houghton-Mifflin, 1972.

Johnson, W. Bruce, Robert P. Magee, Nandu J. Nagarajan, and Harry A. Newman. "An Analysis of the Stock Price Reaction to Sudden Executive Deaths." *Journal of Accounting and Economics* 7 (1985): 151–74.

Johnston, Patrick. "Does Decapitation Work? Assessing the Effectiveness of Leadership Targeting in Counterinsurgency Campaigns." *International Security* 36, no. 4 (Spring 2012): 47–79.

Jones, Seth G., and Martin C. Libicki. *How Terrorist Groups End: Lessons for Countering al Qa'ida.* Santa Monica, CA: RAND, 2008.

Joosse, Paul. "Leaderless Resistance and Ideological Inclusion: The Case of the Earth Liberation Front." *Terrorism and Political Violence* 19 (2007): 351–68.

Jordan, Jenna. "Attacking the Leader, Missing the Mark." *International Security* 38, no. 4 (Spring 2014): 7–38.

Jordan, Jenna. "When Heads Roll: Assessing the Effectiveness of Leadership Decapitation." *Security Studies* 18, no. 4 (December 2009): 719–55.

Kaplan, Edward H., Alex Mintz, and Shaul Mishal Claudio Samban. "What Happened to Suicide Bombings in Israel? Insights from a Terror Stock Model." *Studies in Conflict and Terrorism* 28 (2005): 225–35.

Katzenstein, Peter J. "Coping with Terrorism: Norms and Internal Security in Germany and Japan." In *Ideas and Foreign Policy*, edited by J. Goldstein and R. O. Keohane, 265–95. Ithaca, NY: Cornell University Press, 1993.

Kenney, Michael. *From Pablo to Osama.* University Park: Pennsylvania State University Press, 2007.

Kilcullen, David, and Andrew Exum. "Death from Above, Outrage Down Below." *New York Times*, May 16, 2009.

Kirby, Aidan. "The London Bombers as 'Self-Starters': A Case Study in Indigenous Radicalization and the Emergence of Autonomous Cliques." *Studies in Conflict and Terrorism* 30, no. 5 (2007): 415–28.

Kleinman, Steven, and Matthew Alexander. "Try a Little Tenderness." *New York Times*, March 11, 2009.

Kober, Avi. "Targeted Killing During the Second Intifada: The Quest for Effectiveness." *Journal of Conflict Studies* 27, no. 1 (2007): 76–93.

Kolata, Gina. "Advances Elusive in the Drive to Cure Cancer." *New York Times*, April 24, 2009.

Koschade, Stuart. "A Social Network Analysis of Aum Shinrikyo: Understanding Terrorism in Australia." Paper presented to the Social Change in the Twenty-First Century Conference, Queensland, Australia, October 28, 2005. https://eprints.qut.edu.au/3496/1/3496.pdf.

Kristiansen, Wendy. "Challenge and Counterchallenges: Hamas' Response to Oslo." *Journal of Palestine Studies* 28, no. 3 (1999): 19–36.

Krueger, Alan B., and Jitka Maleckova. "Education, Poverty and Terrorism: Is There a Causal Connection?" *Journal of Economic Perspectives* 17, no. 4 (2003): 119–44.

Kydd, Andrew H., and Barbara F. Walter. "The Strategies of Terrorism." *International Security* 31, no. 1 (2006): 49–80.

Lacey, Marc, and Ginger Thompson. "Next Foreign Crisis Could Be Next Door." *New York Times*, March 24, 2009.

LaFree, Gary, and Laura Dugan. "Introducing the Global Terrorism Database." *Terrorism and Political Violence* 19 (2007): 181–204.

Laitin, David D., and Jacob N. Shapiro. "The Political, Economic, and Organizational Sources of Terrorism." In *Terrorism, Economic Development, and Political Openness*, edited by P. Keefer and N. Loayza, 209–32. Cambridge: Cambridge University Press, 2008.

Langdon, Lisa, Alexander J. Sarapu, and Matthew Wells. "Targeting the Leadership of Terrorist and Insurgent Movements: Historical Lessons for Contemporary Policy Makers." *Journal of Public and International Affairs* 15 (Spring 2004): 59–78.

Laqueur, Walter. *The Terrorism Reader: A Historical Anthology*. New York: New American Library, 1978.

Laqueur, Walter. "The Terrorism to Come." *Policy Review* 126 (August–September 2004).

Lesser, Ian O., Bruce Hoffman, John Arquilla, David Ronfeldt, and Michele Zanini. *Countering the New Terrorism*. Santa Monica, CA: RAND, 1999.

Levitt, Barbara, and James G. March. "Organizational Learning." *Annual Review of Sociology* 14 (1988): 319–40.

Levitt, Matthew A. *Hamas: Politics, Charity, and Terrorism in the Service of Jihad*. New Haven, CT: Yale University Press, 2006.

Levitt, Matthew A. "Hamas Social Welfare: In the Service of Terror." In *The Making of a Terrorist: Recruitment, Training, and Root Causes*, edited by J. J. F. Forest, 120–35. Westport, CT: Praeger Security International, 2006.

Ling, Yan, Zeki Simsek, Michael H. Lubatkin, and John F. Veiga. "The Impact of Transformational CEOs on the Performance of Small to Medium-Sized Firms: Does Organizational Context Matter?" *Journal of Applied Psychology* 93, no. 4 (2008): 923–34.

Locicero, Alice, and Samuel J. Sinclair. "Terrorism and Terrorist Leaders: Insights from Developmental and Ecological Psychology." *Studies in Conflict and Terrorism* 31, no. 3 (2007): 227–50.

Lotrionte, Catherine. "When to Target Leaders." *Washington Quarterly* 26, no. 3 (2003): 73–86.

Lubold, Gordon, and Shane Harris. "Trump Broadens CIA Powers, Allows Deadly Drone Strikes." *Wall Street Journal*, March 13, 2017.

Mannes, Aaron. "Testing the Snake Head Strategy: Does Killing or Capturing Its Leaders Reduce a Terrorist Group's Activity?" *Journal of International Policy Solutions* 9 (Spring 2008): 40–49.

Margolick, David. "Israel's Payback Principle." *Vanity Fair* 509 (January 2003): 40–47.

Matanock, Aila. *Electing Peace: From Civil Peace to Political Participation*. New York: Cambridge University Press, 2017.

Mazzetti, Mark, and Scott Shane. "CIA Had Plan to Assassinate Qaeda Leaders." *New York Times*, July 14, 2009.

McAllister, Brad. "Al Qaeda and the Innovative Firm: Demythologizing the Network." *Studies in Conflict and Terrorism* 27, no. 4 (2004): 297–319.

McCann, Carol, and Ross Pigeau. *The Human in Command: Exploring the Modern Military Science*. New York: Kluwer Academic/Plenum, 2000.

McCormick, Gordon H. "Terrorist Decision Making." *Annual Review of Political Science* 6 (2003): 473–507.

McGeough, Paul. *Kill Khalid: The Failed Mossad Assassination of Khalid Mishal and the Rise of Hamas*. New York: New Press, 2009.

Meindl, James R., and Sanford B. Ehrlich. "The Romance of Leadership and the Evaluation of Organizational Performance." *Academy of Management Journal* 30, no. 1 (1987): 91–109.

Meindl, James R., Sanford B. Ehrlich, and Janet M. Dukerich. "The Romance of Leadership." *Administrative Science Quarterly* 30, no. 1 (1985): 78–102.

Meixler, Louis. "Iraq Inspiring Copycat Beheadings." Associated Press, November 6, 2004.

Melcher, Arlyn J. "Leadership Models and Research Approaches." In *Leadership: The Cutting Edge*, edited by J. G. Hunt and L. L. Larson, 94–108. Carbondale: Southern Illinois University Press, 1977.

Merari, Ariel. "Academic Research and Government Policy on Terrorism." *Terrorism and Political Violence* 3, no. 1 (1991): 88–102.

Meyer, Marshall W., and Lynne G. Zucker. *Permanently Failing Organizations*. Newbury Park, CA: Sage, 1989.

Miller, Greg. "Under Obama, an Emerging Global Apparatus for Drone Killing." *Washington Post*, December 27, 2011.

Mintzberg, Henry. *Power in and Around Organizations*. Englewood Cliffs, NJ: Prentice Hall, 1983.

Mishal, Shaul, and Avraham Sela. *The Palestinian Hamas: Vision, Violence, and Coexistence*. New York: Columbia University Press, 2000.

Moe, Terry. "The Politicized Presidency." In *The New Directions in American Politics*, edited by J. E. Chubb and P. E. Peterson, 235–72. Washington, DC: Brookings Institution, 1985.

Moe, Terry. "The Politics of Bureaucratic Structure." In *Can the Government Govern?*, edited by J. E. Chubb and P. E. Peterson, 267–329. Washington, DC: Brookings Institution, 1989.

Moe, Terry. "Presidents, Institutions, and Theory." In *Researching the Presidency: Vital Questions, New Approaches*, edited by G. C. I. Edwards, J. H. Kessel, and B. A. Rockman, 337–86. Pittsburgh, PA: University of Pittsburgh Press, 1993.

Morris, Aldon, and Suzanne Staggenborg. "Leadership in Social Movements." In *The Blackwell Companion to Social Movements*, edited by D. A. Snow, S. A. Soule, and H. Kriesi, 171–96. Malden, MA: Blackwell, 2004.

Moss, Michael. "In Algeria, Insurgency Gains a Lifeline from Al Qaeda." *New York Times*, July 1, 2008.

Moss, Michael, and Souad Mekhennet. "Rising Leader for Next Phase of Al Qaeda's War." *New York Times*, April 4, 2008.

Moyar, Mark. *Phoenix and the Birds of Prey: Counterinsurgency and Counterterrorism in Vietnam*. Lincoln: University of Nebraska Press, 1997.

Muczyk, Jan P., and Daniel T. Holt. "Toward a Cultural Contingency Model of Leadership." *Journal of Leadership and Organizational Studies* 14, no. 4 (May 2008): 277–86.

Mukherjee, Siddhartha. *The Emperor of All Maladies: A Biography of Cancer*. New York: Scribner, 2010.

Mumford, Michael D., Jazmine Espejo, Samuel T. Hunter, Katrina E. Bedell-Avers, Dawn L. Eubanks, and Shane Connelly. "The Sources of Leader Violence: A Comparison of Ideological and non-Ideological Leaders." *Leadership Quarterly* 18, no. 3 (2007): 217–35.

Myre, Greg. "In Loss of Leaders, Hamas Discovers a Renewed Strength." *New York Times*, April 25, 2004.

Nagl, John A., David H. Petraeus, and James F. Amos. *The U.S. Army/Marine Corps Counterinsurgency Field Manual: U.S. Army Field Manual No. 3–24*. Marine Corps Warfighting Publication No. 3–33.5. Chicago: University of Chicago Press, 2007.

Nepstad, Sharon Erickson, and Clifford Bob. "When Do Leaders Matter? Hypotheses on Leadership Dynamics in Social Movements." *Mobilization: An International Journal* 11, no. 1 (2006): 1–22.

Nesser, Petter. "How Did Europe's Global Jihadis Obtain Training for Their Militant Causes?" *Terrorism and Political Violence* 20, no. 2 (2008): 234–56.

Nessman, Ravi. "Sri Lanka Says War Over, Rebel Leader Killed." Associated Press, May 18, 2009.

Neumann, Peter R. "Negotiating with Terrorists." *Foreign Affairs* 86, no. 1 (January–February 2007): 128–38.

Neustadt, Richard E. *Presidential Power*. New York: Macmillan, 1960.

Nixon, Richard M. *Leadership*. New York: Warner, 1982.

Olson, Mancur. *The Logic of Collective Action*. Cambridge, MA: Harvard University Press, 1965.

Ortiz, Roman D. "The Human Factor in Insurgency: Recruitment and Training in the Revolutionary Armed Forces of Colombia (FARC)." In *The Making of a Terrorist: Recruitment, Training, and Root Causes*, edited by J. J. F. Forest, 263–76. Westport, CT: Praeger Security International, 2006.

Pape, Robert. "The Strategic Logic of Suicide Terrorism." *American Political Science Review* 97 (2003): 343–61.

Pape, Robert. "The True Worth of Air Power." *Foreign Affairs* 83, no. 2 (March–April 2004): 116–30.

Paz, Reuven. *Hamas Analyzes Its Terrorist Activity*. Herzliya, Israel: International Institute for Counter-Terrorism, December 21, 1999. https://www.ict.org.il/Article.aspx?ID=774#gsc.tab=0

Pedahzur, Ami. *Suicide Terrorism*. Cambridge: Polity, 2005.

Perl, Raphael. *Combating Terrorism: The Challenge of Measuring Effectiveness*. CRS Report for Congress, March 12, 2007.

Pfeffer, Jeffrey. "The Ambiguity of Leadership." *Academy of Management Review* 2, no. 1 (1977): 104–12.

Phillips, Brian J. "Do 90 Percent of Terrorist Groups Last Less than a Year? Updating the Conventional Wisdom," *Terrorism and Political Violence* (2017): 1–11. https://doi.org/10.1080/09546553.2017.1361411.

Phillips, Brian J. "Enemies with Benefits? Violent Rivalry and Terrorist Group Longevity." *Journal of Peace Research* 52, no. 1 (2015): 62–75.

Phillips, Brian J. "Terrorist Group Cooperation and Longevity." *International Studies Quarterly* 58, no. 2 (2014): 336–47.

Piazza, James A. "Rooted in Poverty? Terrorism, Poor Economic Development, and Social Cleavages." *Terrorism and Political Violence* 18, no. 1 (2006): 159–77.

Pillar, Paul R. "Counterterrorism After Al Qaeda." *Washington Quarterly* 27, no. 3 (2004): 101–13.

Pincus, Walter. "Zarqawi Is Said to Swear Allegiance to Bin Laden." *Washington Post*, October 19, 2004.

Popper, Micha, and Raanan Lipshitz. "Installing Mechanisms and Instilling Values: The Role of Leaders in Organizational Learning." *The Learning Organization* 7, no. 3 (2000): 135–45.

Posen, Barry R. "The Struggle Against Terrorism: Grand Strategy, Strategy, and Tactics." *International Security* 26, vol. 3 (2001–2002): 39–55.

Post, Jerrold M. "Killing in the Name of God: Osama bin Laden and Al Qaeda." In *Know Thy Enemy: Profiles of Adversary Leaders and Their Strategic Cultures*, edited by B. R. Schneider and J. M. Post, 17–40. Maxwell Air Force Base, AL: U.S. Government Printing Office, 2003. http://www.au.af.mil/au/awc/awcgate/cpc-pubs/know_thy_enemy/post.pdf.

Post, Jerrold M. "Terrorist Psycho-logic: Terrorist Behavior as a Product of Psychological Forces." In *Origins of Terrorism*, edited by W. Reich, 25–42. Washington, DC: Woodrow Wilson Center Press, 1990.

Post, Jerrold M., Ehud Sprinzak, and Laurita M Denny. "The Terrorists in Their Own Words: Interviews with 35 Incarcerated Middle Eastern Terrorists." *Terrorism and Political Violence* 15, no. 1 (2003): 171–84.

Price, Bryan C. "Removing the Devil You Know: Unraveling the Puzzle Behind Leadership Decapitation and Terrorist Group Duration." PhD diss., Stanford University, 2009.

Price, Bryan C. "Targeting Top Terrorists." *International Security* 36, no. 4 (Spring 2012): 9–36.

Price, Bryan C. "Terrorism as Cancer: How to Combat an Incurable Disease." *Terrorism and Political Violence* (June 2017): 1–25. https://doi.org/10.1080/09546553.2017.1330200.

Pynchon, Marisa Reddy, and Randy Borum. "Assessing Threats of Targeted Group Violence: Contributions from Social Psychology." *Behavioral Sciences and the Law* 17, no. 3 (1999): 339–55.

Quandt, William B. *Revolution and Political Leadership: Algeria, 1954–1968*. Cambridge, MA: MIT Press, 1969.

Rapoport, David C. "The Four Waves of Modern Terrorism." In *Attacking Terrorism: Elements of a Grand Strategy*, edited by A. K. Cronin and J. M. Ludes, 46–73. Washington, DC: Georgetown University Press, 2004.

Rapoport, David C. "Terrorism." In *Encyclopedia of Government and Politics*, edited by M. Hawkesworth and M. Kogan. London: Routledge, 1992.

Reid, Edna F., and Hsinchun Chen. "Mapping the Contemporary Terrorism Research Domain." *International Journal of Human-Computer Studies* 65, no. 1 (2007): 42–56.

Rejai, Mostafa, and Kay Phillips. *Leaders of Revolution*. Beverly Hills, CA: Sage, 1979.

Rejai, Mostafa, and Kay Phillips. *World Revolutionary Leaders*. New Brunswick, NJ: Rutgers University Press, 1983.

Richardson, Louise. *What Terrorists Want*. New York: Random House, 2006.

Romero, Simon. "Cocaine Trade Helps Rebels Reignite War in Peru." *New York Times*, March 18, 2009.

Rose, R. S. *The Unpast: Elite Violence and Social Control in Brazil, 1954–2000*. Athens: Ohio University Press, 2005.

Ross, Jeffrey Ian, and Ted Robert Gurr. "Why Terrorism Subsides: A Comparative Study of Canada and the United States." *Comparative Politics* 21, no. 4 (1989): 405–26.

Safire, William. "Sharon Enters Armistice Talks." *New York Times*, February 4, 2002.

Sageman, Marc. *Leaderless Jihad: Terror Networks in the Twenty-First Century.* Philadelphia: University of Pennsylvania Press, 2008.

Sageman, Marc. *Understanding Terror Networks.* Philadelphia: University of Pennsylvania Press, 2004.

Salancik, Gerald R., and Jeffrey Pfeffer. "Constraints on Administrative Discretion: The Limited Influence of Mayors on City Budgets." *Urban Affairs Quarterly* 12 (1977): 475–98.

Sandler, Todd. "Collective Action and Transnational Terrorism." *World Economy* 26, no. 6 (2003): 779–802.

Savage, Charlie, and Eric Schmitt. "Trump Poised to Drop Some Limits on Drone Strikes and Commando Raids." *New York Times*, September 21, 2017.

Schanzer, Jonathan. *Hamas vs. Fatah: The Struggle for Palestine.* New York: Palgrave MacMillan, 2008.

Schechter, Erik. "Where Have All the Bombers Gone?" *Jerusalem Post*, August 9, 2004.

Schein, Edgar H. "The Role of the Founder in the Creation of Organizational Culture." Working Paper #1407-83. Boston, MA: Sloan School of Management, MIT, 1983. https://dspace.mit.edu/bitstream/handle/1721.1/2039/SWP-1407-09320305.pdf.

Schmitt, Eric, and Thom Shanker. "US Adapts Cold-War Idea to Fight Terrorists." *New York Times*, March 18, 2008.

Sciolino, Elaine. "France's Terrorism Strategy Faulted." *New York Times*, July 3, 2008.

Seale, Patrick. *Abu Nidal: A Gun for Hire.* London: Hutchinson, 1992.

Sedgwick, Mark. "Inspiration and the Origins of Global Waves of Terrorism." *Studies in Conflict and Terrorism* 30, no. 2 (2007): 97–112.

Shane, Scott. "Government Hit Squads, Minus the Hits." *New York Times*, July 19, 2009.

Shane, Scott. "Inside a 9/11 Mastermind's Interrogation." *New York Times*, June 22, 2008.

Shanker, Thom. "New Lessons for the Army on Iraq Duty." *New York Times*, February 19, 2009.

Shapiro, Jacob N. "The Terrorist's Challenge: Security, Efficiency, and Control." PhD diss., Stanford University, 2007.

Shapiro, Jacob N. *The Terrorist's Dilemma: Managing Violent Covert Organizations.* Princeton, NJ: Princeton University Press, 2013.

Shepsle, Kenneth A., and Mark S. Bonchek. *Analyzing Politics: Rationality, Behavior, and Institutions.* New York: W. W. Norton, 1997.

Singer, Peter W. *Can't Win with 'Em, Can't Go to War Without 'Em: Private Military Contractors and Counterinsurgency.* Washington, DC: Brookings Institution, 2007.

Slackman, Michael S. "In Algeria, a Tug of War for Young Minds." *New York Times*, June 23, 2008.

Spencer, Alexander. "The Problems of Evaluating Counter-Terrorism." UNISCI Discussion Paper No. 12 (October 2006), 176–201.

Stalinsky, Steven. "'Jihadi Porn' Puts Beheadings Online." *New York Sun*, June 28, 2006.

Staniland, Paul. "Defeating Transnational Insurgencies: The Best Offense Is a Good Fence." *Washington Quarterly* 29, no. 1 (Winter 2005–2006): 21–40.

Staniland, Paul. "Explaining Cohesion, Fragmentation, and Control in Insurgent and Paramilitary Groups." PhD diss., MIT, 2008. http://hdl.handle.net/1721.1/62654.

Stares, Paul B., and Mona Yacoubian. "Unconventional Approaches to an Unconventional Threat: A Counter-Epidemic Strategy." In *Mapping the Jihadist Threat: The War on Terror Since 9/11*, edited by K. M. Campbell and W. Darsie, 85–95. Washington, DC: Aspen Institute, 2006. https://www.usip.org/sites/default/files/stares_yacoubian_threat.pdf.

Stein, Kenneth W. "Yassin's Assassination." *La Vanguardia*, April 1, 2004.

Stern, Jessica. "The Protean Enemy." *Foreign Affairs* 82, no. 4 (July–August 2003): 27–40.

Stinchcombe, Arthur S. "Organizations and Social Structure." In *Handbook of Organizations*, edited by J. G. March, 142–93. Chicago: Rand-McNally, 1965.

Stout, Mark, Jessica M. Huckabey, John R. Schindler, and Jim Lacey. *The Terrorist Perspectives Project: Strategic and Operational Views of Al Qaida and Associated Movements.* Annapolis, MD: Naval Institute Press, 2008.

Sunstein, Cass R. "Misery and Company." *New Republic* 239 (2008): 39–43.

Tamashiro, Howard. "The Danger of Nuclear Diplomatic Decapitation." *Air University Review* 35 (September–October 1984): 74–79.

Tamimi, Azzam. *Hamas: A History from Within.* Northampton, MA: Olive Branch Press, 2007.

Therneau, Terry M., and Patricia M. Grambsch. *Modeling Survival Data: Extending the Cox Model.* New York: Springer, 2000.

Toameh, Khaled Abu. "Analysis: Hamas Desperate for Lull." *Jerusalem Post*, January 6, 2009.

Trager, Robert F., and Dessislava P. Zagorcheva. "Deterring Terrorism: Can It Be Done?" *International Security* 30, no. 3 (2005–2006): 87–123.

"Transcript of Rice's 9/11 Commission Statement." CNN.com, May 19, 2004. http://www.cnn.com/2004/ALLPOLITICS/04/08/rice.transcript/.

Trow, Donald B. "Executive Succession in Small Companies." *Administrative Science Quarterly* 6 (1961): 228–39.

Tucker, Jonathan B. "Historical Trends Related to Bioterrorism: An Empirical Analysis." *Emerging Infectious Diseases* 5, no. 4 (1999): 498–504.

Turbiville, Graham H., Jr. "Hunting Leadership Targets in Counterinsurgency and Counterterrorist Operations." *Joint Special Operations University* 7, no. 6 (2007): 1–102.

Ulmer, Walter F., Jr. "Introduction." In *Leadership: The Warrior's Art*, edited by C. Kolenda, xxix–xxxvi. Carlisle, PA: Army War College Foundation Press, 2001.

United States Institute of Peace. *How Terrorism Ends.* Washington, DC: USIP, 1999.

U.S. Congress. Senate. Senate Government Affairs Permanent Subcommittee on Investigations. *Global Proliferation of Weapons of Mass Destruction: A Case Study on the Aum Shinrikyo*, October 31, 1995, 104th Cong., 1st sess.

Venkus, Robert E. *Raid on Qaddafi*. New York: St. Martin's Press, 1992.

Verba, Sidney. *Small Groups and Political Behavior.* Princeton, NJ: Princeton University Press, 1961.

Victoroff, Jeff. "Mind of the Terrorist: A Review and Critique of Psychological Approaches." *Journal of Conflict Resolution* 49, no. 3 (2005): 3–42.

Walt, Stephen M. "Beyond bin Laden: Reshaping US Foreign Policy." *International Security* 26, no. 3 (2001–2002): 56–78.

Waltz, Kenneth N. *Man, the State, and War*. New York: Columbia University Press, 1959.

Wang, Catherine L., and Pervaiz K. Ahmed. "Organizational Learning: A Critical Review." *The Learning Organization* 10, no. 1 (2003): 8–17.

Wasserman, Noam. "Founder-CEO Succession and the Paradox of Entrepreneurial Success." *Organization Science* 14, no. 2 (2003): 149–72.

Weber, Max. *The Theory of Social and Economic Organizations*. New York: Free Press, 1947.

Weimann, Gabriel. "Virtual Disputes: The Use of the Internet for Terrorist Debates." *Studies in Conflict and Terrorism* 29, no. 7 (2006): 623–39.

Weiner, Nan, and Timothy A. Mahoney. "A Model of Corporate Performance as a Function of Environmental, Organizational, and Leadership Influences." *Academy of Management Journal* 24, no. 3 (1981): 453–70.

Wiktorowicz, Quintan, and John Kaltner. "Killing in the Name of Islam: Al-Qaeda's Justification for September 11." *Middle East Policy* 10, no. 2 (2003): 76–92.

Wilkinson, Paul. *Terrorism Versus Democracy*. London: Frank Cass, 2000.

Wilner, Alex S. "Targeted Killings in Afghanistan: Measuring Coercion and Deterrence in Counterterrorism and Counterinsurgency." *Studies in Conflict and Terrorism* 33, no. 4 (2010): 307–29.

Wood, Elisabeth Jean. "Armed Groups and Sexual Violence: When Is Wartime Rape Rare?" *Politics and Society* 37, no. 1 (2009): 131–62.

Worrell, Dan L., Wallace N. Davidson III, P. R. Chandy, and Sharon L. Garrison. "Management Turnover Through Deaths of Key Executives: Effects on Investor Wealth." *Academy of Management Journal* 29, no. 4 (1986): 674–94.

Wright, Jamie, and Joan Dassin. *Torture in Brazil: A Shocking Report on the Pervasive Use of Torture by Brazilian Military Governments, 1964–1979.* Translated by J. Dassin. Austin: University of Texas Press, 1998.

Wright, Lawrence. *The Looming Tower.* New York: Knopf, 2006.

Wright, Lawrence. "The Master Plan." *New Yorker*, September 11, 2006.

Young, Joseph K., and Laura Dugan. "Survival of the Fittest: Why Terrorist Groups Endure." *Perspectives on Terrorism* 8, no. 2 (2014): 1–23.

Yukl, Gary. *Leadership in Organizations.* Upper Saddle River, NJ: Prentice Hall, 2002.

Zawodny, J. K. "Infrastructures of Terrorist Organizations." *Conflict Quarterly* 1, no 4 (1981): 24–31.

Zimmerman, Doron, and Andreas Wenger. *How States Fight Terrorism: Policy Dynamics in the West.* London: Lynne Rienner, 2007.

Zussman, Asaf, and Noam Zussman. "Assassinations: Evaluating the Effectiveness of an Israeli Counterterrorism Policy Using Stock Market Data." *Journal of Economic Perspectives* 20, no. 2 (2006): 193–206.

Index

Page numbers in *italics* indicate figures or tables.

Abu-Asi, Adel Najin, 87
Abu Nidal Organization (ANO), 79
Abu Sayyaf, 58
Adams, Gerry, 87, 220*n*68
Afghanistan, 16, 20, 94; militia in, 75; al-Qaeda in, 45; U.S. invasion of, 74
African National Congress (ANC), 220*n*67
Algeria, 78
Alibaba, 32
Allaf, Rime, 82
Amman, Jordan, 157, 160, 164
ANC. *See* African National Congress
ANO. *See* Abu Nidal Organization
Ansar-al-Sunnah, 82
anti-American sentiment, 11
Apocrypha, book of, 19
al-Aqsa Martyrs Brigade, 99, 176, 189
Arafat, Yassir, 111, 157, 165, 170, 171
Armed Forces of National Liberation (FALN), 109

Army, U.S., 41, 62
Army of God, 89
Asahara, Shoko, 77, 83
Asal, Victor, 105, 120
assassination, 2, 152, 187; of Ayyash, 163–64; counter-assassination, 19; effect of, 176; incarceration and, 167; by lethal injection, 232*n*10; of terrorist leaders, 100; of Yasin, 168, 170, 184
asymmetric warfare, 77
Aum Shinrikyo, 2, 42, 53; Asahara in, 77, 83; expansion of, 91; organizational structure of, 221*n*78 authority, 76; organizational theory on, 77
autocratic states, 115, 183
Autonomous Decorators, 107
Awda, Abd al-Aziz, 233*n*15
Ayyash, Yahya, 232*n*10; assassination of, 163–64

Baader, Andreas, 52
Baader-Meinhof Gang, 13
al Banna, Sabri, 79
Barber, James, 5
bargaining theory, 13
Barghouti, Marwan, 99, 189
Barsky, Yehudit, 157
Bascompte, Pere, 70
Bass, Bernard M., 54
Battle of Algiers (1966), 78
behavioralists, 34
beheadings, 81–82, 97
Berg, Nicholas, 81, 82
Berti, Benedetta, 175
Bezos, Jeff, 32
bin Laden, Osama, 25, 30, 74; death of, 1, 100; iconic status of, 75; organizational culture within al-Qaeda and, 80; unsuccessful attempt to kill, 20; Zarqawi and, 81
Black Tigers, 83
Blackwater, 38, 62, 215n110; compared to al-Qaeda, 64; as economic firm, 63; murders committed by, 64
bodyguards, 170
bomb making, 96
bosses, 91
Boston Red Sox, 32
Breton Liberation Front, 109
Bryant, Kris, 32
B'Tselem, 173
Buddhism, 53
"bunch of guys" theory, 93, 222n98
bureaucracy, 37, 86, 91; of terrorist groups, 146
Burns, James Macgregor, 35, 77
Bush, George W., 3, 22, 65, 110
Byman, Daniel L., 5, 17, 96, 98, 172, 173, 174, 184

CAIN. *See* Conflict Archive on the Internet
cancer treatments, 186, 187
car bombs, 162, 167
Carroll, Glenn, 36, 38, 101
Cathedral High School, 56
Central Intelligence Agency (CIA), 1; coup in Guatemala engineered by, 20
chain of command, 61
Chandy, P. R., 67
charisma, 50, 51; routinization of, 52; terrorist leaders and, 77; of Yasin, 171
Chicago Cubs, 32–33
Christian apocalypticism, 53
Christian Scientists, 37
Churchill, Winston, 40
CIA. *See* Central Intelligence Agency
civil liberties, 11, 115
civil rights, 83
clandestineness, 3, 33, 38, 42, 46, 57, 70, 113, 181, 211n40; groupthink and, 44; ideology and, 51; institutional constraints and, 48; institutionalization and, 47; organizational learning and, 45; paranoia and, 78; of terrorist groups, 104–5; uncertainty and, 43. *See also* nonclandestine organizations
cocaine, 69
Cohen, Dara, 39
Cold War, 20, 185; Solidarity movement and, 57
Colombian Ministry of Defense, 91
Combating Terrorism Center (CTC), 47, 95, 224n6
complacency, 126
confidence intervals, 119

Conflict Archive on the Internet (CAIN), 110
contingency theory, 35
corruption, 165
Council on Foreign Relations, 152
counter-assassination, 19
counterinsurgency, 63–64
counterterrorism, 1, 75, 94, 145, 186; counterterror analysts, 47; decapitation tactics and, 2, 72; effectiveness of, 173, 189; by France, 78; heavy-handed, 149; International Institute for Strategic Studies and, 82; in Iraq, 48; Israel and, 19, 152; policy, 16; Rapoport on, 120; reconciliation model of, 185; research in, 28; resources for, 188; states capacity for, 104, 114, 183; strategies, 17
Cox proportional hazards model, 28, 117, *123–25*, *130–31*, 181, 188; decapitation methods and, *139–40*; founders and, *136–37*; ideology and, *133–34*; leadership turnover and, *143–44*
Crenshaw, Martha, 16, 44, 49, 52, 86, 88, 146
Cronin, Audrey Kurth, 16, 18, 19, 21, 58, 94, 112, 137
CTC. *See* Combating Terrorism Center

Dabruzzi, Kyle, 93
Dahl, Robert, 6
David, Steven R., 49
Davidson, Wallace N., III, 67
decapitation tactics, 1, 98, 110, *115*, *116*; advantages of, 95, 96; attractiveness of, 80; conceptualization of, 122; counterterrorism and, 2, 72; disadvantages of, 100; discomfort with, 146; against drug cartel kingpins, abysmal failure of, 54–55; duration of effects of, 122; early in organizational life cycle, 102; effects of, 101, 117, 144, 148; failed attempts of, 100; founders and, 134; groups ended and experienced decapitation, *195–98*; groups ended and not experienced decapitation, *194–95*; groups not ended and experienced decapitation, *192–93*; groups not ended and not experienced decapitation, *191–92*; Hamas and, 4; hazard rate and, 121, *128*; in historical context, 19; Israel and, 153, 164; Jordan criteria for evaluating, 145; leadership turnover due to, 142; limitations on analysis of, 29; lingering effects of, 135, 141; mass decapitation, 158; methods of, *139–40*, 141; morality and, 100; mortality rates and, 149; multiple decapitation events, 127–29, 146; organizational death and, 145; organizational decline and, 150–51; organizational performance and, 154; policymakers and, 2, 29, 95; policymakers and theoretical justification behind, 57; primacy of, 22; prominent cases of, 18; questionable effectiveness of, 2–3, 18, 23, 25, 103–4, 144–45, 167, 179, 185; success of, 99; theoretical justification behind, 57; timing of, 96, 127, 132, 158–59, 182
decaptime, 129
Decker, Scott H., 44, 69–70
de Gaulle, Charles, 40
Deikman, Arthur J., 77
della Porta, Donatella, 43
Delta Force, U.S., 74

Democratic Front for the Liberation of Palestine (DFLP), 84
Democratic Party, 51
DFLP. *See* Democratic Front for the Liberation of Palestine
Dichter, Avi, 174
drill instructors, 40
drone strikes, Trump and, 2
drug cartels, 3, 37, 44, 45, 47; chain of command of, 61; ideology and, 65; Kenney on terrorist groups and, 65; kingpins of, 54–55, 69–70; recruiting by, 56
drug trade, 28
drug trafficking, 86
Dugan, Laura, 112

Earth Liberation Front (ELF), 89
East Africa, 16
economic firms, 8, 36, 53, 86, 181; Blackwater as, 63
Eilstrup-Sangiovanni, Mette, 98
ELF. *See* Earth Liberation Front
El Salvador, 109
Encyclopedia of Government and Politics, 120
Enders, Walter, 93
environmental constraints, 37, 38
environmentally responsible practices, 58
Epstein, Theo, 32
Escobar, Pablo, 69
Europe, 106
execution, 138, 167
expectation management, 4
experiential *metis*, 48, 61, 96, 146
external constraints, 88

failure, 88, 90, 100; risk of, 118
FALN. *See* Armed Forces of National Liberation

Farabundo Marti National Liberation Front (FMLN), 109
FARC. *See* Revolutionary Armed Forces of Colombia
fascism, 185
Fatah, 99, 176, 233n15; Hamas rival of, 159; heterogeneous membership of, 153; Yasin and, 155
Field Manual 1 (FM-1), 62
firm-specific capital, 51
first intifada, 156, 159
FM-1. *See* Field Manual 1
FMLN. *See* Farabundo Marti National Liberation Front
foot soldiers, 13, 14, 15
Forbes magazine, 32
foreign policy, 12, 20
Foreign Terrorist Organization, U.S. (FTO), 109
founders, 90; in control, 135; Cox proportional hazards model and, *136–37*; crises involving, 102; decapitation tactics and, 134; hazard rate and, 137, 146; leaving voluntarily, 134; loss of, 127; Yasin, Hamas founded by, 152, 154
fractionalization, 99, 101, 178
fragging, 40
France, 78
Francis, Pope, 32
Free Aceh Movement, 109
Free Masons, 42
FTO. *See* Foreign Terrorist Organization, U.S.
Furtado, Eugene P. H., 51
Fury, Dalton, 74, 75

Gambetta, Diego, 12
gang rape, 39
gang warfare, 86
Ganor, Boaz, 138

García, María Elena, 99
Garrison, Sharon L., 67
Gartenstein-Ross, Daveed, 93
Gaza city, 152, 170
Gaza Strip, 154, 155, 160, 172, 173; Israel and, 174
GDP. *See* gross domestic product
general human capital, 51
George, Alexander, 5
Germany, 11, 43
al Ghoul, Adnan, 164
Gleis, Joshua L., 175
Global Terrorism Database (GTD), 105, 109–10, 162, 169, 220n67; on Hamas, 163, 172
global war on terrorism, 93
God's Army, 201n35
Greece, 107
gross domestic product (GDP) per capita, 126, 148, 150
group decision making, 43
Group for Preaching and Combat (GSPC), 204n84
groupthink, 44, 49; susceptibility to, 80
Grusky, Oscar, 41, 66
GSPC. *See* Group for Preaching and Combat
GTD. *See* Global Terrorism Database
Guatemala, 20
Gulf War, 20
Gupta, Dipak K., 23, 24, 166
Guzman, Abimael, 79, 80, 110; capture of, 99

Hagan, Joe D., 6
Hamas, 4, 27, 28, 83, 97, 98, 151, 184; cease-fires signed by, 163; Cell 101, 233n28; domestic support for, 176; evolution of, 153; Fatah rival of, 159; GTD on, 163, 172; Hezbollah meeting with, 162; low-level members of, 76; military capability, 166; Muslim Brotherhood and, 158; organizational network of, 158; organizational performance of, 163, *163*, 168, *168*; organizational roots of, 234n40; Pedahzur on, 169; PIJ and, 167; PLO and, 170, 175; political wing of, 173; popularity of, 156; recruiting by, 153; resiliency of, 166; security of, 172; size of, 159; social services provided by, 161; suicide terrorism by, 162, 163, 166, 235n55; survival of, 158, 160, 174; Yasin founder of, 152, 154; Yasin return to, 170
hands-on key executives, 68
Haniyya, Isma'il, 174, 175
Harmony database, 47
hazard rate, 122, 145; decapitation method and, 141; decapitation tactics and, 121, *128*; founders and, 137, 146; leadership turnover and, 142; multiple decapitation events and, 127–29; terrorist groups and, 118, 147
Heaven's Gate, 42
Hebrew University, 177
Hermann, Margaret G., 6
Hezbollah, 30, 176; Hamas meeting with, 162; leadership of, 85; Pedahzur and, 84
Hitler, Adolf, 71
Hobbes, Thomas, 78
Hoffman, Bruce, 46, 80, 88, 112
Holofernes (fictional character), 19
Horst, Karl, 64
hostages, 156
House Intelligence Committee, 22
"How al-Qaida Ends," (Cronin), 16
Howeydi, Fahmy, 64
humanitarian issues, 50

hunger strikes, 99
Hutchinson, Steve, 112, 138

ICG. *See* International Crisis Group
ideology, 50, 55, 62, 113, 132, 147, 182; clandestineness and, 51; control for, 122; Cox proportional hazards model and, *133–34*; drug cartels and, 65; hard-core ideological and value-oriented groups, 53; homogeneity of, 79; impact of, 149; values-driven organizations and, 52
incarceration, 137; assassination and, 167; incarcerated terrorists, 83; of Yasin, 155, 158, 159, 164, 172, 175
indoctrination, 13
informants, 62
innocent civilians, 75, 81, 85
innovation, 45
Institute for Defense Analyses, 47
institutional constraints, 37, 38; clandestineness and, 48
institutionalization, 47; lack of, 62; operational security and, 49–50
institutional stickiness, 89
intelligence gathering, 114, 148
internal constraints, 88, 89
International Crisis Group (ICG), 204n82
International Institute for Strategic Studies, 82
International Security, 98
Internet, 222n98
interrogation, 137, 138, 157
Iran, 84, 153, 174
Iranian Revolution, 155
Iraq, 16, 20, 63, 94; counterterrorism in, 48; insurgency in, 81
Ireland, 115

Irish Republican Army, 11
Islam, 79, 85; Islamic fundamentalism, 152; militant Islamism, 83, 84; Muslim Brotherhood and, 154
the Islamic Center. *See* al-Mujamma' al-Islami
Islamic State, 76, 79, 81, 85; al-Qaeda and, 82, 114; radicalization by, 93
Israel, 1, 2, 24, 170, 235n61; counterterrorism and, 19, 152; decapitation tactics and, 153, 164; disproportionate response by, 159; Gaza Strip and, 174; intelligence agents, 155, 175; international condemnation of, 162; Israeli-Palestinian conflict, 97; Israel-Lebanon border, 161; miscalculations by Israeli government, 161; policymakers and, 171; security officials, 158; targeted killing programs by, 23, 30, 144, 169, 184, 232n10; terrorist attacks against, 176; ultra-orthodox Jewish population in, 42; Yasin and, 155–56
Israeli Information Center for Human rights in the Occupied Territories, 173
Israeli Prison Services, 99
Italy, 11, 43, 86

Jabril, Ahmed, 7
Jackson, Brian A., 45
Jama'at al-Tawhid wal-Jihad, 81
Al Jazeera, 64
Jerusalem, 177
jihad, 79, 81, 85
Jihaz al-Ahadith, 160
Johnson, W. Bruce, 67
Jones, Calvert, 98
Jones, Seth G., 110, 113, 126

Jordan, Jenna, 25–26, 107–8, 145, 146, 147, 153, 177
Judith (fictional character), 19
al-Jurah, 154

Kaltner, John, 85
Kaplan, Edward H., 23
Kaplan-Meier (K-M) estimates, 119
Karan, Vijay, 51
Kenney, Michael, 47, 48, 54, 55, 56, 61, 96, 108; of terrorist groups and drug cartels, 65
Kenya, 20
Kfar Darom, 172
kidnapping, 103, 159, 161, 167
KLA. *See* Kosovo Liberation Army
K-M. *See* Kaplan-Meier estimates
Knights of the Torched Bank, 107
Koran, 84; suicide terrorism and, 85
Koresh, David, 71
Kosovo Liberation Army (KLA), 87
Kristiansen, Wendy, 171
Kurdistan Worker's Party (PKK), 83
Kuwait, 165

Langdon, Lisa, 24, 102, 107
Laqueur, Walter, 93
leadership, 3, 4, 15, 25–26; changes, 6, 149, 182; contingency theory of, 35; decision making of, 12; glorification, 99; of Hezbollah, 85; leader-follower dynamics, 180; leadership capital, 9; loss of, 41; media and, 5; motivations and, 6; organizational performance and, 5, 7, 9, 33, 73; participative, 34; of street gangs, 69; succession, 36, 43, 59, 66, 215*n*109; succession, crisis in, 101; succession, involuntary turnover, 67, 69; succession, uncertain, 68; of terrorist groups, 14, 85; transactional, 35, 70–71, *71*; transformational, 35, 70–71, *71*, 72, 77; turnover, 142, *143–44*, 146; values-driven organizations and, 52; violence and, 40, 59. *See also* terrorist leaders
leadership decapitation. *See* decapitation tactics
Lebanese Socialist Revolutionary Organization (Shibbu Gang), 87
Lebanon, 168; Israel-Lebanon border, 161
lethal injection, 232*n*10
Liberation Tigers of Tamil Eelam (LTTE), 76, 83, 209*n*151, 238*n*147
Libicki, Martin C., 110, 113, 126
Libya, 16, 20
Libyan Islamic Fighting Group (LIFG), 109
lone wolf terrorists, 199*n*2
longevity, 111, 112, 114, 118, 120, 122, *123–25*; group size and, 129, 130; timing of decapitation and, 127
Looming Tower, The (Wright), 95
Lord's Resistance Army, 39
Los Angeles Archdiocese, 56
LTTE. *See* Liberation Tigers of Tamil Eelam

Ma, Jack, 32
macro-level factors, 94
Magee, Robert P., 67
Man, the State, and War (Waltz), 5
managers, 51, 52
Mandela, Nelson, 87, 220*n*67
Mannes, Aaron, 24, 26, 102, 107, 117, 207*n*129
Manson, Charles, 71
al-Maqdisi Abu Muhammad, 218*n*41
Marin, Pedro Antonio, 91

martyrs, 19, 178
Marxism, 52
Marxism-Leninism, 8, 83, 113; Turkish Communist party / Marxist-Leninist group, 122
Marzuq, Abu, 160, 164
Mashal, Khaled, 175, 232n10
McCormick, Gordon H., 14
McGuiness, Martin, 87, 220n68
media, 5
Memorial Institute for the Prevention of Terrorism (MIPT), 105, 110, 214n98, 225n15
MEND. *See* Movement for the Emancipation of the Niger Delta
Merari, Ariel, 104
mercenaries, 50
Merkel, Angela, 32
Meyer, Marshall W., 86
MICG. *See* Moroccan Islamic Combatant Group
Middle East, 159
military leaders, 178
MIPT. *See* Memorial Institute for the Prevention of Terrorism
Mishal, Khalid, 164, 172
Mishal, Shaul, 159, 162
Moe, Terry, 36, 37, 38
Mofaz, Shaul, 174
morality, 63, 167; decapitation tactics and, 100; moral culpability, 84; rival groups and, 112; of targeted killing programs, 153
Mormon Church, 24, 37
Moroccan Islamic Combatant Group (MICG), 109
mortality rates, 104, 118, 158, 183, 189; decapitation tactics and, 149; leadership change and, 182; of terrorist groups, 102, 106, 149;
terrorist leaders and, 127; variables affecting, 150
Mossad, 164, 232n10
Movement for the Emancipation of the Niger Delta (MEND), 97
al-Mujamma' al-Islami (the Islamic Center), 152, 154, 155, 156, 176; international donations, 160
Mundra, Kusum, 23, 24, 166
Munich Olympics massacre, 232n10
Muslim Brotherhood, 154, 155, 170; Hamas and, 158; Marzuq and, 160

Nagarajan, Nandu J., 67
nationalism, 86–87, 113, 122; Islamic fundamentalism and, 152; organizational death and, 132; resilience of, 147; Six-Day War and, 155
National Liberation Front, 78
National Military Strategy for the War on Terrorism, 2006, 22
national security, 27, 94, 180
National Security Strategy, 2002, 21
National Strategy for Combating Terrorism (NSCT), 21; 2003, 180; 2006, 22, 27
National Strategy for Counterterrorism, 2011, 180
natural death, 134, 148
Neustadt, Richard, 5, 36
New Age medical practices, 53
Newman, Harry A., 67
Nidal, Abu, 79, 80, 111
Nixon, Richard, 40
Nobel Peace Prize, 8
nonclandestine organizations, 46, 48–50, 66; uncertainty and, 60
noncombatants, 85
nonideological organizations, 51, 53

non-profit-maximizing organizations, 55
nonviolent organizations, 38, 59
Northern Ireland, 115
North Korea, 20
NSCT. *See* National Strategy for Combating Terrorism
null model, 119

Obama, Barack, 1, 3, 110
O'Malley, Pat, 112, 138
oncology, 186, 187
operational capability, 4, 188
operational effectiveness, 173
operational security, 42, 45, 105; ensuring, 90; institutionalization and, 49–50; need for, 78
Operation Infinite Reach, 20
organizational behavior, 6; influence of, 11
organizational characteristics, 75
organizational contexts, 38, 57
organizational death, 122, 132; decapitation tactics and, 145
organizational decline, 128; decapitation tactics and, 150–51; of terrorist groups, 142
organizational inertia, 92
organizational learning, 43, 45, 213*n*74; impediments to, 146; inhibition of, 80; al-Qaeda and, 47; terrorist leaders and, 78, 80
organizational performance, 3, 4, 72, 90; decapitation tactics and, 154; of Hamas, 163, *163*, 168, *168*; leadership and, 5, 7, 9, 33, 73; measures of, 88; Pfeffer on, 8, 9; of terrorist groups, 97; terrorist leaders and, 89
organizational theory, 3, 5, 12; on authority, 77

organizational typology, 34
Oslo peace accords, 160, 163

Pakistan, 100, 218*n*41
Palestine, 23, 24, 155, 161, 165; Israeli-Palestinian conflict, 97; Palestinian refugees, 157
Palestinian Islamic Jihad (PIJ), 83, 97, 159, 161, 166, 233*n*15; Hamas and, 167
Palestinian Liberation Organization (PLO), 111, 156, 157, 165, 168, 176; cease-fires signed by, 163; Hamas and, 170, 175
Panetta, Leon, 1
Pape, Robert, 20
paramilitary teams, 22
paranoia, 78
Patton, George, 71
peaceful da'wah, 155
Pedahzur, Ami, 12, 83, 97; on Hamas, 169; on Hezbollah, 84
Penn World Tables, 114
People's Liberation Army, 109
Peralta, Johnny Justino, 87
Permanently Failing Organizations (Meyer and Zucker), 86
personality, 36
Pfeffer, Jeffrey, 7, 8, 9
PFLP. *See* Popular Front for the Liberation of Palestine
PFLP-GC. *See* Popular Front for the Liberation of Palestine—General Command
PGIS. *See* Pinkerton Global Intelligence Services
Phillips, Brian J., 111, 112, 120
Phoenix program, 20
PIJ. *See* Palestinian Islamic Jihad
Pinkerton Global Intelligence Services (PGIS), 106

PKK. *See* Kurdistan Worker's Party
PLO. *See* Palestinian Liberation Organization
PMC. *See* private military company
Poland, 57
policymakers, 3, 94, 103, 167, 184, 190; decapitation strategies, theoretical justification behind and, 57; decapitation tactics and, 2, 29, 95; decisions of, 19; domestic support for, 98; ending terrorism and, 93; expectation management for, 4; interests of, 10; Israel and, 171; long-term effects of policies by, 25; on rehabilitation, 27; temper of, 23; terrorist leaders and, 22; unwarranted sense of security for, 120; war on drugs and, 69
political organization, 92
political science, 5, 228n62
political utility maximizers, 14
Pollack, Kenneth M., 5
Popular Front for the Liberation of Palestine (PFLP), 7, 13, 84, 113
Popular Front for the Liberation of Palestine—General Command (PFLP-GC), 7, 156
Post, Jerrold, 84, 86, 113
Prabhakaran, Velupillai, 83, 209n151, 238n147
principal-agent problems, 90, 213n73; Shapiro and, 96
private military company (PMC), 61, 62–64
profit-driven organizations, 50, 55, 57; self-interests and, 64
profit maximization, 3, 33, 53, 55, 181
propaganda, 161, 162, 224n6
Proscribed List (United Kingdom), 109
public opinion, 5

Qaddafi, Muammar, 20
al-Qaeda, 25, 180, 202n48; in Afghanistan, 45; beheadings and, 81–82; Blackwater compared to, 64; Bush on, 65; future of, 1; Hoffman on, 46; Islamic State and, 82, 114; Jama'at al-Tawhid wal-Jihad and, 81; organizational culture of, 80; organizational learning and, 47; paramilitary teams dispatched to kill leaders of, 22–23; relevance of, 93; September 11, 2001 and, 85; top leaders of, 97
Qasir, Ahmad, 84
al-Qassam Brigades, 164, 233n28, 236n88
Qatar, 165, 168
Qolbi, Sulthon, 204n82

radicalization, 93
RAF. *See* Red Army Faction
RAND, 110, 113, 114
al-Rantisi, Abd al-Aziz, 97, 162, 169, 171, 172, 174, 178
Rapoport, David C., 27, 119, 120, 121
rational choice, 6
recruiting, 56; by Hamas, 153
Red Army Faction (RAF), 52
"Red Queen" theory, 112
regime type, 115, 126
religious cults, 57
religious organizations, 53
religious terrorist groups, 84, 103, 126; longevity of, 112; resilience of, 147
Republican Party, 51, 106
resiliency, 101
retaliation attacks, 25, 146
Rethemeyer, R. Karl, 105, 120
Revolutionary Armed Forces of Colombia (FARC), 58, 76, 89, 113; expansion of, 91

revolutionary movements, 9
Revolutionary Popular Vanguard (VPR), 231n2
Rice, Condoleezza, 206n117
right-censored data, 117, 207n129
right-wing groups, 122, 126, 132
Romney, Mitt, 106, 107
Royal Institute of International Affairs, 82
Rumsfeld, Donald, 16–17

Sageman, Marc, 93
Salafism, 83, 202n48
Salim, Jamal, 165
Sandler, Todd, 93
Saudi Arabia, 165
second intifada, 169, 173
Sela, Avraham, 159, 162
self-interests, 70, 71; profit-driven organizations and, 64
self-radicalization, 15
Senate Government Affairs Permanent Subcommittee on Investigations of the Committee on Governmental Affairs, U.S., 91
Sendero Luminoso, 110–11, 113
separatism, 86–87, 112, 122; Islamic fundamentalism and, 152
September 11, 2001, 1, 10, 16, 64; planning for, 25; al-Qaeda and, 85
Shallah, Ramadan, 233n15
Shanab, Abu, 170
Shapiro, Jacob N., 52, 96, 98
Shaqaqi, Fathi, 233n15
Sharon, Ariel, 169
Shehada, Salah, 170
Shibbu Gang. *See* Lebanese Socialist Revolutionary Organization
Shin Bet, 174
Shining Path, 2, 24, 28, 58, 79, 99, 110
Sierra Leone, 39

Six-Day War, 155
60 Minutes, 74
Skull and Bones, 42
slavery, 83
social benefits, 55
social clubs, 53
social dynamics, 11
social identity theory, 38
socially responsible practices, 58
social movements, 9
social service organizations, 92
social utility maximizers, 14
Solar Temple, 53
Solidarity Gas Canisters, 107
Solidarity movement, 57
SOPs. *See* standing operating procedures
South Africa, 87
South Asia Terrorism Portal, 110
Soviet Union, 20
span of control, 90–91
Sri Lanka, 76
standing operating procedures (SOPs), 61
START. *See* Study of Terrorism and Responses to Terrorism
state characteristics, 149
statistical significance, 126
Stevenson, Jonathan, 82
street gangs, 40, 56; leadership of, 69
"Structure of Terror, The" (NSCT), 21, *21*
Study of Terrorism and Responses to Terrorism (START), 214n98, 225n15; National Consortium of, 110
Sudan, 165
suicide terrorism, 13, 97, 171; Black Tigers and, 83; blame for, 85; by Hamas, 162, 163, 166, 235n55; Koran and, 85; Qasir and, 84; rates of, 23; women and, 205n85
Syria, 16, 153, 168, 174, 175

tactics, techniques, and procedures (TTPs), 46
Taliban, 45, 74
Tamimi, Azzam, 162, 166
Tanzania, 20
targeted killing programs, 2, 18, 177; effects of, 152; by Israel, 23, 30, 144, 169, 184, 232n10; morality of, 153
Taslim, Fajar, 204n82
Terra Lliure, 70
terrorism, 185, 187; causes of, 10–11, 12, 15, 16; ending, 92–93; frequency of, 102; global war on, 93; incarceration and, 137; inflated threat of, 107; lack of consensus definition of, 107; literature on, 10; misleading conclusions about, 106; organizational history prior to turning to, 158; threat posed by, 16. *See also* suicide terrorism
Terrorism and Political Violence, 120
Terrorism Knowledge Base (TKB), 105, 109–10, 214n98, 220n67, 225n15
terrorism research, 104
terrorism scholars, 67, 119, 190
terrorist attacks, 22, 153, 155; against Israel, 176
terrorist groups, 3, 7, 72, 77; ally groups, 111, 118, 183; bureaucracy of, 146; clandestineness of, 104–5; constraints faced by, 12; decapitation tactics and, *115*, *116*, 117; decline of, 101; definitions of, 120; dynamics, 94; ending of, 18, 93, 94; foot soldiers of, 13, 14; groups ended and experienced decapitation, *195–98*; groups ended and not experienced decapitation, *194–95*; groups not ended and experienced decapitation, *192–93*; groups not ended and not experienced decapitation, *191–92*; group-specific characteristics, 122; hazard rate and, 118, 147; individual-level factors for joining, 15; Kenney on drug cartels and, 65; lack of data on, 104; leadership change and, 182; leadership of, 14, 85; longevity, group size and, 129, 130; longevity of, 111, 114, 118, 120, 122, *123–25*; mortality of, 4; mortality rates of, 102, 106, 149; motivation of, 70; operating in perpetually hostile environments, 91; organizational "black box" of, 29; organizational collapse of, 2, 145; organizational decline of, 142; organizational inertia and, 92; organizational performance of, 97; recruitment to, 14–15; religious, 84; replenishment of, 55; resiliency of, 98; rival groups, 111, 112, 126, 129; separatist, 220n68; size of, 90, 113–14, 149; survival times of, 117, 119, *119*; timing of decapitation and longevity of, 127; use of violence by, 163. *See also* religious terrorist groups
terrorist leaders: arresting, 138; assassinations of, 100; charisma and, 77; decision making by, 95; failure and, 88; follow-on leaders, 137; as founders, 90; incentives of, 85; mortality rate and, 127; organizational learning and, 78, 80; organizational performance and, 89; paranoia of, 78; policymakers and, 22; role of, 87; secret identity of, 97, 98; transmission of important organizational information by, 91; unique aspects of, 92; Yasin as, 154
Terrorist Organization Profiles (TOPs), 106, 110, 120, 214n98, 225n15; bias and, 107

Terrorist Perspectives Project, 47
terror stock, 23
Thaci, Hashim, 87
3-D model of organizational types, 57–58, *58*, 59
TKB. *See* Terrorism Knowledge Base
TOPs. *See* Terrorist Organization Profiles
torture, 157
Trump, Donald, 3, 110; drone strikes and, 2
TTPs. *See* tactics, techniques, and procedures
Turkish Communist party / Marxist-Leninist group, 122

Uganda, 39
uncertainty, 43; nonclandestine organizations and, 60
Unification Church, 42
United Arab Emirates, 165
United Kingdom, 109, 115
United Nations Resolution 1373, 228*n*56
United States (U.S.), 16, 85, 153, 164, 168, 185; Afghanistan, invaded by, 74; anti-American sentiment, 11; Army, 41, 62; counterterrorism strategy of, 1, 94; Delta Force, 74; foreign policy of, 20; international condemnation of, 162; national security, 27, 180; presidents of, 36–37, 48; public bureaucracy of, 37; resources used for killing bin Laden, 100; targeted killing program expanded by, 2; war on drugs by, 69

values-driven organizations, 3, 33, 38, 50, 56, 70, 181; goals of, 53; ideology and, 52; leadership and, 52; morality and, 63; values-based judgments, 57

Van Winkle, Barrick, 44, 69–70
Vietnam, 20
Vietnam War, 40
violence, 3, 33, 57, 60, 70, 76, 181; acts of, 106; group cohesion and, 39, 41; leadership and, 40, 59; nonviolent organizations, 38, 59; terrorist groups use of, 163; threat of, 39
voluntary turnover, 67
volunteer groups, 53
VPR. *See* Revolutionary Popular Vanguard

Waltz, Kenneth, 5, 6
war on drugs, 69
wealth, 126
Weber, Max, 35, 76
Weibull model, 117
West Bank, 160, 165, 173, 174
West Point, 47
Who Governs? (Dahl), 6
Wiktorowicz, Quintan, 85
women, 89, 205*n*85
World War II, 20, 49
Worrell, Dan L., 67, 68
Wright, Lawrence, 95

Yale University, 42
Yasin, Sheikh Ahmed, 97, 163, 166, 177, 233*n*28; assassination of, 168, 170, 184; charisma of, 171; Fatah and, 155; Hamas founded by, 152, 154; incarceration of, 155, 158, 159, 164, 172, 175; Israel and, 155–56; release of, 165, 167; return to Hamas, 170; as terrorist leader, 154; torture of Yasin's son, 157; trial of, 161
Yemen, 16, 165
Young, Joseph K., 112
Yukl, Gary, 36

al-Zahar, Mahmoud, 165, 174
Zarate Willka Armed Forces of
    Liberation, 87
Zarqawi, Abu Musab, 81, 82, 218n41,
    219n42

Zawahiri, Ayman, 82, 218n41, 219n42
    224n6, 224n6
Zawodny, J. K., 49
Zucker, Lynne G., 86

GPSR Authorized Representative: Easy Access System Europe, Mustamäe tee 50, 10621 Tallinn, Estonia, gpsr.requests@easproject.com

www.ingramcontent.com/pod-product-compliance
Lightning Source LLC
Chambersburg PA
CBHW020534030426
42337CB00013B/844